Of Rhubarb and Roses

The Telegraph
BOOK OF
THE GARDEN

Edited by Tim Richardson

Contents

Introduction

What to expect, trawling through every piece of garden writing in the *Daily Telegraph*'s history?

I'm not sure quite what I was anticipating, but I know it was not diatribes against melon frappé or the best places to find wild chives on the Lizard peninsula. I'm not sure, either, that I was quite ready for the fact that a garden column appeared in the newspaper every single day from the late 1950s on. The result was bulging file after file brought up from the *Telegraph*'s distant archive, each filled to bursting with carefully snipped clippings. Snow, drought, storm, new plants launched, old plants rediscovered, the latest furore at the Chelsea Show – the garden columnist falls upon everything that makes one year different to the last, for with a cyclical subject such as horticulture there is the ever-present danger of repeating oneself. The *Telegraph*'s writers have avoided this for the most part, though I was amused to come across at least four versions of a 'May I introduce you to euphorbias?' piece by the same author. One of the fascinations of gardening is the way the same issues arise year after year while always seeming different, somehow – perhaps because of the vagaries of the seasons.

Then there are the news stories, deferential in earlier days – 'Duke of Norfolk Wins Gold Medal at RHS Show' (1961) – rather more sensational later: 'Conflict Among the Marrows' (1984). In more recent years the daily columns have been replaced by a Saturday gardening supplement which has become required reading for keen horticulturists, the repository of a wide range of writing on the topic. This variety is in part simply the result of more space being available: once the 'what to do in your garden this week' and question-and-answer areas are taken care of, there is an opportunity for writers to venture into more specialist horticultural topics and newsworthy items, as well as garden design and history, opinion and comment. It is the latter topics which have proven the most fruitful breeding ground for the plums picked for this anthology – writing that is idiosyncratic, original, piquant or esoteric.

The *Telegraph*'s first regular garden writer was H. H. Thomas, who was a well-known horticulturist in his own right. He contributed the odd news story through the 1930s and in 1937 he was given a regular column. The war put paid to this – in fact, there was hardly anything about gardens printed in the paper during the war years, a reminder of quite how grim it was – and the column did not commence again until 1953. Gordon Forsyth took over the year after and in the late 1950s he was joined by Fred Whitsey, who can fairly be described as the doyen of *Daily Telegraph* garden writers, contributing by far the most in terms of pure wordage, right up until his death in 2009. From the 1950s until the 1990s the stable of *Telegraph* garden writers remained small, with Gordon Forsyth and Robert Pearson notable for their reliability and down-to-earth good sense, Denis Wood for his connoisseurial bent, and Fred for his range of interest and extraordinary (I use the word advisedly) ability to add a fresh spin to well-worn horticultural topics. He was as happy discoursing on the gardens of the Italian Riviera as he was on how to hold a spade properly; in that sense he was perhaps the model for the modern garden writer. The tyranny of the daily column can lead to a kind of madness, however, as the writer desperately casts around for new ways of expressing himself. I have included here one of the most remarkable instances of this: Fred's 1967 column on compost, which begins with him on the masseur's couch, of all places, and concludes with a (favourable) comparison between the lore of manure and the work of George Bernard Shaw.

I used the word 'himself' just then, and some will have been pulled up by it, understandably enough. But the fact is, the *Telegraph*'s garden writers were all male until the 1980s, which is perhaps reflective of the times. In fact, the tone and content of the garden journalism in the newspaper is a good touchstone for the way gardening has changed over the years. (By the way, as a matter of policy I have not edited out references to chemicals which are now illegal, or excised recommended nurseries which are now defunct, on the grounds that such references are redolent of the times. Also, in the interest of authenticity, I have retained plant names as they existed at the time of publication – some will have changed since, but interested readers will be able to identify any new names via the internet.)

From the 1950s to the 1970s, many of the columns exhibit rather a 'man-to-man' attitude, with advice on lawn care, the use of chemicals, pruning, double-digging and other physical work along the lines of 'jobs for the weekend'. Sometimes there is even a feeling that the reader is being ordered about; that a smooth and weed-free lawn is every Englishman's duty and that the list of jobs really ought to be ticked off as completed unless one is at death's door. The best writers tend to leaven this potential tyranny of the reader with a little humour, however, or with a frank admission of their own failures and shortcomings.

At this time the aesthetics of the garden were either incidental or couched in terms of plants that are 'worthwhile', 'rewarding' or 'good value', with the emphasis strongly on shrubs. Herbaceous perennials, which have come to dominate garden writing today, were seen almost as fripperies, 'companion plants' to shrubs that were only worthy of noting in group lists of up to a dozen. A whole column on campanulas, for example, was a rarity indeed at this time. Trees were another popular topic – also an area of horticulture traditionally favoured by men. Gardening was much more about the broad sweep, as opposed to the fine detail, and it is noticeable how much smaller the range of plants then being discussed was, compared with the ever-expanding range of flowers with which today's serious gardener is expected to be familiar.

In the mid-twentieth century there was already a strong tradition of garden writing by women, of course, with Margery Fish and Vita Sackville-West only the most celebrated. But it was in the 1980s, when Gertrude Jekyll's books fell out of copyright and were reprinted, and authors such as Rosemary Verey and Penelope Hobhouse came to the fore, that herbaceous gardening for colour effect became de rigueur again. That led to a change in emphasis at the *Telegraph*, with herbaceous perennials suddenly deemed a worthwhile topic, and the Arts and Crafts spirit resurgent in English gardens. Rosemary Verey's piece on winter colour can be seen in this light, as can Robert Pearson's peroration on the use of grey- and silver-leaved plants (the fabled 'white garden' being conceived originally as a grey garden). The style of more recent garden columnists – notably Stephen Lacey, Ursula Buchan and Mary Keen, and in the *Sunday Telegraph* Elspeth Thompson – reflects this admixture of practical lore and horticultural connoisseurship. The love of roses had always been there, of course, and this anthology includes classic articles by Graham Stuart Thomas and Vita Sackville-West. And in recent years fruit and vegetables have become quite as fashionable as the latest star plant to hit Chelsea, as a new generation of allotmenteers and community gardeners comes of age.

Writing about flowers without recourse to cliché and sentiment is unexpectedly challenging, and Vita herself summed this up better than anyone in her foreword to *Some Flowers* (1937):

It is very difficult to write about flowers. I discovered this truth
only when I started to do so. Before I tried my hand at it myself, I
had done nothing but rail against those who were trying to do the
same thing. I found myself losing my temper frequently with the
nauseating sentimental phraseology which seems to impose itself on
all those otherwise sincere and honest gardeners who feel impelled
to transmit their knowledge... In a very short space I had to combine
the descriptive with the practical – petals, in fact, with slugs;
loveliness with manure; lavishness, with instructions for pruning.

The best writers can achieve this balance between practical advice
and lyrical appreciation – in the case of newspapers, all to a strict
deadline. This can lend the writing a freshness and spontaneity that
is sometimes missing in garden books. There is room here, too, for
individualistic or controversial opinion, since newsprint is still regarded
as being more ephemeral than the pages of a bound tome. Germaine
Greer and Sir Roy Strong – who come from different planets,
horticulturally speaking – are united at least by their ability to 'shoot
from the hip' in this way, their writing imbued with a strong sense of
personality. Of course, this notion that what appears in a newspaper is
'here today, gone tomorrow' has always been something of an illusion
(for one thing, the piece may end up in an anthology such as this). But
today the situation is almost reversed, now that most *Telegraph* garden
pieces also appear online, and therefore achieve a greater permanence,
and reach a far wider readership, than would have been the case in the
decades before the advent of the internet.

I suppose this theme of writing to order looms large for me today,
since the deadline for this introduction is suddenly upon me and I
find myself writing during a weekend away. As it happens the place
is Sissinghurst and the borrowed desk I am sitting at was Vita's, my
view through casement windows that of burnished orange echinacea,

crimson salvias, clipped yew and the beatific, wondering smiles of the visitors gliding by. Their expressions make me think, 'Does anything in life give as much pleasure as a beautiful garden?'

Last night, the white garden at midnight was a revelation. But that is not a subject to be enlarged upon now; I am going to write it up in the next day or two. It will, I hope, become another garden article fit for publication in the pages of the *Daily Telegraph*.

Tim Richardson

August 2013

1.

'Act rashly
whenever possible'

The Life of the Gardener

The seven ages of the gardener

By Anne Scott-James

This week some 180,000 of the keenest gardeners in Britain will glide through the turnstiles at Chelsea. Each will have a different target according to his tastes and interests. Some will hurry to the show gardens rich in brickwork and rhododendrons, others will crowd round the tropical rainforest, others again will be eager for a demonstration of the latest weapons in the pest war – perhaps a breakthrough in the form of a nuclear spray.

Each will have reached a particular stage in the development of a gardener, for I believe that there is a natural progression in a gardener's taste throughout his life – a toddler will not care for rare conifers, nor a prosperous man in middle age for buttercups and daisies.

Of course, many gardeners will not run the whole gamut, for they will find their ideal quite early in life. These men and women will create a garden in a certain style and stay with it, concentrating on good maintenance. But for those who live to old age through a variety of experiences, the course runs something like this.

Stage 1

Think back to your childhood, thoughtful parents having given you a plot of your own. Your favourite plants are quick growers which shoot up overnight, like radishes and Virginia stock. You are lucky with seeds and Daddy is slightly crusty because your radishes came crisp and fresh

to the table while his own first sowing failed. He points out that he did
your thinning and weeding. You like planting small bulbs, especially
yellow crocuses. You enjoy using the hose. You are a careless flower
picker, pulling the heads off primroses and adding one of mother's
rare fritillaries to your bunch of dandelions.

Stage 2

You have your first garden, which is probably a rectangle, but are not
yet interested in plants or design. You plan a garden which is mostly
lawn with geometric beds cut out for flowers, vegetables at the far end,
and a small metal greenhouse. You buy some elementary gardening
books and colourful catalogues which stuff your mind with planting
clichés – pink tulips with forget-me-nots, pansies with Hybrid Tea
roses, forsythia with everything. You consider a climbing rose against
the house, but decide against, as it will harbour earwigs and look untidy.
You buy some gargantuan bedding plants.

Technically, you learn fast and buy the best equipment. Your lawn
is better kept than it will ever be again, your hedge of *Lonicera nitida*
is trimmed to perfection, your roses never meet a greenfly. Your
vegetables are large and healthy – one parsnip will feed four – and you
are in danger of creating a tomato mountain.

Stage 3

You are now a social animal, possibly upwardly mobile, certainly
either married or otherwise paired off. The most important part
of your garden is the terrace, furnished with amazingly expensive
garden furniture, including a barbecue. This amenity has come a
long way from the simple little grill of Creole origin. Tiled in the
Portuguese manner, it has its own accessories and is hung about with
harpoons and pokers. There are garden umbrellas and some tubs of
flowers.

Beyond the sociable terrace, the scene varies. There may be a lawn and specimen magnolia, or a rose garden with trellis and arches, or a swimming pool with water so blue that it puts the Mediterranean to shame. There are no plants of particular notice.

Stage 4

You are in your late 30s or older and have changed a good deal. You have become aware of design and read John Brookes and Roy Strong. You know about siting a statuette or Lutyens seat as a focal point and how to cut up a flat garden by changing the levels or making a winding path to create mystery. Your plant knowledge is sophisticated and extends to foliage plants, ground-cover plants, winter plants and green-flowered plants. You prefer species to cultivars.

For plant associations you follow Graham Thomas. If your garden is large enough you plant a white-and-green enclosure, following Sissinghurst. You make an Elizabethan herb garden with brick paths and tiny box-edged beds filled with medieval herbs you will never use. You are a devotee of shrub roses, especially the old French kinds which get blackspot and flower once only.

You have now joined the vast unofficial society of garden visitors and learn much from the beautiful and varied gardens which are open to the public. You drive miles to obscure nurseries which sell choice plants which are rather short of roots. You read Robin Lane-Fox. You appreciate that Latin names are not an affectation, but an essential means of communication. You try to squash the silly woman who says with a conceited laugh 'plain English is good enough for me'.

Stage 5

You are even more aware of design. You feel the need of a vista and make a laburnum tunnel. You are attracted by historic formal gardening and plan an alley bordered by espalier fruit trees. You admire the play of light on water and make a pool fringed with *Iris laevigata*. You repaint the base of the swimming pool sea-green instead of blue. If you are making your first pool you tuck it out of sight and plant a yew hedge all around it, for it is now an anti-status symbol, a sop to the children who are oblivious to cold.

Your range of plant material is still expanding, especially upwards – every inch of the house is smothered in climbers. You grow a few rows of gourmet vegetables, such as Little Gem lettuces and Pink Fir Apple potatoes, realising that sprouts and onions are cheaper and better in the shops.

Stage 6

You are in the grip of ecology. You join in the preservationist societies and nurture plants which are disappearing from the wild.

This does not deter you from collecting plants abroad, although you castigate the grandchild who has been caught picking celandines on the village green. You encourage nettle for the butterflies and grow a patch of ragwort. You exchange rare plants with friends. You have a wild garden which proves more labour intensive than you expected.

Your little copse underplanted with spring flowers is a real pleasure, but your new meadow garden, urged on you by conservationists, has not yet proved its worth, the little orchids and poppies and cornflowers being engaged in a losing struggle against thistles and docks. You will have to hand-weed or keep a sheep.

Your colour taste becomes ever more subtle; the accent is on variegated plants, silver sub-shrubs and soft white roses which look their best in twilight.

Stage 7

You claim to feel young and healthy, but your knees and back are not very skittish. By a miracle your taste has changed so that you genuinely prefer the kind of gardening you can most easily do. You go into reverse about growing hundreds of different plants and filling every bit of earth with ground cover and you pare down your range to a very few good plants.

You get rid of rampant fillers like the periwinkles which smother your hellebores and learn to admire certain genera, such as primulas or hostas. You acquire a taste for trees grown singly and apart, as in an arboretum.

Above all, you want to go on learning, for this is one of the eternal joys of gardening. You have a secret scheme for an elegant conservatory leading to the fresh adventure of a warm, delightful plant-filled room. Here you will experiment with more tender and exotic plants than you have grown before; here you will study newly acquired books from your botanical library; here you will entertain in a scented paradise.

15 SEPTEMBER 1998

Do it, but do it your way

By Mirabel Osler

Gone are the lax days of August when the garden slumped and there was nothing to be done about it. In fact, it was a wonderful time of year when the greenery encroached on my thoughts, filling me with frivolous conjectures. One of the maddest of these is my dream of making an immense bridge spanning my back garden as an alternative to going upstairs and leaning out of the bathroom window whenever I want an aerial view of the design. But all that is over: now it's back to earth and forward planning.

September is the dreaded moment for looking at all those indecipherable, bossy messages telling me to get rid of an unkempt patch of Jerusalem sage, to stop buying more lacecap hydrangeas and, most crucially, to order bulbs before the end of winter.

Bulbs and trees have a natural symbiosis, so if you are facing your first gardening autumn, they are a good place to begin. If you haven't a tree, plant one. Plant two or three! Trees have priority over everything else; followed by the bulbs to go beneath them. Because the bulb genus is so large, you can experiment with them till you find the ones you like; those that suit your spirit as well as your garden. Gradually, I've come down in favour of tulips – Viridiflora and Parrots – their combination of streaks, edgings and feathering give me a chance to mess about as though I were using a paint box. Bulbs have an added advantage in that, when you've made a gaffe with, say, a dollop of sugar-icing pink ones in the wrong place, it can be rectified. This is not so easy with trees, although I have moved one of mine five times in four years.

I wish when I'd started to garden that someone had breathed confidence into me and told me to go for what I wanted and not be intimidated by notions of respectability. I know now that one can try anything. If it doesn't work, no matter. Try something else. Gardens are probably the most forgiving area of one's life. Relationships can't be transplanted, cut to the ground, manipulated and grouped together in any unorthodox manner you fancy in the way that plants can.

I knew of one gardener who chose plants by first considering how they died. She needed to be certain that by the end of the year she would be left with coppery leaves, sculptured seed heads and curiously shaped pods. Customary gardening dogma would have had her tidy them up; instead, she left them in situ. This may sound a droll way of gardening, but it worked. Because it was what she wanted she had the gumption to go for it, totally disregarding every tenet of gardening decorum.

In a small back garden, one unconventional gardener has made up for his lack of space by having nothing but pots and staging on which to display them. Like floral bookshelves, they rise up the walls – plants that require more sun take the top shelf, while those needing gloomy humidity lurk along the floor. There's just room for a table and chairs, making it as functional as those galley kitchens where, by swivelling on your heel, you have everything to hand.

One last plea for innovation. Play with colours, push out the frontiers of accepted practice, and act rashly whenever possible. Try shaping shrubs such as spirea or rosemary – even rue – into green boulders, and don't let shortage of space restrict your choice of roses. A rose called the 'Rambling Rector' has appeared by mistake in my garden; rather than evict him I shear him back every year so that his inclination for philandering is kept in check.

14 APRIL 1990

The Dixter approach: spring

By Christopher Lloyd

Easter is when the reluctant gardener pokes his nose out of doors like a dormouse emerging from hibernation and decides that conditions have now improved sufficiently to venture into the garden again.

You and I, of course, have been spasmodically busy throughout the winter, but I must admit to becoming more like the dormouse with the passing of the years. I have evolved a rationale to convince myself of the wisdom of not clearing, digging or indeed doing anything in my borders, apart from planting some bulbs, until this time of year.

The days are usually warmer – or at least longer. The birds are nesting and singing agreeably. There is an infectious sense of bustle and activity abroad in which the plants are sharing. The bulbs are through, so there is no longer the danger, as in autumn, of spearing them inadvertently with a fork (although there is of stepping back and squashing them). Most importantly, you can now see exactly where and what all the plants are – and if you left their tops on throughout the winter, you will also know how tall they grow.

I never clear plant debris till now. It has dried out during the winter and is light and easy to remove to the compost heap. Phlox stems break off with the snap of a freshly baked cracker. The aconitums are already lying on the ground and simply need to be gathered, while the tougher cardoons and *Artemisia lactiflora* need cutting. Do this as low as you can get with the secateurs, leaving no stumps. I am most particular about this. Stumps have jagged edges which will tear your skin next time you are working among them, and they become hollow and offer shelter to earwigs.

Ladybirds are out in force by now and are one of the most effective weapons against aphid infestation. Last year, after an incredibly mild winter, we were told that there would be a superabundance of pests. But there was also an abundance of ladybirds. Just as the aphids seemed to multiply dangerously, they vanished.

All the same, there are times in spring when I feel bound to take action against aphids to protect the young growth on a few of my plants, notably the hellebores, euphorbias, lupins, honeysuckles and certain viburnums such as *Viburnum carlesii* and *V. opulus* (the guelder rose), whose leaves otherwise become hopelessly deformed. I do not spray my roses at all.

But to return to border-tidying: there are some plants with which you should never lose patience. It is sometimes tempting to give a yank to an old peony or euphorbia stem, or to a derelict leaf of *Helleborus orientalis*, but these will come away from the plant together with the young shoot bud at the base, and you will be filled with remorse for what you have done.

Those hellebore (Lenten rose) leaves certainly need removing, together with their stalks. Kniphofias, with their long, lanky foliage, are always a nuisance, but it is safe to shorten them back by half. They are among the plants which seldom need to be disturbed – once in seven or eight years, perhaps – but if you do want to make another patch, now is the time. Use single crowns – they will soon make multiples.

The woody-stemmed *Kniphofia caulescens*, which is chiefly valuable as a dramatic foliage plant, makes a pineapple bouquet of glaucous foliage and looks all the better for being divided and reset as single crowns every other year. It can be used as a corner-piece in the same way as yuccas and bergenias.

Bergenias themselves tend to be replanted far too seldom. Having the reputation of no trouble, evergreen ground cover, they are just left to get on with it from year to year, becoming ever more woody and flowering only at the margins of an old planting. Give them a break. Dig the whole lot out and replant with single pieces, so that the tuft of leaves is at ground level with no stem showing.

Most ground cover will benefit from being replanted in improved soil from time to time: *Geranium macrorrhizum* is a good example (the one with a strong aroma of oil of geranium), though you could leave this until it has flowered. It will often show its appreciation by flowering again during the summer.

Split and replant your pulmonarias after they have flowered. Their mottled or silvered foliage is often their main asset and this improves greatly after thinning and resetting. The same goes for varieties of *Lamium maculatum* such as 'White Nancy', 'Chequers' and 'Beacon Silver'. The first seems immune to mildew, which afflicts the others. *Stachys lanata* (lamb's lugs) is very susceptible to mildew and I advise growing something else to do the same job – *Artemisia canescens*, for instance, with its tangled whorls of silver-grey wire.

A garden notebook is essential for keeping a record of what you have planted, where and when. It offers an alternative to labelling plants. I do not like the look of labels; if they are made to last they are expensive, if not, they constantly need replacing – and if they outlive the plant they are a reminder of its demise. A name in a notebook can soon be memorised and noting the dates of planting will remind you when to replant.

Spread the work of replanting evenly over ten years so that a few phloxes (or hostas, hemerocallis or whatever) will be split and reset in improved soil each year. In this piecemeal way, you ensure that your borders will never have an off year.

Some perennials such as sunflower (helianthus) and the Michaelmas daisy, *Aster novi-belgii*, carry more imposing flower panicles if they are replanted every year, using single shoots and spacing them 12in (30cm) apart. The best and safest time to replant many subjects that would resent disturbance in the autumn is just as they are starting into new growth. This is notably true of ornamental grasses and bamboos which are shrubby grasses. You must keep their roots damp at every stage and water them in generously.

A good time to mess about with ferns is just as their new fronds are about to unfurl. Those like dryopteris and polystichum (the male shield ferns), which make dense lumps of tightly knit crowns, are quite hard work to divide, but they look much better once separated into single crowns, with the fronds on one crown no longer interfering with those of its neighbours. These ferns can be imaginatively grouped near to simple, broad-leaved perennials like hostas and bergenias.

You might think this is a bad time to be disturbing the Rhizomatous Bearded irises – so soon before they should be flowering in May and June – but that depends; if their colonies have become a tangled, unproductive mass, they will scarcely flower anyway. If you replant now, using only the strongest pieces from the outside of the old colony, your irises will have the whole growing season in which to re-establish, and they will flower well next year. But if you wait until after their problematic flowering this year and replant them in July they will not be strong enough to make much of a show in 1991.

There is a strong temptation to replant irises too deeply, to ensure that they are firm enough to stand up against the wind. But you must never lose sight of the piece of rhizome beneath each fan of leaves. It must remain at the soil surface. The iris can be made to take in sail by cutting down the leaf fan by half.

If there is a problem with perennial weeds in your borders, you really must attack them for a whole growing season before replanting with your own perennials (which harbour weeds among their roots). Wait until couch grass, ground elder or bindweed are growing strongly, then treat them with glyphosate (Murphy's tumbleweed, for example), but do not exceed the recommended dose.

The idea is for the plant to take the chemical into its whole system, so that roots as well as top are killed. If you just burn off the top by exceeding the dose, the roots will grow again. Tough customers such as ground elder may show up again later in the season and require a second treatment. But glyphosate really works and is a great boon to the hard-pressed gardener.

Problems with the secateurs-in-handbag brigade

By Oliver Pritchett

We were at the scene of the crime. It was by this wall, in a sunny position, that *Mutisia decurrens* was last seen alive about three weeks ago. Now there was just a bare patch of earth. We were at the Royal Horticultural Society's gardens, at Wisley in Surrey, and Tony Lowe, general secretary of the National Council for the Preservation of Plants and Gardens, was pointing to another example of the botanical crime wave. *Mutisia decurrens* – a sort of climbing daisy – had been abducted.

Many perfectly respectable people – perhaps even *Sunday Telegraph* readers – have, from time to time, helped themselves to a cutting, a few seeds or a small plant from a public garden. Mr Lowe regards such people as The Worst of Garden Pests.

In a powerful article in the Council's newsletter, Mr Lowe writes: 'This pest is not only a parasite but a braggart. How often have you heard a friend proudly boast that he "acquired" that plant while on holiday or while visiting such and such a garden. Were you to brand him a common thief and put him in the same category as a supermarket shoplifter he would be offended for he is a gardener, a superior breed, and anyway "It's been done for years – everybody does it." Do they? Should they? Should we encourage the petty thief?'

Mr Lowe has certainly raised a startling point. I had always supposed gardening enthusiasts to be the most law-abiding people. Is it time perhaps to start a crimewatch radio programme called *Gardeners Interrogation Time*? I looked at those respectable, comfortable people in the Wisley rock garden. Which one was Chummy? Were those people married couples or villains working in pairs?

Many offenders go to gardens armed with plastic bags, secateurs and small hand forks, Mr Lowe said. Or they take a teaspoon for digging up small plants. Jane Taylor, his deputy, added: 'One gets suspicious of ladies with capacious handbags, and capacious macs.'

'It has become an accepted crime,' Mr Lowe said.

'It is almost a national sport,' Jane Taylor added. 'Pillars of the WI who would never dream of entering your house and taking the silver will strip your garden bare.'

There are two categories of plant and cutting removers. There are those who admire a plant and discreetly take a cutting, then there are the more organised, expert thieves who go for the rare plants and know exactly what they are looking for. 'They are very knowledgeable and acquisitive,' Jane Taylor said. 'It is a sort of stamp-collecting mentality.'

Wisely holds the National Collection of snowdrops – more than 300 varieties – but the list of them is guarded carefully and some of them are kept out of the way in a 'stockade'.

I asked Mr Lowe if ever he felt tempted when he went into a garden. 'I go round with my hands in my pockets,' he said. 'The temptation is enormous.'

We strolled round the marvellous Wisley gardens, admiring its attractions. With so many secluded areas you can see how easy it would be to take something without being noticed. We paused by some lovely flowers and a label which said 'Colchicum – Violet Queen'. Mr Lowe kept his hands in his pockets.

In the Alpine House there was a notice warning that an electronic alarm system was in operation and asking visitors to keep to the path. The dwarf cyclamen bloomed unmolested.

Other precautions have been suggested. Mr Lowe, in the newsletter, proposed that a mesh buried three inches under the soil would become entwined with the roots of the small plants so that digging them up would become a messy operation. Bamboo rods can also be planted through a plant's root ball system. The layout of public gardens can be organised to keep rare plants out of secluded areas and to allow for a 'cordon sanitaire' between walkways and flower beds. Such crime-prevention gardening calls for a new garden designer, a sort of Culpability Brown.

The most fascinating solution was suggested by Jane Taylor. It suggests a whole new specialisation in Deterrent Horticulture. If you sow *Loasa vulcanica* round your precious plants you will find that it not only has a pretty flower but also a nasty sting for anyone who tries to tamper with it. Members of the blumenbachia family will serve the same bodyguard function. She also suggested *Fascicularia pitcairnifolia* for its helpful spikes, toothed the wrong way like a shark's mouth, or perhaps a nice vicious *Aciphylla*. Faced with all these italics, I had, for a moment, an unworthy urge to go and steal a Latin dictionary from a public library.

John Simmons, the curator of the Royal Botanic Gardens at Kew, agreed that the theft of plants was an increasing problem. 'Alpines are particularly vulnerable,' he said. They now have closed-circuit TV in the Alpine House and glass screens to protect the orchids, cacti and carnivorous plants. 'It is a natural appetite in society to have something which is rare and scarce,' he said. 'It's a bit sad, really.' Kew has its own police station, manned by 22 members of the Royal Botanic Gardens Constabulary; it also has electronic security devices and a contract with a security firm. Mr Simmons also said that Kew had, from time to time, been a victim of people systematically taking rare and important plants and knowing exactly what they were looking for.

John Sales, chief garden adviser to the National Trust, says the problem of theft increases as the number of visitors grows.

Some people who steal a cutting cannot be bothered to copy out the complicated name from the label so they steal the label as well. 'There is a different morality applied to gardens as opposed to houses,' he said.

The solution, he said, was in the strategic placing of rare plants and of having more wardens who would not just watch over visitors but try to help and educate them.

'In the National Trust we feel very anxious about putting up lots of notices to tick people off in advance and make them feel unwelcome,' he said. 'We want them to enjoy their visit and not to feel got at.'

Interestingly enough, some of the worst offenders appear to be coach parties organised by gardening clubs. 'It is almost a game with them to see who can come away with the most cuttings,' said Michael Calnan, another gardens adviser to the National Trust.

The National Trust has even had urns stolen. And there is a story of a lady who was caught in the act of digging up a plant. When she was challenged she said: 'It's quite all right – I'm a member.'

A couple of days ago on the TV programme *Gardeners' World*, Clay Jones was seen in Lanhydrock, in Cornwall, demonstrating how to take a cutting from a camellia. Within two weeks that particular plant was entirely stripped by enthusiastic gardeners.

The thing about plants and cuttings is that they should be a gift not loot, a mark of a friendship not a guilty secret, part of an exchange not swag. As Jane Taylor said: 'If you want a plant, give a plant. If you go to a garden take some beads for the natives.' In the meantime, beware of *Fascicularia pitcairnifolia*.

15 APRIL 2006

Loony gardening

By Lila Das Gupta

How do we calculate when Easter falls? It's the first Sunday after the first full moon following the vernal equinox. It's strange to think that one of our most important religious festivals is governed by the moon, because we pay so little attention to it in other parts of our lives. But for a select group of gardeners, it governs everything they do.

One of the best known proponents of 'moon gardening' is John Harris, head gardener at the 200-acre Tresillian estate near Newquay in Cornwall. John has been preparing his beds, sowing and harvesting his crops by the phases of the moon for more than 40 years. And before you write him off as loopy, think again: once he has planted his crops in the Victorian walled vegetable garden, he never waters them – drought or no drought, they're on their own.

John's affinity with plants started long ago. His father died when he was 11, and, as the eldest child, he took on the family allotment. By the time he left school at 15 he had acquired four plots. Then in the 1950s, he became an apprentice on a big estate under a head gardener who put the fear of God into his underlings. Everything had to be done just so.

You can see the effects of this traditional training on the Tresillian estate. The lawns are immaculately kept, the beds neat and tidy, and beyond this the 35 acres of garden have been skilfully restored in a naturalistic way. Even Mr Harris's potting shed is a sight to behold; all the old tools are beautifully kept – clean, oiled and ready for use.

But beneath this conventional exterior lies a man whose knowledge of folklore has won him a dedicated band of admirers. He has advised water-starved farmers in northern India, trained ex-offenders, and regularly broadcasts on BBC Cornwall (also available on the internet), where he gets callers from as far afield as Denmark and Australia.

John says he took up moon gardening after studying the ways of Native Americans. The theory is that the moon exerts a gravitational pull on the earth's water table, which is highest during a full moon. So, vegetables that produce below the ground – root crops such as potatoes, carrots or beetroot – are best planted in the new moon, and crops above ground – spinach, corn or tomatoes and the like, or any flowers – should be planted in the moon's first quarter, when the water table is rising.

In addition to lunar planting, John also uses a 'deep bed' system in the vegetable gardens, which means plants require no additional watering. In the autumn, a 90cm by 90cm (3ft by 3ft) pit is dug and the soil removed. The bottom is then filled with twiggy material, followed by a layer of green kitchen waste, more aerating material, and then some manure, and so on.

No layer is ever more than a few inches thick. The bed is never trodden on, so it won't become compacted, and is made slightly lower than the surrounding earth, so that it can catch rainwater from the top as well as water raised by the moon from below. In a garden or vegetable plot at home, John thinks it is enough to dig one spit deep, as this will still be beneficial to your fruit and vegetables. Most of this work is completed by the end of autumn, but there is still time to prepare beds for crops that go in later, such as marrows, pumpkins and squashes.

At Tresillian, the varieties grown are exclusively 'heritage', many supplied by seed specialist Thomas Etty (www.thomasetty.co.uk).

'Kentucky Wonder' (1850) and 'Pea' or 'Frost' beans (1828) are recommended varieties of climbing French bean. 'Lazy Housewife' (1810) is also available in dwarf variety. Everything is organically produced, relying on companion planting for pest control; for example, Mexican marigold (*Tagetes minuta*) will deter eelworm when planted among potatoes.

If you are ever lucky enough to be visiting the south-west, I suggest you book on one of John's tours. He is a remarkable and engaging man who offers insights into so much more than gardening.

The lingua flora

By Stephen Lacey

I failed my Latin O-level at the first attempt and I only passed the second time because, miraculously, the piece set for translation was one I had done just a few weeks before. Seventeen years later, I find that half my conversation is in Latin. I have to write it and read it. For Latin, blended with Greek and other tongues, is the language of plant names and, without it, keen gardeners are unable to communicate.

Novice gardeners assume that botanical Latin is used only to impress and to keep them in their place; and, sometimes, they are right. I know quite a few sweet old battleaxes who counter visitors' tentative queries by drowning them in a torrent of six-syllable names. These ladies are definitely using the language to intimidate not to enlighten.

The way to trip them up is to question their pronunciation. No one is on safe ground when it comes to speaking Latin. There is an 'accepted' way of pronouncing it but few people have studied it thoroughly and, in any case, there are any amount of anomalies.

People educated at public schools stretch and raise the vowel sounds and speak it with an accent which they like to think Roman patricians would have used. My Oxford tutor, called upon to speak on ceremonial occasions, coloured his Latin with a heavy Italian accent and pronounced 'c' like 'ch' when appropriate, his theory being, he said, that the Romans came from Italy.

Most of the time, botanical Latin is used because there is no alternative. There are common English names for only a small percentage of garden plants and many of these simply identify a group, not an individual. All forms of digitalis are called foxgloves; all forms of oenothera are called evening primroses.

Even less helpfully, the common names can vary from locality to locality, from country to country. A plant maybe called 'southernwood' by one person, 'lad's love' by another and 'old man' by another. Call it *Artemisia abrotanum* and we all know what is meant and can look it up in a reference book.

'Do you have a gas plant?' I was once asked by an American gardener. No, I replied, imagining this to be another expensive installation – perhaps for heating fish ponds or garden seats in cold weather – which all Americans have and I haven't. In fact, he was talking about *Dictamnus albus*, that inflammable perennial which we call burning bush, or dittany, or fraxinella.

Getting to grips with botanical Latin looks a daunting task but you can take it gently, gradually committing to memory the names of the plants in your own garden; and you will find that the more names you learn, the easier it becomes and the quicker you will absorb new ones.

As important as the determination to learn is the presence of a stooge. You must have someone to practise on, a person who will be suitably impressed each time a new mouthful of Latin is disgorged. Ideally, he or she will be entirely ignorant of plants and will never have studied classics. You do not want to be corrected continually, you want only admiration and encouragement.

To help you get started, you will need a reference book with phoenetic spelling. I recommend *The Dictionary of Plant Names* by Allen J. Coombes (Collingridge), a pocket-sized book which you can whip out while your stooge's back is turned. As well as giving the accepted pronunciations for a long list of garden plants, it also tells you what the names mean and their derivation.

Funnily enough, understanding what I am saying has played no part in the learning process for me. I would be hard pressed to translate or explain half the Latin I speak. I learn plant names just as I learn people's names, by matching words and faces.

The old drinks' party trick of repeating the name of your new acquaintance as you talk to him works well for plants, too, by the way.

30 APRIL 2011

Why I hate gardening

By Anne Wareham

I hate gardening. I have four acres of garden to make and care for practically single handed, and the work involved is – work. I recently sat in a hall full of worthy garden professionals and RHS members who were debating 'Is gardening still core to the British way of life?' Speaker after speaker got up and extolled the virtues and delights of gardening. I felt as if I were on a foreign planet.

Outside it had been pouring with rain for weeks. Everything was sodden and disintegrating, and I needed to get out there because there were things that had to be done. It was cold, wet and horrible – and so would I be by the time I came in.

Can anyone seriously enjoy planting bulbs? I wasn't made with a hinge in my back, and my left hip is beginning to protest loudly at the pressure exerted by plunging the bulb planter. A quarter of garden work is probably planting things; half of it is cutting things down, cutting them back and pulling them out. This is relentless: I no sooner cut things down than they're up again. It's as bad as weeding, which at least, as a glyphosate user, I can do standing up. How on earth can the organic lot, condemned to their knees in a truly endless task of pulling things out, enjoy gardening? Are they deluded? Don't they notice? Are they endlessly worshipping their weeds?

Gardening is talked-up housework that you have to do outside. It has everything in common with housework, even some of the tools. I have a vacuum cleaner that I use indoors and out since it sucks up wet as happily as dry. Gardening has a great deal of the same objectives as housework and is mostly depressingly judged on the same kind of criteria – is it neat and tidy and is it weed-free, alongside is it neat and tidy and is it dust-free? It has the same sort of status except among the seriously sad.

Gardening is boring. It is repetitious, repetitive and mind-blowingly boring, just like housework. All of it – sowing seeds, mowing, cutting hedges, potting up, propagating – is boring, and all of it requires doing over and over again.

If there are enjoyable jobs, they're mostly enjoyable for the result not the process. There is no actual intellectual content to the task itself, even if there may be in the planning and designing.

So, if there is something wrong in my world, if an editor has snubbed me or a call centre driven me round the bend, I find myself obsessing. I think we are supposed to be delighting in being out in the open air, communing with nature, but me, I'll be obsessing, writing rude letters in my head. Wishing I were comfortably indoors writing rude letters.

There was even talk in this RHS debate about the great virtues of double digging. Double digging is not only bad for your back (and boring): it is totally unnecessary. It's a kind of horticultural joke and does more harm to the soil than good. Why are we promoting masochism?

The RHS has also been terribly keen on getting children interested in gardening, indeed this is a preoccupation among many gardeners and garden professionals. I have absolutely no idea why. It's a hopeless career for all but the totally dedicated.

And as a hobby? Who pursues that which was shoved at them in youth? And why does it matter whether they do or don't? I asked why it was important to get children gardening on Twitter and got a variety of answers: to make them love the earth; it's good exercise; so parents can have help weeding and spend time outside without the children complaining (why would the children care where their parents are as long as they're off their backs?); to teach patience, and many other, unspecified lessons.

I have a wide range of followers on Twitter, including artists, foodies, interior designers, historians and politicians, and what was striking was that while the gardeners on Twitter broke out into a hot clamour of tweets about all the different reasons why children should garden, not one non-gardener thought it mattered at all.

And I still, despite all the clamour, don't understand why there is such evangelical zeal. What other pursuit, however worthy, is inflicted on children in this way? Plenty of time to discover the delights and horrors of gardens when you're grown up.

There are enemies out there in the garden, too. Not just the neighbours, who have to restrain themselves from throwing bricks at our garden visitors because they find them so irritating. No – the 'wildlife'. In this part of the world we have rabbits, deer, wild boar, squirrels, panthers, rats – you name something that the British Isles fosters and which is damaging to gardens, and we have it. Just down the road in the Forest of Dean they have rambling sheep wandering the roads and gardens; some people get visitations from cows, and this doesn't do the vegetation much good at all.

And a shadow hangs over all: how will I cope with all this gardening in 10 or 20 years' time? What kind of nightmare have I created for myself because I cannot contemplate leaving this place? I find it hard enough to go away for the night. And should I care that it will all change after I'm gone, when it might well get gardened by idiots or built over? I know I'm not supposed to, but I do.

I realise that at this point I'm supposed, by the rules of rhetoric, to relent and acknowledge in a gently humorous way that I am really one of the gang, and I do really like getting out there and dirty. Well, sometimes it's not as bad as I think it will be.

Mostly it offers a sense of relief from the oppression of knowing a job needs doing and is sitting there waiting. Usually, job done, I come in with a sense of relief, and that is a pleasure. And a sense of exhaustion, which can be another kind of pleasure. The best bit is the hot bath.

What I do like is a garden, and I have no other means of obtaining one. In a gardening world obsessed with plants and with the delights of gardening, this puts me in a very small minority. But for me the point is the product.

Not a showplace for plants. Not an outdoor gym. Not even a nature reserve. A garden, designed and planted to give delight to the eye and the realisation of a fantasy about what could possibly be made with the shape of the land, with plants, with the work of the seasons and the weather. This is the point of it all and it is worth all the rest – just. I think. Maybe. Yes.

Things I don't do

Turn my compost heap
Wash my pots
Clean my garden tools
Edge the grass
Grow my own vegetables
Dig up plants and divide them
Put out slug traps
Spike, weedkill, aerate, topdress, remove moss from, worm-kill, water or roll the lawn
Graft
Dig
Lime
Clean the greenhouse

Remove any leaves from borders
Remove anything from borders – just leave it to rot where it grew
Label plants
Mulch at some particular time of year

Things I don't often do

Feed plants in borders
Sharpen my tools
Deadhead
Prune
Stake (except vampires)

 20 JANUARY 1990

Every flower a friend and every tree a lover

By Anne Scott-James

There is no place like a garden for intensifying human emotions. In my own garden, I never plod methodically through my tasks, thinking dull thoughts. I am either in a happy dream, imagination soaring into the flowery realms of paradise, or I am in black despair over plans which have failed. Or I am laughing at some gardener's joke, or cursing blunt tools or impertinent caterpillars. Indeed, I must look pretty mad to anyone peering over the hedge as I groan or chuckle while I prune or plant. The point is, in my garden I am more than usually sentient.

Therefore, a good gardening book must, to my mind, be a blend of information with feeling. The information is important. I cannot bear sloppy books, with stale precepts or inaccurate spelling of plant names. Luckily, there are plenty of gardening books which are quite excellent on facts, though this alone does not make them great. It is the author's power to communicate the moods and experiences of the gardener's world, with its affinity to both men and nature, which lifts a book above the crowd.

The garden book I have read most often is *Elizabeth and Her German Garden*, by Elizabeth von Arnim, a brilliant, beautiful, egotistical woman, also something of a sexual wrecker, who married first time round a bad-tempered Prussian count whom she refers to throughout as the 'Man of Wrath'.

Elizabeth made her garden in the 1890s in north Germany, a flat, sandy land of cornfields, birches and pines, so cold in winter that the Baltic freezes and transport is by sleigh. The house was an old convent 'with dandelions up to the very door', the nearest town an afternoon away. The locals were either eccentric or stodgy. The gardener carried a spade in one hand and a revolver in the other.

The nearest female neighbour was 'an expert on sausage-making, the care of calves, and the slaughtering of swine', whose children had white plaits and thick legs. But Elizabeth called this unpromising environment her kingdom of heaven.

She had a genuine passion for the natural world and here she made a garden of a wildish kind, full of roses, poppies, pinks, columbines and lavender, with 'every flower and weed a friend and every tree a lover'.

She spent whole days in the garden, eating 'meals so simple that they could be brought out to the lilacs on a tray'. Visits from her censorious husband in the city were dreaded, though she seems to have loved her three little daughters at that time, gratifyingly charming in black stockings and sunbonnets. Elizabeth's prose is so acidulous, yet poetic, that this is one of the best bedside books in the world.

Humour of a kindlier nature draws me to *The Gardener's Year*, by the Czech playwright, Karel Capek, published in English in 1931. Capek owned a small suburban garden and he recorded the everyday experiences which may seem trivial to the outsider, but are momentous to the 'real gardener' for whom the book is written. His first plant was a house-leek; his first discovery was that a plant can grow 'from under the seed upwards, lifting its seed on its head like a cap. Think if a child should grow carrying its mother on its head'. He sows a lawn with expensive seed and up comes a crop of thistles. He waters the garden and the hose attacks him like a monster from the sea.

Capek finds that gardeners recognise each other by some secret sign in any environment, even a dentist's waiting-room. Two men in dress suits at the theatre do not discuss the play, but artificial manures, aphis, asters and Dutch lilies. This is gardening as I know it.

Moving from the ridiculous to the sublime, I am carried away by *On the Eaves of the World*, by Reginald Farrer. Farrer was a plant-hunter, not the greatest of his time as a collector, but the best as a descriptive writer, whose travels in remotest China and Tibet during the First World War must surely raise the blood pressure of the tamest tourist. The discovery of a new plant raises him to ecstasy.

'Through the foaming shallows of the copse I plunged, and soon was holding my breath with excitement as I neared my goal, and it became more and more certain that I was setting eyes on *Paeonia moutan* as a wild plant … Here in the brushwood it grew up tall and slender and straight, in two or three unbranching shoots, each of which carried at the top, elegantly balancing, that single enormous blossom … of absolute pure white, with featherings of deepest maroon radiating from the base of the petals from the boss of golden fluff at the flower's heart … For a long time I remained in worship, and returned downwards at last in the dusk in high contentment.'

The 17th century was a century of delight and the word is often used by William Lawson in *A New Orchard and Garden*, the first classic of the small garden, written in 1618 in the same lovely newborn prose as King James's Bible.

Lawson was a Yorkshireman and his book is a practical manual illustrated with useful woodcuts, but the didactic message overflows into the pleasures of nightingales, sweet-smelling flowers, shady walks, trees in blossom and fishing in the garden stream.

The book ran into some 10 editions in the 17th century and I am the lucky possessor of a facsimile of the third edition, printed in Monotype Cochin on handmade paper and bound in vellum, published by the Cresset Press in 1927. It took me three years to find a copy and it cost a bomb, but was worth every penny. It is a joy to handle and to read. This, and earlier editions, can be enjoyed at specialist libraries.

The Education of a Gardener, by Russell Page, is a thoughtful, indeed a difficult, book which must be read with concentration. It falls into a rare category of garden literature, a book on the aesthetics of landscape gardening, and it is very good indeed. First published in 1962, it was a landmark in this century of plantsmanship, a book by an architect about scale, light, shape and colour in relationship to plants; about the placing of water and stone; the importance of trees. Though the gardens which Russell Page created were of the grandest, his judgments hold truths for every gardener.

Once upon a time, when I was young, I was up to the neck in the classics. In the course of a strenuous life, most of my knowledge has slipped away, but so long as I can read I will return from time to time to Homer and Virgil, usually in that prop of old age, a Loeb edition. I list Virgil's *The Georgics* as my last book.

Though ostensibly didactic, *The Georgics* are really about the pleasures of farming and gardening, a hymn to country life. In Virgil, natural things are so alive that they are almost capable of human feeling – the moon blushes, the birds enjoy their chicks, the olive tree is lively, the soil rejoices or mourns. His poetic images stay forever in my mind and I never fail to think of Virgil's 'joyful bees' when I hear bees buzzing on my lavender, muffling the din of Concorde streaking overhead.

19 MARCH 1943

VISITOR DROPS IN

Mrs Harold Nicolson (V. Sackville-West, the poet), had a surprise visitor at her country place, Sissinghurst Castle, Kent, the other day. A Royal Air Force pilot landed his airplane in a nearby field and asked permission to see over the Castle.

He told her that when he spotted it from the air he recognised it from photographs which were published in a magazine last year. So he came down to have a closer inspection.

Mrs Nicolson showed him the house and grounds. But she forgot to ask him to sign the visitors' book, and is unaware of his identity.

The distinctive feature of Sissinghurst Castle is its soaring red-brick tower. The rest of the place was in ruins when Mrs Nicolson bought it about 12 years ago. It has been skilfully restored. There is a beautiful garden, which Mrs Nicolson planned and looks after herself.

Both the Nicolson sons are overseas with the Army. Mrs Nicolson is the local organiser for the Women's Land Army.

FAMILY PHRASES

To the editor of The Daily Telegraph

Sir, – The phrase 'through leaves', mentioned by the Hon. V. Sackville-West in her broadcast as an expression in her family to denote pleasure or satisfaction, reminded me of the expression 'sloshy', used in our family with exactly the same meaning.

It was derived from the childish enjoyment of biting into a sloshy, juicy William pear, causing, unless the utmost caution were exercised, the juice to run down over one's chin. It might be 'Oh, how sloshy', or 'that will be sloshy', or just a murmured 'sloshy' if something you were doing was going well.

Yours faithfully,

E. C. Allfree

Birchington, Kent

2.
'Ruby-petalled flowers hang like jewels'

Joy in Variety of Blossom

Advice from the greatest flower connoisseur

By Graham Stuart Thomas

For all the inspiration of the wonders put on show by the specialist growers who gather at Chelsea, few people would be content with a garden of their own devoted to one genus of plants, regardless of how many varieties could be assembled. We gardeners like our gardens to yield flowers and interest throughout the year: our delight is found not only in variety but also in blending plant forms and the colours of flowers and foliage.

Early in the year we welcome the joyous daffodils but these reveal their greatest beauty when combined with blue and purple flowers, the scillas and grape hyacinths in particular. The same is felt when, at the end of June and early July, the old French roses of the 19th century are in full flower. It seems inappropriate to call them old fashioned because fresh blooms come every day and week, year after year. Yet, because nothing to resemble them has been raised since, they are unique in the floral world in shape, colour, scent and vigour, and undoubtedly have a period touch. But I think they need other plants with them: they need contrast of shape and a blending of colours.

The old roses make large rounded bushes and cover their rather dark, dull foliage with hundreds of blooms at midsummer. Their colours embrace a few whites but the majority are of some shade of pink, mauve-pink, grey-purple and maroon, with a few striped ones thrown in, like candy among pearls. There is a richness to be obtained from a planting of the old Gallica, Alba, Damask, Centifolia and Moss sections, shrubs of some 4 to 6ft, which cannot be obtained from any other group of plants – but their season is short, a few weeks at most.

However, we must not forget that the same may be said about many of our favourite shrubs – forsythias, azaleas, rhododendrons, lilacs and many others – and few have the range of colouring and scent of the old French roses. They burst upon us at the very crown of the year, soon after the longest day, to herald in all the richest scents that crowd our senses and those of the insects. (This is what we have done on a large scale in the garden of Mottisfont Abbey, Hampshire, where the National Trust's collection of old roses has been assembled.)

It is pretty obvious that we shall have to be careful in our selection of companion plants for flowering with the old roses. White, pale yellow and lavender-blues are the principal requirements, to act as soft contrasts and complements to the pervading mauves and pinks. We need also contrast of line and tint of foliage; any plant with grey or glaucous leaves will prove to be admirable foils to the rose's foliage and flowers – such as various artemisias, Jackman's Blue rue, pinks and carnations and Stachys byzantina (*S. olympica*). And the bearded irises give us one old stalwart in lavender-blue whose bright grey leaves remain in beauty till autumn.

This brings me to the importance of line. Most of the roses – and indeed many other shrubs and plants – are of a rounded, rather dumpy outline, with a copious spotting of small leaves and flowers. Not only do they need the mellowing effect of grey foliage, but also tall spikes such as are provided by *Campanula latiloba alba*, *Dictamnus albus*, the Madonna lily (plant only in early August), irises of the orientalis section and, so important, white foxgloves. The foxgloves are not perennials but sow themselves abundantly, sometimes in the right places. Many seedlings – they take two years to flower – will revert to the usual rosy-purple tint. Although lovely, this is not what we want for our colour scheme. Fortunately when the young plants are in full growth in April it will be found that those which are going to be white have paler green leaves than the purplish ones which have a smear of grey-mauve on the backs of the leaf stalks.

The uplift provided by these erect plants can be supplemented by white-flowering shrubs, such as Philadelphus 'Belle Etoile', and also the vertical slender spikes of *Sisyrinchium striatum* with small straw-yellow flowers. As for lavender-blues, we need hardly look further than *Campanula persicifolia* and its white form, the catmints (nepeta), the purple-leafed sage (salvia) and *Salvia haematodes*, which rises to 4ft.

Armed with such a palette as this, our group of old roses can be enhanced at flowering time. Groups of short-growing, late-flowering plants, notably *Aster thomsonii nanus* and *Anaphalis triplinervis* and a few colchicums and fuchsias, will carry on until autumn.

For spring there are all the smaller bulbs, to extend from the snowdrops in February, through crocus season, to *Scilla* 'Spring Beauty' and many short daffodils.

The beauty of it all is that there never need be a dull moment in such a scheme. Nor do the roses seem to be discouraged by such competition. The grape-purple of 'Cardinal de Richelieu' and 'Capitaine John Ingram'; crimson of 'Surpasse Tout' and 'Henri Martin'; pink of 'Céleste' and 'Maiden's Blush' and mauve of 'Belle de Crécy' and 'President de Sèze' will enchant us every year.

And here is a bonus for everyone: the equally beautiful varieties of the Portland and Bourbon sections flower again towards autumn.

Wildflowers as garden plants

By Noël Kingsbury

I was told a tale once about an Indian maharajah who, on visiting an English country house, was delighted to spend an afternoon being shown round his host's garden. At the end of the tour the host asked him what he had liked most. 'The little white flowers scattered across the grass,' was the reply. The host was delighted but uneasy because, as far as he was concerned, the daisies in the lawns were weeds and a sign of poor groundsmanship.

Whereas once any wild plant that appeared in the garden was regarded as a weed, attitudes have now changed and many gardeners actively encourage wild flowers. Often, particularly in country gardens, wild flowers introduce themselves, forming attractive and spontaneous combinations with garden plants. They add a distinctly relaxed touch that is impossible to achieve with bedding plants, let alone by deliberate planning. But beware – there is a fine line between attractive effects and having a garden overrun with wild flowers: they may need occasional management to keep them within bounds.

Daisies (*Bellis perennis*) are common lawn weeds and you only have to leave areas of grass uncut for a couple of weeks in late spring to let them flower. They may be joined by the china blue Persian speedwell (*Veronica persica*) – an attractive combination. In my garden I find this pair often crop up in flower beds where they make a good accompaniment to bulbs and early herbaceous plants such as pulmonarias. Since their growth is light they don't pose any serious competition to other plants. Later, in June and July, the purple flowers of self-heal (*Prunella vulgaris*) can be a colourful feature in lawns and borders, but its growth is more vigorous and you may wish to thin out plants that take up too much space in borders.

Primroses (*Primula vulgaris*) often appear by themselves in country gardens in the wetter parts of Britain, or a few plants can be bought from a garden centre and left to self-sow in shaded places. Their green-yellow flowers are a welcome sight in spring before they become semi-dormant after June, a fact that makes it feasible to combine them with large late-flowering border perennials.

In the wild, primroses, often grow alongside bugle (*Ajuga reptans*) whose dark leaves and blue flowers look lovely next to it. Bugle will also survive the competition from summer-flowering perennials and, being evergreen, it can be used to bring a sense of life to what would otherwise be bare earth between border plants in winter. Both can be planted under shrubs, especially in combination with bulbs such as dwarf narcissi and scillas.

Lesser celandine (*Ranunculus ficaria*) is one of those plants that can drive a tidy-minded gardener to distraction. It forms carpets of dark, heart-shaped leaves in damp shady places in early spring, and can seem impossible to eradicate. But why bother? The leaves are so low they do not offer any competition to garden plants and the brief show of yellow star-shaped flowers in spring is always welcome, especially in the dark places that the plant seems to like. In any case, the foliage will have died away by May or June.

Bluebells (*Hyacinthus non-scriptus*) are most spectacular en masse but are worth encouraging in smaller gardens where they will thrive in light shade, among shrubs for example. You can buy seed or bulbs but it will take some years for numbers to build up and form the dense mats that give real impact. Country gardeners often find a few in the wilder nooks and crannies. Encourage them by ensuring they have enough light to grow but not so much as to allow grasses to thrive. Beneath the outer canopies of deciduous trees is the best place. Their worst enemy is the bramble, which must be dug out or continuously cut back until it disappears.

Wild garlic (*Allium ursinum*) is a less romantic and more aggressive woodland-edge wild flower, though the drifts of white can be welcome in drier shade. However it can be a problem if not wanted, particularly around bulbs or low-growing perennials, and must be dug out. But it is rarely a problem in country gardens, alongside mature shrubs or established and strong-growing later-flowering perennials such as hardy geraniums or asters. The leaves make a fine mild-flavoured soup – reason enough to keep a patch going.

Red campion (*Silene dioica*) is one of the most brightly coloured wild flowers and featured in many of the show gardens at Chelsea this year. Its deep-pink flowers liven up many a West Country lane. It is less likely to appear uninvited in your garden but is easy to grow from seed and, once established, will generally spread itself around. It forms a short-lived and insubstantial plant and self-sowing is rarely a problem. It combines well with late-spring perennials such as the pinks, violets and blues of *Aquilegia vulgaris*, and looks particularly striking with yellow-green *Euphorbia polychroma*.

More common and sometimes more troublesome because of enthusiastic self-seeding is herb robert (*Geranium robertianum*), whose red leaves and pink flowers in early summer can often be tolerated alongside shrub roses, and robust upright perennials such as campanulas. If it becomes too much of a good thing you can easily pull out or hoe off the seedlings.

Of all garden wild flowers foxgloves (*Digitalis purpurea*) are perhaps the most popular as they create a strong vertical among more clumpy perennials. Some gardeners, though, are frustrated because they will not set seed. This is probably because foxgloves prefer lighter soils. Digitalis take up quite a bit of space and if they become prolific it may be necessary to ruthlessly thin them out.

If wild flowers don't appear by themselves they can be grown from seed or bought like other garden plants. There are now several mail-order companies specialising in seed or plantlets of a wide variety of wild flowers and established plants can now be found in some garden centres. Car-boot sale plant stalls should be avoided though, as there are still some people around who dig plants up from the wild to sell.

25 AUGUST 1990

Scents to remember

By Stephen Lacey

Some of us are by nature sniffers and tweakers. But, generally, society prefers us to keep our smelling instinct firmly repressed. We are permitted, and encouraged, to smell wine and perfume, but smelling leather, paint, wooden furniture or old books attracts the label of eccentric, or worse.

Restaurateurs, shopkeepers and dinner party hosts are likely to take offence if you raise their food to your nose before putting it into your mouth. The assumption is not that you are seeking a fuller sensual experience, but that you are checking to see if it is edible. Sometimes you are, but it would be nice if they would not assume it.

Mercifully, smelling plants is free from taboo. In fact, it is considered quite normal. I poke my nose into everything – flowers, leaves, fruits, bark, roots and seeds. You never know what you are going to encounter and it is a challenge trying to decide what the scent smells like.

Sometimes you get a nasty surprise. I was having a National Trust tea in the conservatory at Dyrham Park, near Bath, last week and staring at a tall potted oleander. I knew oleanders were scented, but oddly enough I had never actually sampled one, so I walked across and pulled a flowering stem to my nose.

Imagine sticking your head into a pot of ground pepper and inhaling deeply. I sneezed, my eyes started watering, and my throat started burning. It was several minutes before I was breathing comfortably again. 'Sweetly scented' is the description given in my reference books. I must have caught the flowers at the wrong moment.

At nearby Lacock Abbey (also National Trust), I had a pleasanter surprise. A bean tree was in full bloom. I took it to be *Catalpa x erubescens*, since the more common Indian bean trees, *C. bignonioides*, finished flowering a few weeks ago. It was a splendid sight, with large lime-green leaves and erect panicles of white flowers marked in crimson and orange-yellow. But the biggest treat of all was the scent. It was astonishingly rich, the sort of perfume you might expect in a tropical rather than a hardy tree.

Back home I consulted Alan Mitchell's *Field Guide to the Trees of Britain and Northern Europe*. Mitchell is one of the very few gardening authors who take the trouble to describe scents; many do not even mention them. Against this catalpa he writes: 'Intensely fragrant with the scent of Lilium speciosum', the popular florist's lily. Spot on.

Mitchell is a reliable guide for my nose, though we do not always agree. He thinks the giant fir, *Abies grandis*, has leaves fragrant of oranges; to me they are definitely grapefruit. Western red cedar smells to him of pineapple; to me it is of pear drops. No two people ever detect quite the same flavours, which makes it all the more entertaining to go on sniffing sorties with someone else or to compare notes with a book when you return.

Some scents are quite hard to track down, even when they come floating to you on the air. In the Savill Garden, Windsor, this spring I kept catching wafts of what I decided was pumpkin pie. I just couldn't find the source, even with the help of one of the gardeners.

The scent was too resinous for a flower; it had to be from a leaf or a bud; it was not sweet enough to be balsam poplar. In a large woodland garden like this, there are 1,000 possibilities.

Then I remembered having read somewhere that the southern beeches (nothofagus) were strongly aromatic in spring. Was there one nearby, I asked. Yes, *N. antarctica*, 30 yards away. Eureka!

Occasionally, you don't even realise that it is a plant giving off the scent. Now and again I have been noticing a soapy smell outside my greenhouse.

Since it is close to the washing line and wash-house I have never taken much notice of it. But earlier this summer I thought, wait a minute, this scent seems very seasonal and is always in the same small area. I wonder if it is a plant. And, sure enough, it turned out to be the developing flower heads of Jerusalem sage, *Phlomis fruitcosa*.

Other scents you may not even know you have got. For years I have been growing a diminutive version of lamb's lugs called *Stachys citrina*. I happened to be telling someone about one of my favourite scents, the chocolate of *Cosmos atrosanguineus*, when he asked me if I knew this stachys. Yes, why? Tweak the leaves when you get home, he said. I did, and I sampled it again this morning. It is like savouring a box of Bendicks Bittermints. Ambrosia to a chocoholic like me.

10 JUNE 1978

The rise and fall of the lupin empire

By Fred Whitsey

Peering over garden fences as I drive about and studying what I can see of roadside gardens while I am waiting for the lights to change, I get the idea that lupin growing these days is largely concentrated in gardens that get precious little attention. Once the lupin was universal. Today I see it planted very rarely in those carefully contrived schemes aimed at in the gardens of those who take their gardening with gusto and a little seriousness.

Perhaps it grew too tall and too wide. Perhaps it wasn't much to look at once its great moment of June flowering was over. Perhaps it too often 'went back to blue' instead of staying those bright cottage colours, often two of them in the same spike. All of which is doubtless true, to the detriment of the well-loved lupin.

Taking the points in reverse order, coloured varieties only 'went blue' because they were allowed to set seed and self-sow. The seedlings were inferior in colour but not in vigour and ousted the parents who were weakened by the strain of seeding. Buy a plant of a coloured variety, however, snap off the spent flower heads before the seedpods ripen, and the same plant will be with you for several seasons, provided that you protect it from slugs in the spring just as you would your lettuce plants.

As for the bulky, leafy appearance that succeeds flowering, you have to put lupins at the back of the border, with the oriental poppies, so that they throw up into relief the later-flowering kinds. A good maxim to follow anyway in planning borders: start with the early flowers at the back, letting one after another take the stage until the last, like the *Aster amellus* – still flattish plants at this time of year – have the front to themselves at the end of the season.

As for the size of the plants, this has been cured for everyday gardens by the breeding of a strain to be found as seed in the shops under the Garden Pride label called Monarch Dwarf Lulu Mixed.

The great point about this valuable product of the Hurst plant-breeding station in vegetable-covered Essex is that the plants have the same colourings but only grow to about half the height of the Russell strain bred by old George Russell, the railwayman from York who mixed up many lupins on his allotment and produced one of the wonders of the gardening world.

The snag is that whereas once you could buy many dozens of lupins 'to colour', as the nurserymen used to put it, all with pet names of their own, today you could count those available on one hand. Nor can you buy plants of our little Lulu knowing what colour you will get. So you have to flower the seedlings in small pots, identify them and at once dispossess each plant of its single small spike of flowers to let it build up into something worth planting.

Fortunately the seed, of which you get little in a packet – it is expensively produced – can be sown individually in small pots. This makes for both quickness of raising and easy classifying once you have seen the true nature of the goods.

The same breeder of new flowers has applied the same principles of reduction to the delphinium, which is also grown on a much smaller scale than hitherto because of its ungainly proportions.

In this case you again have a plant half the size of those lofty great spires that you had to stake as individuals, to hold them up against wind and rain and prevent them from being turned into writhing serpents. A better name in this case: Blue Fountains.

The fact that you can only get the seed mixed hardly matters unless you are the most exacting of purists. A packet of seed will give you a nice mixture of blues, and perhaps some plants with flowers in violet and white, too. Bred into the strain is the capacity for giving what delphinium experts delicately call the 'bees' – the part of the flower at the heart that enshrines the sexual organs – in contrasting colourings, often black.

Not that I am in any possible way disparaging those who have taken the delphinium to their hearts and compete in exhibitions with it. The valiant Delphinium Society is celebrating its golden jubilee this year and can look back on 50 years that have not only seen the advancement of the flower through its stimulus but also, I would think, its preservation through the 'wild garden' era when labour-saving was all the rage and when it could have gone into eclipse.

The society has also encouraged the cultivation of delphiniums from seed, and was one of the first authorities to pinpoint the difficulty arising from the way that the seed so quickly loses its viability unless stored from the day of its ripening in refrigerators. Warmth is nothing to this plant and the seed actually germinates at temperatures as low as lettuce does.

Though the seed is smaller than that of lupins, it is worth handling it with tweezers and sowing into small pots and potting on the seedlings if necessary.

The traditional time for planting out both lupins and delphiniums from seed is in the autumn, but given the value of the plants from the carefully selected seed available and the appalling hunger of slugs for the shoots, I would have thought it better to keep the seedlings in the comfort of a cold frame for the winter. Here you can more easily keep an eye on both the plants and the slugs, and then plant out in spring. To look after the watering problem you can always leave off the light except for the worst of the weather and sink the pots in that.

Budding beauties

By Elspeth Thompson

Look, Mummy, it's opened!' cried Mary, my nearly-three-year-old daughter, as we sat down to breakfast the other day. In front of her in a jar of water was the sprig of horse chestnut we had snapped off a tree in the park a week or so before (just one is permissible for this purpose every year, I feel). Back then, it had been hard to persuade a small child that this bare twig, with its sticky brown buds, was worth taking home. But, sure enough, after a few days of central heating, the dark scaly covering of the top bud began to split, revealing a fragment of fuzzy grey-green leaf.

Day by day the amount of green grew, until that morning, when all three leaves emerged, still folded on the end of soft silvery stalks and looking for all the world like an old man of the woods, stretching with clenched fists after a long sleep. It may sound fanciful, but anyone who has seen the 19th-century German photographer Karl Blossfeldt's study of exactly this subject will know what I mean. We have a copy of his photograph of a horse chestnut bud opening on our landing and it makes me smile whenever I see it.

It is a delight to share the joys of spring with my daughter. Buds bursting open after the long cold months of winter are such a potent symbol of change and renewal, and she senses my excitement on a walk in our local woods, where the bare branches are suddenly tinged with green.

The hazel is just beginning to break, with snips of tightly ribbed green on the tips of the branches; then will come the hawthorn and birch, and lastly the beech, like scraps of bright green silk in the sunlight, and the untidy greenish-yellow tassles of oak.

In our country garden I cut a few twiggy branches to bring inside to speed up the opening – combining a little light pruning with decorating the house. Add some sprigs of forsythia if you have it – to my mind those bright yellow flowers look better in a vase than in the border, and it is fun to watch the knobbly brown buds open in the warmth. On Easter Sunday, we hang our collection of painted eggs from the branches.

All over Britain, gardens are burgeoning with buds about to burst. Watching them is one of life's great pleasures. You'll need patience to see anything to compete with the speeded-up time-release photography on television, but there are real treats to be had.

Opium poppies on a sunny spring day can split their glaucous green buds to shake out the finest tissue-paper frills, and I have never forgotten the thrill of seeing a hibiscus flower unfurl one early morning on a balcony in Rome.

Some buds are almost as beautiful as the flowers themselves. Those of the pasque flower (*Pulsatilla vulgaris*), just emerging around Easter, are encased in hairy silver sepals as soft as down – a delicate foil for the velvety mauve petals within. Another of my favourites is the nectaroscordum, whose curious greenish-pink flowers are held in a tall tissue-thin sheath, twisted at the top like the minaret of a mosque.

In my London front garden, they rise high above the silver-leaved plants, the buds growing fatter day by day until you can detect the outlines of the flowers within. One sunny day is all it takes for the tissue to tear and drop those subtly streaked bells in a dangling, dancing dome – sometimes with the top of the tissue left balancing, like a jaunty cap, on top. As the flowers fade, crisp up and die, they close and point upwards again, as if trying to become buds once more.

Roses, of course, are beautiful in every stage of growth. Often the buds are of a stronger hue than the full bloom – pink buds often opening into white and, in the case of the China rose 'Mutabilis', tawny orange buds becoming first apricot and then coppery cream flowers. And who has not wondered at a peony bud, so round and tight and fat, and had to suspend disbelief that it could possibly contain all that blowsy ballgown abundance? It really is a magical time.

 **9 MAY 1970**

The oldest cottage flowers of all

By Denis Wood

May is the month in which to sow the seeds of certain old-fashioned flowers which are nowadays seldom available as plants. They have been known in English gardens at least since the 17th century and are some of the old cottage garden flowers with an artless charm that so many others have lost.

Two are for borders or clearly defined beds. *Dianthus barbatus*, sweet William, grows to about a foot. The clove-scented flowers in July are crowded in nearly flat corymbs like small pinks joined together in one tuft. It may be difficult now to obtain plants of sweet Williams, but the seeds are available in self-colours of crimson, white, pink and scarlet and 'harlequin', in which several shades of colour exist in one flower head.

My favourites are the auricular-eyed (or auriculaeflorus) sweet Williams, usually available only as a mixture. Generally, I am against mixed colours, preferring myself to do any mixing that I consider ought to be done, but sweet Williams and polyanthuses are exceptions.

Sweet Williams are unfortunately prone to rust and at the first sight of this they should be sprayed with a copper fungicide and careful attention paid to good cultivation, that is, making sure that the soil is well supplied with fertilisers and that the plants do not become dry. Any leaves affected with rust should be picked off and burnt.

Also flowering in July are Canterbury bells, *Dianthus Medium*. Note the capital M. The word does not mean middle but, according to David McLintock in his *Companion to Flowers*, the word traces back to the Medes. The Canterbury bells available as plants in October or March are usually of the calycanthema variety, duplex of cup and saucer, in which one bell grows in the other.

Plants are usually obtainable as the inevitable mixed, but seeds can be bought of self-colours, white, lilac and rose. For myself, I much prefer the old plain single Canterbury bells, which I believe are now entirely unobtainable as plants, although the seed can still be bought. They have a comforting, if rather blousy, prettiness which appeals to me.

The other three plants are for unplanned wildernesses, in my case the thinner parts of my mini-copse. Sweet rocket, dame's violet or queen's gilliflower are names for *Hesperis matronalis*. About 2 to 3ft tall, it has spikes of four-petalled, mauve, purple or white flowers in June, which are fragrant, particularly in the evening. They have a tall slender country grace. Seedsmen offer white and violet-purple single varieties which will thrive in ordinary soil and multiply from seeds.

I cannot find that the old double 'rockets' of the 17th century are offered in any catalogues, and I believe that they may only now survive in some old gardens, perhaps in Scotland. These were plants for beds and borders rather than the wilder parts of a garden, and, I believe, required to be renewed annually from cuttings; and, by contrast with their single-flowered brothers, they need a rich soil. I should be interested if anyone could tell me where plants can be obtained.

Honesty, *Lunaria annua* (or *biennis*), like the rockets, another member of the cruciferae, is from 1 to 1½ft tall, typically purple, but there are blue and white forms. In April and May I am always surprised by the unexpected purple colour of the flowers so early in the year among the daffodils.

Last, the only true native of the five, *Digitalis purpurea*, the Foxglove. Up to 5ft tall, the shaded mauve-purple flowers have pink and brown-spotted throats and are borne in a dense spike in early summer. With their tall, erect bearing they have a fawn-like detachment when seen as a receding host in the dappled shade of thin woodland.

There have been disastrous 'improvements' on this fine native plant and anyone intending to raise it from seed should make sure of getting the true native, *purpurea* or *purpurea alba*.

All these are generally treated as biennials, that is, the seed is sown this month in the open ground or better, in boxes in cold frames. The young seedlings are pricked out about 6in apart into rows in spare ground and put into flowering positions in October; they will flower the following summer.

Being cottage garden plants they have long been out of fashion and we should not forget our debt to seedsmen like Thompson & Morgan of Ipswich who continue to make seeds available to a discerning few who are not content to be decorators only but willing to take the trouble to raise the plants for themselves.

In fact, it may be that possession of a cold frame and a few square metres of spare ground could mark the first steps in the making of a real gardener.

Looking far beyond the usual suspects

By Beth Chatto

What is an unusual plant? If you are new to gardening almost everything may be, except delphiniums, chrysanthemums and Michaelmas daisies. I often wonder why more unusual plants are not more generally seen in gardens since they are often easy to grow as well as attractive.

For those who have graduated into the wider realms of gardening I may be writing of plants they already know, but I do not intend to deal with plants which are unusual because they are awkward. I like plants which, given the right conditions, flourish outside in our mischievous climate without constant attention.

There are many interesting and unusual varieties of plants which are already well known. Take *Alyssum saxatile* for example. The bright mustard-yellow form has become commonplace and under-valued because it is so often planted with too much competing colour. But I prefer the pale lemon-yellow alyssum 'Citrinum' and alyssum 'Dudley Neville' which has clusters of soft apricot flowers. Seldom seen is the variegated form of A. 'Dudley Neville' whose soft grey-green leaves are broadly edged with cream. They show up handsomely among the more feathery silvers and greys.

I particularly like the double flowered form of white arabis, *Arabis caucasia* 'Flore Pleno', when in spring its stems of creamy white rosettes look like miniature double stocks. Aubrietia is in flower at the same time, but what do you use to follow? The drought-resisting mountain phlox provides carpets of colour, all shades of pink, blue and white, lovely as edgings to borders, fine on a rock garden. For those whose soil is not too dry and in partial shade, there are other delights from the phlox family. *Phlox stolonifera* spreads in cool, leaf-mouldy soil, making modest ground cover all the year until the end of May, when it erupts with heads of exquisitely soft blue flowers held just above the leaf carpet. There is a white form called P. 'Ariene'.

Where conditions are still not too dry I have been glad to discover the hardy fuchsias, especially those with pretty leaves. *Fuchsia genii* looks much like an ordinary variety with red and purple flowers, but the foliage is golden. To look its best it needs some light, but not so much direct sun that the delicate leaves are scorched.

In late summer and autumn *Fuchsia magellanica* 'Versicolor' is one of the most beautiful foliage plants. Each year it will throw up tall graceful stems, more than a yard high, set with drooping branches whose leaves are a suffusion of grey, rose and cream. The slim ruby-petalled flowers hang like jewels among them. Once established these fuchsias are quite hardy, but a bucketful of dead-leaf litter poured over them in late autumn will ensure the safety of the underground buds.

Small flowered violas can nestle beneath the fuchsias, perhaps the old-fashioned viola 'Maggie Mott', soft blue and deliciously scented, or 'Irish Moll' whose small velvety brown faces have olive-green shadows. They have been used as bedding plants under roses, though I should have though it would be a bit too hot for them in many rose beds. Most of the violas like rather cool conditions. All the forms of *V. cornuta*, which are so pretty, like large blue or white unscented violets on tall stems, will stand sun provided they have a cool root run, or have sun for only part of the day.

Returning to the dry sunny garden, have you seen *Crepis incana* sitting among scented mats of thyme? It is a very well-behaved dandelion, a choice plant for a sunny well-drained site. It is likely to rot in a garden which lies cold and wet in winter. It makes low rosettes of toothed grey-green leaves which send up rather stiff branching stems in mid-summer, supporting a bouquet of soft rose-pink dandelion flowers fit for a bridesmaid. Even the thymes which surround it could be unusual; perhaps thymus 'Doone Valley', which I love in early spring when its new growing tips are dark red, opening to make flat carpets of dark-green leaves partly touched with gold. There are thymes with entirely gold leaves, with grey leaves edged with pink and cream, leaves that smell tantalisingly of crushed lemon or caraway seeds – not to mention the flowering thymes.

The common antirrhinum has two unusual relatives. Both are perennial. The first is linaria 'Canon Went', a slender thing with tall stems up to 3ft high, closely set with small narrow grey leaves. For weeks in summer they are topped with fine spires of tiny pink flowers. Quite different is *Linaria triornithophora*. This lengthy name means 'bearing three birds'. Actually it bears many more than three: the unopened buds clustered round the branching stems look much like flights of tiny budgerigars. They love a hot dry spot, opening snapdragon flowers of rich purple tipped with yellow. Occasionally you find a shrimp pink seedling, a delicious colour.

There is good reason why *Gunnera scabra* is not frequently seen. Apart from liking really wet soil, one plant covers as much land as some people have for an entire flower bed, its great upturned umbrella-like leaves can be as much as 4ft across, and children love to shelter beneath them from a shower of rain.

Lysichitum too, the yellow American swamp arum, loves to surge up through a metre of wet mud by the pond side and is not too easily accommodated. But both these noble plants are the making of a garden which can take them.

I have recently found the lovely green-flowered *Galtonia viride* – not the earlier-flowering *Galtonia princeps* and *Galtonia candicans*, which carries pure white flowers like great snowdrops in late July. *Galtonia viride* has the same smooth stems, up to 3ft tall, from which hang pale-green wide-open bells, like jade.

The late summer and autumn days are enlivened by a strange, non-prickly, thistle-like plant which can be found under two names. I first knew it as *Cnicus atropurpureus*, but its real name is *Cirsium rivulare*. It needs no staking out but holds heads of rich wine-coloured flowers high on 4ft stems. It appears quite remarkable rising among the silver foliaged plants, which look so well in autumn. It should definitely not be placed near dahlias, where one or the other would be outclassed.

None of these unusual plants is difficult. Somewhere in the temperate world most were found growing wild, and we in our gardens must try to create something of the conditions to which they were born.

～ 17 AUGUST 1997 ～

Can the sweet pea be rehabilitated?

By Roy Strong

I have an affection for sweet peas, *Lathyrus odoratus*, not that I've grown them, but I'm beginning to think that we should. So often one is put off by one's earliest encounters with a plant. Every year on my wife's birthday, the cottager who loyally fed our cat when we were away used to come up the drive with a bunch of them. They scented the house for days and Julia adored them, but I always remember passing his little garden and seeing the trenching and staking that had gone on to produce this annual floral feast. Not, I thought, flowers for the hard-pressed gardener. So they've belonged to that garden category which is headed 'borrowed landscape', that is something which you don't own or do yourself but enjoy at someone else's expense and labour. In the case of sweet peas, they are generally savoured peeping over a wall or hedge in passing, in our case on the outskirts of Cirencester, where every year a small row of cane wigwams sprouts like soldiers on parade in springtime to be garlanded in pastel shades of pink, violet, blue, cerise and white until the frosts of October spell their death knell.

The most spectacular display of sweet peas I have ever seen was at a dinner given in the Raphael Cartoon Court of the Victoria and Albert Museum by Geoffrey Howe when he was Foreign Secretary. Every blossom from the whole of the south of England must have been felled for that floral explosion. It was only later that I came across a comment by that great Victorian plantsman E. A. Bowles, whose verdict on them as flowers for the dining table reads as follows: 'A dinner-table decorated heavily with Sweet Peas spoils my dinner, as I taste Sweet Peas with every course, and they are horrible as a sauce for fish, whilst they ruin the bouquet of a good wine.' Flower arrangers please take note.

A vase of them is welcome in a guest bedroom, as we experienced the other day. Outside in the wide herbaceous borders of the garden capacious towers of twigs had been made supporting not the blooms in the vase, which were modern hybrids, but their ancestor, the highly perfumed *Lathyrus odoratus* which was grown up until the beginning of this century.

Now there's a great deal of snobbery about sweet peas. The original variety produces highly scented flowers in shades of white, red, pink and blue. I recall when I was filming at Highgrove a few years back, the Prince of Wales and Lady Salisbury hymning what they referred to as the pre-Spencer varieties as if the poor sweet pea had formed a misalliance with a kitchen maid. Vita Sackville-West, who writes as though she had swum the Channel with the horticultural *Almanach de Gotha* between her teeth, similarly has a down on the modern hybrids. These, with their frilled petals, first appeared in the garden of Countess Spencer at Althorp at the beginning of this century and they're what most people grow. You have to watch out that they retain the scent of their ancestor, but even Vita admits that the modern varieties are sturdier, have more flower heads and a wider colour range. So *chacun à son goût*.

Accounts of how the sweet pea got here are confusing. It is a native of southern Italy and Sicily and its arrival is attributed to seeds sent by a Father Cupani in 1699 to Robert Uvedale, a great character who ran an upper-class boys' school at Enfield and at the same time maintained one of the earliest hot-houses in the country. 'His flowers', it is recorded, 'are choice, his stock numerous, and his culture of them methodical and curious.' Two decades later the botanist Thomas Fairchild was recommending that sweet peas were planted in London squares on account not only of their beauty but also of their smell, which was 'something like honey, and a little tending to orange flower smell'. The architect Sir William Chambers was making use of them for his shrub borders in the 1770s and by the close of the century the sweet pea was a standard ingredient of what was a revival of the flower garden. In a rare plan of a circular island bed at Hartwell House in 1799 there is the sweet pea. And it didn't sink from favour during the Victorian era, William Robinson in *The English Flower Garden* referring to it as 'perhaps the most precious annual plant grown'.

Where does this leave me as I look at the lurid pages of the seed catalogues which tell me there is a National Sweet Pea Society? I'm pleased to see that the pre-Spencer varieties can still be obtained, labelled Edwardian Collection or Old-Fashioned Varieties, but for their descendants the drive is as always for larger flowers and stronger colour, although scent is not altogether neglected. The Bouquet Series is heralded as 'a complete rethink in sweet pea breeding', whatever that means. But with all that demand for a rich soil, a hole stuffed full of manure and compost plus the staking, maybe I'll remain peering at them over the garden fence and leave them for the enthusiast.

21 JUNE 2003

A study in scarlet

By Germaine Greer

Five o'clock on a nacreous June morning, and I'm on my feet as usual, wondering if I dare sneak a half-hour off to step through the hedge, skirt the beet field and walk into the middle of the field of blazing scarlet poppies that I've been greedily gazing at from my workshop windows. I duck out the front gate and set off.

Stomp as I might to flatten the nettles under the hedge, they manage to sting me all up inside my skirt. As I go lolloping along one foot up and one foot down at the edge of the weed-free beet field which has been ploughed to within an inch of the hedge, I suddenly find myself in a warm bath of winey scent flung by what I take to be a white dog rose. Aha! the cognoscenti will say, knows she not that *Rosa canina* is scentless? Yes, she does, so what can the scented white single roses that grow in these hedgerows be?

When I looked into the hedge I found there were four briars growing close together and they were all slightly different. All had dark-green compound leaves with either five or seven saw-edged leaflets and single, five-petalled flowers set above flask-shaped ovaries and adorned with elaborate sepals, each of which ended in a long twisting point as well as carrying two little green side-whiskers, known as lateral lobes. One had a white flower with very open lax petals and no scent whatsoever; the other bore pink cup-shaped blooms with a faint scent.

The other two both had blossoms of the faintest peach colour, one with big lax petals, the other more cup-shaped. Both were strongly but differently scented. In other respects they were straight dog roses, no oil glands, strong, downward curving thorns that were flushed pink on young growth, flanged stipules nearly as long as the leaflets on every leaf and protecting the clusters of flowers in bud, all petals notched, styles like a golden starburst around a green boss.

All rose species hybridise easily, resulting in what Polunin in *Flowers of Europe* calls 'a difficult complex of microspecies', which is just what rose-breeders need. A hedge made of the best-smelling not quite dog rose, which I shall call Rosa x Farmer Hamilton, would smell wonderful and at the same time repel invaders as effectively as the dog rose. I found a piece of pink string in my pocket and tied it to a twig so I could identify it in July and take a few dozen cuttings to beef up the fox defences. I shall almost certainly forget to take the cuttings when the time comes.

On I wend to the poppy field, with legs a-tingle from the nettles, and a few new thorn tracks leaking blood across my arms. Tits and finches carrying beakfuls of protein swerve past my head on the way to their nestlings in the hedge. A hare sits up amid the beet rows, his jaws still going, watches my asymmetrical progress for 10 seconds or so and then falls to again. Rooks caw at me out of the early morning blue. And then the poppies are all around me, gazing up out of their bowls of purest red with their stiff-lashed eyes, each mascaraed anther ending in a tiny purple-black blob, surrounding a receptacle as dark as themselves.

I can't remember ever seeing this field allowed to lie fallow for so long, nor do I remember seeing poppies in it before, but so much viable seed was still lurking in the soil after nearly 20 years of herbicide for it to burst forth this year in a veritable red carpet, made redder by the contrast with occasional bright-green towers of self-seeded beet set with nascent blossom. Between the poppies are mats of *Viola tricolor*, the true heart's ease; here and there a froth of German chamomile rides on the tide of scarlet, over which swing the pendents of occasional wild oats or stiff blue wheat-stalks or silvery barley. Some of the poppies have blond eyelashes or black basal blotches and stand revealed as children of those in my garden.

Something is wrong. Too many of the poppies are turning pink, but not the subtle shades of the hybrids in my garden. They look bleached or blasted. Their stems are too bunched, their buds coiled on themselves in an awkward way. Some of the blossoms have even collapsed and make white-edged turban shapes. For a good 10 minutes I don't get it, even when I see plants knocked flat and the tracks of a vehicle carved through the scarlet.

The whole field has been sprayed, yesterday probably, with Roundup. Even as I stand unbelieving in the sunlit dew, the greens turn sour, and the heads of the poppies sink towards the dust.

What are the best plants of the past 200 years?

By Roy Lancaster

Keen gardeners, especially those in the public eye, are often asked for lists of their favourite garden plants. It is an enjoyable exercise and highlights the huge number of plants that are presently available. So when the RHS first invited members to submit ideas to help mark its bicentenary this year, it occurred to me that here was an opportunity to tap the vast experience and expertise of its plant committees, whose members include respected and gifted amateurs as well as lifetime professionals. The idea for a select list of 200 plants representing 200 years was born and members of all 17 of the plant committees were asked to submit their five Desert Island Disc candidates. The only criterion given was that the plants be available in the current RHS Plant Finder.

Encouraged by the response, Christopher Weddell, the society's senior horticulturist, drew up a list of the 200 plants receiving the most votes. Included in this list are trees, shrubs, climbers, conifers, perennials, annuals, bulbs, rock plants, house and greenhouse plants, and fruit. About 124 of them already have an RHS Award of Garden Merit. And no genus or group (i.e. maples) was allowed more than three entries. Contributors were also asked to give reasons for their choice and to provide a short description of each.

Predictably, given the specialist and often idiosyncratic interests of some contributors, the list contains its share of the rare and unusual. *Crataegus orientalis*, the Oriental thorn, has been chosen by Fergus Garrett, Christopher Lloyd's gardener, who enjoys this small but hardy tree for its 'lovely shape, big flowers and the most wonderful fruit'. Christopher Lloyd includes *Melianthus major* in his selection. He admires this South African foliage plant for its handsome, glaucous leaves with heavily toothed margins.

John Blanchard, the daffodil specialist, describes *Oxalis squamata* as 'an outstanding Chilean alpine with an exceptionally long flowering season', adding that it is 'a good-tempered garden plant and lovely to see in the wild'. Peter Cunnington, of Ness Gardens in the Wirrall, also chose a plant of wild origin. The beautiful blue-trumpeted *Gentiana sino-ornata* reminds us that this is the centenary of Scottish plant hunter George Forrest's first expedition to China, which gave us so many popular plants.

Many of the plants on the list are long-established and reliable garden favourites, such as *Lilium regale*, the Regal lily, a 'Chinese' Wilson introduction and a favourite of Pamela Schwerdt, formerly head gardener at Sissinghurst. She values it for being 'stylishly scented and a good contrast of shape with other things out at that time'.

In the same camp is *Geranium psilostemon*, chosen by Victoria Wakefield, creator of the wonderful garden at Bramdean House in Hampshire, which is famous for its perennial borders, roses and sweet peas. She admires its superb colours, autumn leaf tints and excellent contribution to border planting.

The list does not ignore plants of culinary value, such as raspberry 'Autumn Bliss', of which Alan Buller, grower, exhibitor and judge of fruit and vegetables, asks: 'Who needs any other?' Joan Morgan, joint author of *The New Book of Apples* (Ebury Press) and probably the only person to have tasted and annotated almost every one of the world's apple varieties, praises the pear 'Fondante d'Automne' for its texture and flavour, adding: 'One of the best October pears with good regular crops. Reliable in the English climate.' Joan also chooses 'Golden Noble' as 'the classic English cooking apple, a good cropper and easy to grow on any soil, ideal for all traditional dishes, apple pie, sauce, baked apple etc.' Interestingly, Eric Spander and Harry Baker, both members of the Fruit Group Committee, included penstemon 'Sour Grapes' and *Plumbago auriculata* respectively in their selections, which shows what catholic tastes most committee members – even those of the more specialist persuasion – possess.

Two native plants were also included on the list, although I was not surprised given their beauty. One is the pasque flower *Pulsatilla vulgaris* chosen by, among others, Brian Mathew, ex-Kew botanist and bulb expert, who favours it for its long-lived, low-growing, compact habit, its hardiness, its large showy flowers and its attractive seed heads. Both Anne Blanco White and Cy Bartlett of the Joint Iris Committee praise *Iris foetidissima*, our native gladdon. Cloudy in colour compared with most others yet, in Anne's opinion, 'good value almost anywhere but especially the small garden' with its double impact of colourful winter seeds and lush clumps of shining evergreen foliage.

Which plants did I submit? I'll mention two. First, an old favourite, *Magnolia liliifolia*, 'Nigra', a choice shared with Anne Boscawen of High Beeches Gardens in Sussex. I have three examples of this compact, bushy magnolia in my garden, which is suitable for all but shallow chalk soils and gives a great deal of pleasure each year in spring and again in late summer with its erect deep-purple-stained white blooms.

My second choice is *Daphne bholua*, 'Jacqueline Postill', one of the most reliable and productive of winter-flowering shrubs. I enjoy it for its sweetly fragrant rose-stained flower clusters, contrasting with glossy evergreen leaves from January or earlier through to late March or April. It has strong erect growth, thrives best in a sheltered site – preferably in lime-free soil – and enjoys sun or half shade. Not only is it a show-stopper when in flower, it also has a history, having been raised by master propagator Alan Postill and named after his New Zealand-born wife. This type of plant grows wild in the Himalayas, where its perfume fills the woodland glades in months of autumn and winter.

It is the stories and personal anecdotes about favourite plants that make this list so special and a fitting celebration of the society's contribution to our gardens.

28 JANUARY 2012

Be your own florist

By Sarah Raven

Put the current national obsession, grow-your-own, together with make-your-own and it's not surprising that growing cut flowers and using them to make arrangements for your home is the next fast-growing hobby.

Mr Fothergill's, which packs 70 million packets of seed a year for home gardeners worldwide, is predicting cut flower seeds to be the big growth area in the next three years. It has seen sales increases of around 15 per cent in the past 18 months across all cut flower species, after a few years of fairly static growth. Key sellers have been sweet peas, zinnias, rudbeckias and calendulas, as well as other cottage garden favourites.

Lots of factors, aside from fashion, are pushing this along. Shop-bought flowers are expensive in normal times, but in a recession we feel it more. We are also increasingly anxious about air miles, with so many of our commercial cut flowers air-freighted from Africa and South America – and usually boring varieties at that. Home-grown is so much nicer, in so many ways.

If you are giving over a small area of the garden or veg plot to cut flowers, it's worth growing the very best, and going for things which will flower for ages, providing buckets of colour for free.

What most of us want is a gentle drip-drip production over many months, rather than a huge glut of flowers all coming together. This is easy to do if you have the right succession of cut-and-come-again plants, grown in the right seasons.

For spring picking, try old-fashioned, tall-growing wallflowers, such as *Erysimum cheiri* 'Blood Red', 'Vulcan' and 'Fire King' to give you scent and rich colour. As biennials, these must be sown in May to flower the following year, so if you're starting from scratch this year, buy small plants of the new perennial wallflower, 'Winter Orchid', which will flower more quickly and for longer. This has shorter stems, but is unusual among perennial wallflowers in that its flowers are fragrant. It's a nectar-rich flower, ideal for butterflies and bees. All or any of these are invaluable for mixing with daffodils, anemones or tulips through spring.

At this time of year my favourite things are bishop's flower (*Ammi majus*), which looks like a more delicate form of cow parsley. It flowers for much longer and lasts better in the vase. The black cornflower (*Centaurea cyanus* 'Black Ball'), and orange and crimson marigold (*Calendula officinalis* 'Indian Prince') are two other backbone cutting patch plants, and you'd be missing out without the big and blowsy *Malope trifida* 'Vulcan', the ever-flowering annual scabious (*Scabiosa atropurpurea*) and sapphire-blue *Salvia viridis* 'Blue'.

This goes with every colour and lasts well over a week, once cut. Sweet peas, the quintessential cut-and-come-again plant, also need to make their way in there somewhere, with unmissable varieties such as 'Matucana', 'Painted Lady' and 'Prince Edward of York' winning the show in terms of scent.

These are all hardy annuals, which should be sown in the next few weeks inside, or from mid-April straight into the garden. They could ideally be supplemented by a few cut-and-come-again biennials, but you need to have already sown these last May or June.

Biennials I love include the white foxglove, *Digitalis purpurea* 'Alba', and the apricot-pink 'Sutton's Apricot' as well as sweet rocket (*Hesperis matronalis*) and Iceland poppies (*Papaver nudicaule*), which can be treated as annual or biennial.

For later in the year, think of sowing plants such as *Cosmos bipinnatus* 'Rubenza', 'Purity' and 'Dazzler', or a general colour mix. Sown in March, these flower from June until November if our autumn is warm. It's also good to have some of the classy varieties of snapdragon, the tall, single-colour florists' forms such as 'Liberty Crimson' and 'Giant White' to give you elegant vertical spires to cut through the froth.

Last year I fell in love with the cheery, petite annual toadflax, *Linaria maroccana* 'Little Sweeties', which looks lovely in a drinking glass beside the bed. I'm mad about zinnias – either the delicate-coloured, smaller–flowered cultivar, 'Sprite Mix', or the chunky, almost dahlia-like 'Giant Dahlia' in its single colours or as a mix.

For foliage right through the year, flowering (honestly) from March to November, there's nothing better than *Euphorbia oblongata*. Sow this as soon as possible. The great, flat, acid-green plateaus of this plant act like a sieve: three or four stems gathered together in a vase provide a structure into which you can drop all your other flowers. They'll be held fast, the euphorbia acting almost like a living block of florists' foam.

Then there's *Cerinthe major* 'Purpurascens', or honeywort, a plant beloved by bees, which also needs sowing soon, and you've got a good foliage base for most colours. Cerinthe flowers for 8-10 weeks, but if you leave the late-winter sown plants where they are for the seed to ripen, they'll self-sow and you'll get a second crop later this year. Both euphorbia and cerinthe are best sown inside to start them off.

For late-season foliage, 'Bells of Ireland' (*Moluccella laevis*) is everyone's favourite and rightly so. It lasts well in water and is also good dried. Add also the chenille tassels of the green love-lies-bleeding (*Amaranthus caudatus* 'Viridis'), which looks good as a background foliage, but almost more magnificent on its own in a large vase.

If you have soil that is free-draining and quick to warm up, you can sow most seed straight into the garden. If you have heavy soil, it's safer to start indoors …

1. Don't sow too early. Wait until late February/early March for a few early plants but leave everything else until the beginning of April. An early-April sowing allows six weeks from sowing until the end of the frosts in mid-May (although this varies according to where you live). This is the perfect length of time for quick-growing annuals to form decent-sized plants ready to plant out.

2. Sow as thinly as you can. The less competition from close neighbours the better. I now sow almost everything in modular divided trays or expanding peat pellets called Jiffy 7s for exactly that reason.

3. To germinate, most seeds want a warm, moist, dark environment. I place my seed trays of half-hardy annuals on a propagator bench set at about 20°C. I cover them with empty plastic compost bags to keep in moisture and warmth and block out light. Check trays morning and evening. At first signs of germination, uncover trays and put in a place of maximum light. Once germinated, good light levels, cool air temperatures

(just above freezing) and warm roots are ideal. All-round light is also important in forming strong, bulky plants.

4. Do not let your seedlings get potbound. Pot on as soon as you see white roots appearing at the holes in the bottom of the pot.

5. Pinch out and plant out into the garden as soon as the frosts are over. With any plants that are beginning to look leggy, rather than bushy – one, central, spindly, vertical stem shooting up to the skies – pinch out the tip.

6. As soon as the frosts are over, plant out seedlings in the garden at the distance recommended on the back of the seed packet. For two weeks water in well, with a drown, not a sprinkle, so they establish a deep root system which will hopefully reach the water table.

Sowing outside - ground preparation

In an ideal world, the ground would have been dug over some time in the autumn or winter to integrate organic material, e.g. well-rotted manure. If you garden on poorly drained clay soil, add grit or washed sharp sand as well. Get rid of all annual and perennial weeds as you dig. Once dug, try not to tread on the soil directly. To distribute your weight evenly over a large area, stand on a plank.

Sowing

1. Don't sow outside too early. You know when this sowing moment has arrived without looking at the calendar: all over the garden, seedlings are appearing. If nature's doing it, you do it too.

2. Sow into soil with a fine consistency, with no lumps bigger than a large marble. Choose a dry day, following a dry spell of a day or two, to prepare the ground for sowing. Thump any large lumps of soil with the back of a metal rake. They'll shatter when

dry, but remain cloddy when wet. Work out where your lines are going to be and fine-tune the soil in these places only. Rake in one direction, removing lumps bigger than a plum to the side. Repeat at right angles.

3. Sow in straight lines marked out with a garden line or two canes and string, sowing as thinly as you can. Take individual seeds (if large like calendula) or a pinch of seed (if small like tobacco plant) from your palm and sow it as finely as you can into shallow drills. The ideal spacing is 5cm/2in apart – impossible with tiny seeds. For small seeds – sow quickly a small pinch at a time – in a sweep of your arm – so you get finer distribution than meticulous and slow.

4. Thin seedlings out when they are about an inch tall, leaving one good plant every 10cm/4in (see back of pack for exact distance).

5. Thin again to the final planting distance as instructed on the packet. Give them plenty of room.

Aftercare

1. If there is no rain, water twice a week. Really wet the ground to a depth of several inches, but do so gently so as not to displace the seed. Sufficient watering encourages the roots to follow the water and the plants will form deep, strong roots. After a couple of weeks, stop watering unless there's a prolonged period of drought. Strong, deep roots should have reached the water table on most soils by now.

2. Keep the seedling bed weed-free. Weeds, like other seedlings, will compete for light, food and water and do your plants no good. Get rid of weeds with a hoe. After hoeing, I spread a 5cm/2in layer of mulch over the soil.

3. Stake any cut flowers which grow taller than 45cm/18in.

O Rose, thou art lovely

By Fred Whitsey

Even before the sun came at last, walking along the paths of the little vegetable plot was an experience of summer. From behind the box-edging that lines them, old roses lean forward and invite you to sniff and admire. The days were cool, the nights cold, but still the air was filled with such scent as almost to make you believe that familiar calumny that no new rose smells like the old ones. Why are they there with the vegetables then? For several good reasons.

So individual is each variety, so beautifully shaped and marked, that you need to have them at close quarters, beside a path, where you can pause, look and ponder, trying to recall the name and perhaps the rose's history, for the names are almost as fascinating as the flowers. Most of them spend their season's flowering in one glorious flourish and then, it must be owned, don't look much afterwards. As well, then, to have them out of the way in some spot where they will not take a stage better left to others. Anyway, so irresistible are they that wherever you put them in carefully contrived schemes with pinks and penstemons, lavender, sage and rosemary, that you always want more. It comes easy to filch vegetable garden space for them.

What is it that divides old roses so sharply from the newer kinds? Although some go far back into antiquity, it cannot be a matter of dates. What, indeed, characterises an old rose? Scent alone will not do as a definition, since it must also be owned that in this quality they vary considerably. It really comes down to a difference in style, expressed in the form of the flowers and in the subtlety of the markings they carry.

Whereas a modern rose at its most poised moment will be pointed or rounded, revealing its centre only when long past its best, an old rose will be flattened, neatly quartered or globe shaped, often revealing an 'eye' that it has no wish or need to conceal. As time overtakes it the flower will gently fold back its petals, losing no more of its perfection then than does a fully ripe plum. It is then, too, that the most engaging colourings, those suffusions of carmine and violet, enter.

When you get into old roses you soon have to learn that though bewilderingly there are hundreds of varieties they fall into four main groups, differing in the way they grow. The Gallica type, which include the famous striped Rosa Mundi and the crimson Tuscany, are stocky plants inclined to spread by their welcome suckers. In the alba section, of which the most famous member is the soft pink Celestial, are bushes with greyish foliage that reach up to 5ft. These two are the most easily managed as garden plants. Midsummer is their only season.

So it is with the Damask roses, usually more lanky bushes of which the white 'Mme Hardy' and the pink 'La Ville de Bruxelles' are celebrated. They are known for having especially good perfume, as well as for the exquisite way in which the petals arrange themselves in quartered fashion.

A third group is the Centifolia type, the cabbage roses that produce so many petals the flower can hardly contain them or the stems hold it erect. This is the group to which the lovely 'Fantin Latour', such an affecting shade of pink, belongs, together with the smoky purple 'Tour de Malakoff'. The moss rose, whose calyx is clad with sticky, feathery glands which gives it this name, is an offshoot of the Centifolias and is exemplified by the deep crimson 'William Lobb' and cream 'Blanche Moreau'.

It is these last two, together with the repeat-flowering Bourbon type like the curious 'Variegata di Bologna' and the massive-flowered 'Mme Isaac Pereire' (later on the scene), that can prove unwieldy as garden plants if they are left to themselves. In most gardens where they are grown they are given some sort of prop.

From the Damasks and Centifolias, the mosses with them, you cut away flowered wood when the bloom has gone and raise up the supports on their legs which hold a disc of broad wire mesh. The new tall stems grow up through this and are restrained temporarily. Then they are shortened by a third or even half in winter. (Only in winter can you prune the Bourbons or you would remove the wood that will bear the second crop).

Indeed, you can prune old roses harder than is commonly supposed. The bounty of flowers they carry, if only through three heady weeks, is so lavish that a little of it can safely be sacrificed in favour of good garden deportment and to fit them into smaller plots than the public gardens in which they are most often seen.

What is beyond dispute is their vulnerability to those pests and diseases that threaten all roses, even those bred to be resistant. To get rid of both at one squirt you can safely mix Murphy's Tumblelite and Tumblebug, while the PBI Bio firm put up a spray ready mix called Multirose which also has a foliar feed in it.

TEN THINGS YOU DON'T NEED TO WORRY ABOUT

By Ken Thompson

1. Don't waste money on expensive gadgets such as compost aerators and tumblers, or on dubious herbal compost activators.

   The beauty of compost is that nature has been turning green waste into compost for at least 400 million years and needs almost no encouragement from you to go on doing it. You don't even need a bin, other than for the sake of tidiness. All you really need is patience – and anyone will make compost in the end. People who claim not to be able to make compost probably can't catch a cold or lose money at the races either.

2. When pruning floribunda and hybrid tea roses, don't waste time carefully cutting every stem to an outward-facing bud.

   Just cut roses back hard, without worrying about each cut; if you have a lot of roses, you can even use a hedge trimmer. Consider this: when did you last worry about 'outward-facing buds' when trimming a hedge, and has not worrying about them ever done your hedge any harm?

3. Don't buy boxes for wildlife to nest and/or hibernate in. Garden centres now sell a range of wildlife homes designed to attract everything from hedgehogs to bees. With the

honourable exception of those for birds, most don't work and even the few that do aren't worth buying. The only 'wildlife homes' proven to work are those designed to provide nesting holes for solitary bees, but it's simple to make your own for nothing. Drill some holes (4–10mm diameter) in any old piece of untreated wood and hang somewhere sunny. That's it.

4. Don't just weed out every seedling in your garden on principle.

Among the seedlings and small plants that appear spontaneously in your garden, most will be weeds, but not all. Many of your garden plants are itching to self-seed if you only let them, so take an intelligent interest in young seedlings and keep any that look interesting, at least until you're sure what they are.

5. Don't waste money on buying blackcurrant and gooseberry bushes, or on raspberry canes.

I can begin to see why many people aren't attracted by growing veg; after all, you do need a few proper tools, various parts of the process can be cold, or wet, or muddy (or all three), a lot can go wrong, and there is always the possibility of everything being eaten by slugs. But home-grown fruit is easy: plant, pick, eat more or less sums it up. But before you dash off to the garden centre, credit card in hand, check if anyone you know already grows what you want. Raspberries sucker so freely that anyone who grows them will already be digging up new canes and throwing them away, so they may as well give them to you. And stick a few currant or gooseberry prunings in the ground about now and most will be rooted by spring.

6. Don't erect a fence until you have considered the rival attractions of planting a hedge.

A hedge will neither rot, nor blow down in the next gale. Hedges are cheap, especially if you buy bare-root plants at this time of year, make good windbreaks, are permeable to wildlife, last forever and can provide food and nest sites for birds.

7. Don't waste time and money trying to eliminate moss from your lawn.

Consider why there's moss in your lawn. In a generally damp climate like Britain, moss is a natural component of any short grassland and can only be significantly reduced by a great deal of work, including (but not limited to) improving drainage and removing any trace of shade. Whatever you do, moss will always increase in winter. If you really can't stand moss, have you considered moving to the Mediterranean?

8. When planting a new shrub, ignore any instruction to add organic matter to the soil in the planting hole.

Roots may initially grow well in such a hole, but they often struggle to break out into the surrounding soil. Also the modified soil will tend to dry out in summer, and the hole will tend to fill up with water in winter. Plant a new shrub into unaltered soil, and add the organic matter as a top dressing after planting.

9. Don't just squash any creepy-crawly on principle.

At any one time, there are probably several thousand species of insects and other invertebrates that call your garden home. Even an experienced naturalist wouldn't know what all of them are, or exactly what they do for a living, and some of the ugliest are among the most useful. Hoverfly larvae are strong candidates for the least attractive animals in the garden, but few creatures are quite as good at hoovering up aphids.

And finally …

10. Learn from your mistakes.

Don't let a know-all like me tell you what to do in the garden, or when to do it, if your experience tells you otherwise.

3.

'The Dukes of Marlborough and Devonshire have been locked in annual combat over their white Muscat grapes'

The Challenging World of Fruit

14 APRIL 1973

A taste for tomato

By Denis Wood

To taste the essential flavour of raw tomatoes the fruit must be picked ripe and warm from the plant while it still holds its delicate sharp taste, like the smell of the foliage.

Eaten thus it is an entirely different vegetable from what is bought in shops which, unless locally grown, will have been picked when the fruits are pink or even green, their ripening, such as it is, taking place in the course of transit by boat and lorry, and in shelf life.

For many commercial growers, taste is a consideration secondary to thickness of skin to withstand the battering of travel, and uniformity of size to take the eye of market buyers.

When cooked, tomatoes impart their own distinctive flavour to any dish in which they appear, dishes sometimes described as 'à la Provençal'. This flavour is subtly insistent, as indispensible as a viola in a concerto, giving colour to the harmonies but never obtrusive. Tomatoes lend character to all stews, particularly boeuf Bourguignon, and even steak and kidney pie. They can too often, be constituents of unimaginative mixed salads for which they are prostituted by being crudely sliced unskinned or even put in whole.

For me they should always and in all circumstances, be blanched and skinned by dropping them first into boiling water for three minutes and then in cold water, until cool enough to be peeled and quartered, the pith removed, and sprinkled with sea salt and sugar.

When prepared in this way and served with the herb basil they are fit for a king.

A devoted connoisseur hankering after his own tomatoes in May or June, will have a greenhouse heated to 65°F and show in it seeds in boxes or pots in January or February, giving them an intermediate shift into 3in, preferably peat, pots, before putting them into final positions, which can be 8in to 10in pots, or boxes on the staging or prepared borders on the ground inside the greenhouse.

The developing plants are loosely tied to canes or to wires fixed against the glass. Good varieties for a heated greenhouse are 'Alicante', Suttons' 'Seville Cross', an F1 hybrid, and also 'Kingley Cross', another F1 hybrid bred by the Glasshouse Crops Research Institute.

For a man without a greenhouse there are out-of-door varieties which will produce good fruits from August until the first frosts. One of the best for flavour is 'Marmande', a continental irregular-shaped tomato, of the kind so delicious in markets in the south of France, Spain and Italy. It has solid flesh and few seeds.

'Outdoor Girl' is another good one with more orthodox round fruits, and 'Alicante', already referred to, notable for its thin skin, is a splendid variety which can also be grown under glass.

Last year, about the end of May, I was able to buy plants of 'Outdoor Girl' and also of 'Eurocross', both of which, being short of space, I put in between some cistuses on a warm wall, and cheek by jowl with heliotropes, tobacco plants and *Salvia grahamii* against the house wall itself. Apart from the rather aggressive-looking canes needed to support them, the effect was interesting and became really attractive as the fruits reddened.

It is, I think, a mistake to be too conventional about what goes where in a garden; narrow borders of flowers for cutting have long been part of a kitchen garden and now perhaps the reverse process can be tried. Beside tomatoes I had vegetable marrows among flowers, and very gay their short-lived orange trumpets were. Globe artichokes can be used in a mixed border and look splendid, and so can the herb fennel with its tall feathery spikes, in particular the bronze-leafed one.

Two small-fruited tomatoes which will crop well out of doors are 'Small Fry', an F1 hybrid with bright scarlet fruits, only 1in to 1½in across, and 'Sugar Plum', also known as 'Gardner's Delight', which is given the accolade 'supreme' in Thompson & Morgan's flavour guide of tomatoes. Bush tomatoes can often be fitted into a garden where canes and supporting wires are difficult to arrange. A good one is Suttons' 'French Cross', an F1 hybrid with the flavour of 'Marmande'.

When it is not possible to buy plants of such as 'Alicante', 'Marmande' and others in late May, they can be raised at home by sowing seeds in a cold greenhouse or frame in March, or in April in the north.

Soon after germination the young plants can be moved into 3in pots, preferably peat pots. The more heat that can be hoarded in the greenhouse or frame the sooner the plants will develop. The temperature can rise to 72°F before it is necessary to open ventilators or slide the frame-lights open. They must be hardened off by progressively increasing the ventilation at night as danger of frost recedes, before being planted out towards the end of May.

Secrets of the rhubarb triangle

By Caroline Beck

W hen, three years ago, I took over an abandoned allotment in County Durham that was waist deep in weeds, what made me sign on the dotted line were the red stems and crinkled bronze leaves of rhubarb poking up among the nettles. And every year, when I see rhubarb force its way up through the soil, I long to eat a sweet, home-made crumble.

Perhaps the reason rhubarb is so beloved of northern gardeners is that our cool, damp climate produces the sweetest, most succulent stalks and steals a march, for once, on our southern neighbours. It grows particularly well in West Yorkshire and the 'rhubarb triangle' – sandwiched between Morley and Rothwell, to the south of Leeds, and Wakefield – has made the crop into something of a local celebrity.

Most of the long strawberry-pink stems with yellow etiolated leaves in the shops at the moment come from here. The industry grew up at the end of the 19th century. The heavy clay soil made growing easy, fuel to keep the forcing sheds warm was supplied by the Yorkshire coalfields and 'shoddy', a by-product of the local wool industry, was used as a mulch for the tender rhubarb crowns.

Before the Second World War, there were more than 200 growers in this area; now it's down to just 10. One of the biggest is E. Oldroyd & Sons, a family-run business that has been growing rhubarb for more than a century. It's an expensive and labour-intensive activity. The crowns have to be grown outside for two seasons before being brought into large forcing sheds and kept in the dark. Warmth and moisture trick the plant into thinking it's spring. And then up it grows, red and sweet. Harvesting the crop begins around Christmas, starting with 'Timperley Early', and because natural light must be excluded from the sheds, picking is done by candlelight.

Until the early 1960s the 'rhubarb express' train would take crates of the crop from Wakefield to the fruit and vegetable markets of Covent Garden and Spitalfields every night. Now, with tours of the candle-lit forcing sheds proving a tourist attraction, plans are afoot to revive the train – but in reverse, bringing tourists in from the south to Wakefield.

Janet Oldroyd, a fourth-generation rhubarb grower, regularly gives talks about the crop and what she doesn't know isn't worth saying. 'Let's get this over with,' she says. 'Rhubarb is a vegetable and not a fruit.' Although her experience is at the commercial end of the market, she has tips for amateur gardeners, too. 'You should plant fresh rootstock in a deep hole enriched with plenty of well-rotted muck. It's going to be there for some time, so make sure there are no perennial weeds.'

She recommends replacing the plant every eight years and moving it around the garden to prevent a build-up of disease. 'If you have a stalk that's persistently flowering, pull it up and get rid of it.'

Janet gets impatient with people who phone her up saying they've forced their rhubarb and that after a few years it's looking sickly. 'Of course it is,' she says. 'We throw away our rootstock after forcing because it weakens the plant so much. If you're going to force it, you need to rest it. Don't pick it for the summer before or the summer after.'

For gardeners, she recommends two new varieties, *Rheum x hybridum* 'Stockbridge Arrow', a maincrop variety with a high yield and an excellent flavour, and 'Cawood Delight', which has an intense red colour and good flavour but a low yield. 'Queen Victoria', named after the rhubarb-loving monarch, also has a good flavour but, according to Janet, is very well named, because 'she's a temperamental old bugger'.

The only way to harvest rhubarb is the 'pick-and-twist' method. Don't cut stalks with a knife because this can introduce fungal infections. Instead, hold the stalk near the bud at the base and pull and twist firmly.

Just 20 miles outside the rhubarb triangle, the Royal Horticultural Society's northern garden at Harlow Carr, near Harrogate, holds one of two national collections of rheum. It grows more than 120 named cultivars, representing one of the biggest collections in the country.

Allan Kavanagh, volunteer custodian of the National Plant Collection of culinary rhubarb, recommends planting the crowns of a named cultivar in the autumn. Crowns with at least three nobbly buds are the best, planted just below the surface of the soil to encourage them to put down strong roots. Although rhubarb loves moisture-retentive soil and, happily, northern gardens can oblige, don't choose a waterlogged site. If the soil is heavy, plant on a mound to help drainage. Don't pick for the first year because this will weaken the plant. Some stems can be picked the following season and after this you need never want for rhubarb again.

Although it is relatively pest-free, slugs can be a problem – especially when forcing pots are used. A gardener friend who hates losing her earliest crop to slugs recommends putting gravel around the outside of the forcer.

Rhubarb lost its popularity after the war. The sweet-toothed British had eaten it in abundance during the rationing years because it was often the only pudding available. I have childhood memories of being virtually force-fed stringy, overboiled rhubarb by my thrifty grandmother. When smarter, more colourful pineapples, oranges and bananas came in from the tropics, rhubarb was consigned to abandoned allotments and kitchen gardens.

Its revival is thanks in part to the trend for produce that hasn't clocked up more miles than Concorde. With some judicious planning, a few varieties can supply you with stalks from February to the first heavy frosts. 'Early Superb' or 'Timperley Early' are both good for forcing but will produce stems in late March or early April if left to their own devices. The second earlies start cropping in May. Many growers consider the best of these to be the 'Champagnes', which have a good red colour and are sweet and tender. 'Early Champagne', 'Hawke's Champagne' and 'Stein's Champagne' are all delicious. For rhubarb addicts, 'Glaskin's Perpetual' and 'Zwolle Seedling' will produce until late summer or early autumn.

Rheum can also be used in the ornamental garden and its large architectural leaves and fondness for moisture make it ideal for ponds and bogs. *Rheum palmatum* combines well with other damp and shade lovers, such as hostas, irises, hellebores and primulas, where their dramatic foliage and flower spikes add texture and height to planting.

23 OCTOBER 2010

How to grow the perfect grape

By Sarah Raven

There were only three entries for the glasshouse grapes at this year's RHS autumn show; the competitors were two dukes and a Ms M. Walshaw. The Duke of Marlborough went home empty-handed, MsWalshaw bagged a First for a single bunch and the Duke of Devonshire won top prize for the pair with two bunches of his Chatsworth-grown 'Muscat of Alexandria'.

The lack of take-up for this particular class is not surprising. Growing Muscats is a huge achievement and represents months of work, love and worry. They're expensive to produce, but one must remember that these are unbelievably luscious fruit, halfway to a plum, each grape so fat and full you feel it needs a bra. Each one a pure liquid sugar capsule. More of us with greenhouses should at least have a go.

To win competitions you need huge bunches with broad shoulders; every grape must be in good condition, no blemishes, no bruises, and the bloom – the smokiness that covers the skin – must be perfectly intact.

The grapes at Chatsworth are managed by garden custodian Ian Webster, who walks through the grape houses most days. The thought of all the work he does is inspiring but leaves me feeling faintly exhausted. I ask Ian how much of his technique applies to those of us who grow more usual varieties such as 'Black Hamburg' or even the garden-centre variety 'Italia', which I have in my greenhouse. If you want perfection, he says, all of his expertise can be applied to home-grown grapes – but you won't need to use any heat.

Ian starts the grape year in early January, opening up all the doors and vents of the vinery to 'let the cold pour in'. The gardeners have to remove the top 2in of soil from the raised beds every winter to refresh it. The soil is then pH-tested and lime is spread in areas that fall below 6.5. Ideal grape-growing soil is between pH 6.5 and 6.7. The soil is replaced by a mix of about two-thirds loam and one-third sharp sand (no peat) with some charcoal added to keep the soil sweet. This is spread over the beds and lightly watered in. After a week it is top-dressed with blood, fish and bone, and again lightly watered.

So, with the doors open day and night, Ian then chooses the coldest day to prune the vines. If done in too mild a spell, the cut wood bleeds and weakens the plants. All new growth is reduced back to usually one bud per spur (which gives you bigger bunches), or sometimes two buds, with all others entirely removed and the spurs tied in firmly, using Flexi-Tie. Next, Ian – using a blunt knife – scrapes all the loose bark from the main vine stems and around the spurs. This does two things – it gets rid of overwintering pests and, by loosening the bark around the spurs, allows the new shoots to grow through more easily the spring. The whole place then has a massive spring clean, with every pane of glass, every metal strut, scrubbed down with Jeyes Fluid. With grapes and all their potential pests and fungal diseases, you have to be scrupulously clean.

There is then a pause until March, when heat is turned on in one of the houses to bring the grapes into harvest earlier than is natural. The temperature is brought up gradually (to 18°C) and the floor damped down, increasing the humidity and creating a perfect microclimate to force fruit for the middle of August. By doing this in one house and not the other, the fruit then comes in succession. Ian closes all the ventilators and keeps the doors closed, ventilating only on the very hottest days. Any draughts on new growth can spell disaster.

When the growth reaches 6in, raffia ties are spaced 6in apart between the support wires. The growth is thinned down to one shoot (or sometimes two per spur) and these laterals are tied to the raffia. Without this, the new growth naturally reaches towards the glass and will be scorched.

The vines start to flower in mid April – the whole glasshouse fills with a sweet honey scent – and Ian needs to ensure that every truss gets good pollination. He walks down the vines and 'taps the rods' to distribute the pollen, doing so every day for a week while they're flowering.

Once the berries are set, they swell very quickly to the size of a pea – and must then be thinned. At least half of the berries in every bunch are taken out with scissors to allow the others to develop. That's one

Tips for growing grapes at home

Ian recommends three varieties for growing at home: 'Black Hamburg', 'Mrs Pince' (a black variety) and 'Foster's Seedling White'.

Grapes are hungry plants so feed regularly with a balanced feed such as blood, fish and bone every six weeks or a liquid feed (such as seaweed fertiliser) every three weeks.

Beware of extreme fluctuation in temperature – try to keep it constant by regulating ventilation.

Remember to renew any string ties that are tying up the rods every year.

Pollinate around midday when the atmosphere is dry.

When thinning, do not touch the grapes, use a small stick with a V notch in the end to steady them, and small pointed scissors.

Do not walk on the vine root area; this can cause compaction and damage the crop.

Never spray the foliage or grapes with water during the growing season.

A neglected vine can be restored with heavy pruning, but only in the depths of winter when it is very cold.

Always try to have the greenhouse floor dry in the evening and overnight.

Clean up shoots and prunings after thinning and de-shooting in summer or they will spread disease.

heck of a job, but has to be done for fat and healthy fruit and it also helps to reduce the chances of powdery mildew. And at least half the total number of bunches are removed altogether to prevent the vine from becoming exhausted. Ian says that if you fail to do this, the plant will take a while to recover.

You also need to stop the new growth at least two leaves behind the bunch – and keep stopping them in the next few weeks. Any young shoots coming in the axils below the bunch should be removed, too. This encourages all the goodness into the one bunch per spur.

As the season goes on, ventilation is increased. At this point you have to watch your fruit like a hawk 'walking the crop over' – keeping your eyes peeled for the greyish dust on a berry with powdery mildew, or the cobwebs of red spider mite, or cotton wool on any joints of mealy bug. At Chatsworth they use sulphur vapour to prevent the outbreak of fungal diseases and biological control for the likely pests in a greenhouse. Good old-fashioned jam pots – with a drop of water added – keep the wasps at bay.

Finally, the grapes swell and begin to colour in August, when Ian floods the beds with water and then covers them with white polythene. This holds the moisture in the soil but also stops the damp rising into the fruit and encouraging botrytis. There is no water on the beds from that moment until the following spring. In the later-cropping house, the beds are covered with reflective silver sheets, which throws any light up on to the fruit and gives the grapes more colour.

Zesty grape and almond cake

Serves 10–12 as a pudding

Serve this as a pudding with crème fraîche, or as a cake. It keeps well – for four or five days, like a polenta cake, but lighter and moister.

Ingredients
225g (8oz) soft butter
130g (4½oz) caster sugar
100g (3½oz) light soft brown sugar
4 large eggs
150g (5¼oz) plain flour

150g (5¼oz) ground almonds

300g (10½oz) Muscat grapes (halved and deseeded)

Zest of 1 lemon, 1 lime and 1 orange

2 tsp baking power

1 tbsp demerara sugar

1 heaped tbsp flaked almonds

Method

Cream together the butter and caster and light soft brown sugars until pale and fluffy.

Add the eggs one at a time, beating well and scraping the sides of the bowl after each one.

Mix in the citrus zests.

Sift flour, ground almonds and baking powder together and then fold into the mixture.

Spoon the mixture into a loose-bottomed cake tin (9in) lined with baking parchment and scatter the grapes evenly on top.

Sprinkle on the demerara sugar and flaked almonds and bake for about 50 minutes at 175°C/337°F/gas mark 3½ (add 10°C/25°F if non-fan oven) until risen, golden and springy to the touch.

Roasted fennel and grape flatbread

Makes 2 flat breads which each serve 8

This is one of the easiest breads to make. Just shove all the ingredients together, leave to rise, roll out and leave for a short second rising and bake. We had this with fried sea bass fillets and a tomato, chive and chilli salsa. This recipe makes two loaves. You can store one easily wrapped in tinfoil and left in a cool place for 2–3 days and then heat through in a warm oven for 10 minutes.

Ingredients

480g (1lb 1oz) strong white bread flour

21g (¾oz) fresh yeast

2 tsp Maldon salt

4 tsp caster sugar

100ml (3½fl oz) extra virgin olive oil, plus 8 tbsp

2 fennel bulbs

2 tbsp chopped fennel

1 tbsp fennel seeds

300g (10½oz) Muscat grapes (halved and deseeded)

Method

Place flour, salt, sugar, olive oil and yeast into a mixer with a dough hook attachment.

Turn onto a slow speed and gradually add warm water to form a dough, mix for 5-6 minutes. If you don't have a mixer, just mix and knead by hand.

Turn out into a greased mixing bowl, cover with cling film and leave to rise in a warm place for an hour, until it has doubled in size.

Meanwhile, thinly slice the fennel, season quite generously, drizzle with olive oil, wrap in tin foil and roast in the oven at about 180°C/350°F/gas mark 4 (add 10°C/25°F for non-fan oven) for 30 minutes until soft and aromatic. Leave to cool.

Toast the fennel seeds in a dry frying pan until they crackle and pop. Then crush roughly in a pestle and mortar and leave to one side.

Turn the dough out onto a floured worktop and divide in half.

Roll each piece out into a circle about 1½in thick, place on a greased baking sheet and leave to rise a little for about 15 minutes. Then use your thumb to make deep impressions on the surface. These will help to trap the olive oil and prevent your bread from rising too much.

Brush 2 tbsp olive oil over each flatbread, scatter the roasted fennel, halved grapes, chopped fennel and roasted fennel seeds evenly and brush each with another 2 tbsp olive oil.

Leave to rise for another 20 minutes, then bake at 190°C/375°F/gas mark 5 (add 10°C/25°F for non-fan oven) for about 15 minutes.

Cool on a wire rack. While cooling brush again with the remaining olive oil. Serve warm or cold.

✖ 26 OCTOBER 1993 ✖

Dukes duel with Muscats

By Richard Spencer

The sound of grapeshot echoes in the air as the flower of England's nobility leave the battlefield of the Royal Horticultural Society.

The Dukes of Marlborough and Devonshire have been locked in annual combat over their white Muscat grapes. Devonshire's are bigger – but Marlborough's are of better colour. And that carried off the trophy this year.

It was a reversal of fortune. The judges at the RHS Great Autumn Fruit Show awarded the big prize (£20) on points to the Duke of Devonshire last time round. His Grace was philosophical in defeat, but pessimistic about his future chances.

'Miffed is the word,' he said last night. 'I think from now on he is more likely to win than I am.'

Devonshire is feeling particularly irked because without his encouragement his rival might never have entered the stakes in the first place. It was during a shoot at Chatsworth some four years ago that he mentioned he had heard the Blenheim Muscat hit the mark. The gauntlet was promptly taken up. From then, not even the presence on the judging panel of his former gardener Mr Dennis Hopkins, could help. Devonshire's were 'symmetrical, complete and well-balanced,' he said, but Marlborough's 'even more meritorious'.

꧁ 2 OCTOBER 2004 ꧂

The incomparable fig

By Ursula Buchan

Sooner or later, every fruit enthusiast hankers to grow a fig. There's something irresistibly exotic about those pear-shaped, ribby, green or purple fruit, with their luscious, pink, scented flesh, hanging voluptuously from the branches of handsome trees clothed in enormous green leaves. But it is easy to be put off.

Figs were one of the first fruit to be domesticated, and were an important food for the Egyptians and Mesopotamians. Though they have been grown in this country since the Romans introduced them, they won't thrive everywhere outdoors: figs need long, hot summer days to ripen fully and are vulnerable to damage from hard winter frosts. However, on the plus side, they're self-fertile, easier to prune than a peach, not too beset by pests and diseases, and a breeze to propagate. You can grow them in a greenhouse anywhere in the British Isles. Best of all, you can grow them in a large pot, provided you have somewhere frost-free for it to stand in winter.

An outdoor fig is most likely to reward you reliably if you live south of the Trent. All the better if you can provide a tall wall or fence, facing south or south-west, on which to fan-train the tree, and which can be protected temporarily from frosts, if necessary. Reads Nursery in Loddon, Norfolk, holds the National Collection of Figs and Stephen Read has customers in Northumberland – however, he admits that they don't do well in Yorkshire. I know of a number of fruitful trees growing outside in Northamptonshire, where I live, so it's a matter of asking round the neighbours in order to assess your chances of success. In any case, as our summers (generally) get longer, hotter and sunnier, and our winters milder, we can surely be more adventurous.

Figs produce not one but two crops of fruit a year in hot climates: in this country, only one will ripen successfully outdoors. The fruitlets are initiated at the end of shoots in late summer, and will be ready to pick by the following August or September, depending on variety. A second crop is initiated in spring, but these will only ripen successfully under glass. The fruit stores for a few weeks at most in a cool place and, if picked before it is ready, will never ripen off the tree.

What to grow

The most commonly available and hardy variety is *Ficus carica* 'Brown Turkey', which has purple-brown fruits about 5cm (2in) long, but fig aficionados do not rate it as the best-tasting. Stephen Read particularly recommends 'White Marseilles' and 'Saint Johns' – both early and 'melting, juicy, nectar drops' – to grow inside or out, and 'Brunswick', with its handsome, finely cut leaves, for a wall. For growing under glass he would plump for 'Rouge de Bordeaux', which has a heavy crop from mid-August, or 'White Marseilles' and 'Sultane', to give a first crop in July and a second in late September and early October.

How to grow

Fig trees are best grown with their roots restricted to encourage fruit rather than leaf growth. Dig a hole, roughly 60cm (2ft) square and deep, and line it with paving slabs, which should stand just proud of the surrounding soil. Fill the bottom with brick rubble, then a good John Innes No. 3 compost. Plant your tree in spring, cutting it back to about 40cm (15in) tall.

Sideshoots will develop in summer – tie these in. Keep the tree well watered especially as the fruit swell, feeding fortnightly with a high-potash fertiliser. If you are keen and energetic, protect the young shoots of fan-trained plants against frost with fleece or polythene sheeting, rolled down from a lath fixed to the wall. Mulch the roots.

Potted figs grown as bushes or half-standards do best in a 40cm (15in)-diameter pot or even a half-barrel, in John Innes No. 3. Watering is ceaseless in anything smaller. Bring it inside to a greenhouse, cellar, garage or well-insulated shed when frosts threaten.

Propagate by hardwood cuttings.

Pruning

The best way to get a good crop is to ensure that there are many short-jointed shoots in summer, at the end of which the fruits will develop.

In June, after they have made five leaves, pinch out the young shoots on fan-trained figs and those grown as bushes in containers. After the leaves have fallen in autumn, remove any fruitlets that won't ripen. Prune all diseased and dead wood in spring, and tie in young shoots on fan-trained trees, cutting back any that are surplus to one bud. Thin the oldest wood every three years.

Pests and diseases

Blackbirds are very fond of figs, so net the tree as the fruit is ripening. Wasps can also be a problem. The only remedy for coral spot is to cut out the infected wood with secateurs or a pruning saw.

Fruits of merrie England

By Denis Wood

One day I will make a poet's orchard and leading up to it I will have as a sort of ante-chamber a little uphill plot hedged with hawthorn, and with a stream running across one corner. Here I will plant trees not often seen now but which were once cultivated for their fruits, and which all have individual beauty and interest, making them useful also as single specimens in a garden.

Down the left, that is in the south-west corner, I would have three or four quinces by the little stream because they enjoy having their roots near water. They grow into rounded bushes or trees on short trunks, often twisted in outline and full of character. The dark-green leaves are felted a little on the undersides and in May there is a cloud of flowers which are white or whitish-pink.

The fruits are the shape and size of pear-shaped apples, golden-yellow. They have a strong smell which is pleasantly curious to catch on the air in passing but pervasive and sickly indoors, and other fruit should not be stored with them for fear of catching the smell. They are cooked with apples to give sharpness to a pie and they make a very good jelly, one that really 'cools the gums' as an old country woman used to say.

Medlars deserve to be cultivated for the unusual beauty of their flowers and their crooked wayward outline. The flowers are large five-petalled, white or pale pink, within some lights a tinge of yellow on account of the yellow stamens in the centre. A tree will grow to 25ft.

Even that great connoisseur, Edward Bunyard, in his *Handbook of Fruits* (1925) blenched at the prospect of eating them, though he quoted Prof. Saintsbury as considering them to be the ideal fruit to marry to port. A man with courage enough to want to eat the fruits will leave them on the tree until the end of October and then store them in a fruit room until they are 'bletted' – that is beginning to go rotten. They are shaped like small brown apples clasped by the calyx, and showing the ends of the seed vessels through an open end.

Medlars will succeed in ordinary, good, well-drained soil, and need a position in the open in full sun, for preference in the lee of a screen from cold winds.

John Evelyn devotes a whole chapter to mulberries in his 'Silva' of 1664, in the course of which he refers to the attempt made by King James I to establish mulberry plantations here to encourage a silkworm industry, which was soon abandoned. Probably the cold and damp conditions of most of this country are unsuitable for the White mulberry, the one whose leaves provide food for silkworms.

The mulberry of gardens is the Black mulberry, *Morus nigra*, which originated in west Asia and has been cultivated for centuries. It grows to 20-30ft with a width in maturity greater than its height. It has been called the 'wise tree' because its leaves appear so late in the year at the end of May when danger of frost is usually over. Its leaves are large and closely packed, so that in full leaf the tree makes a dense mass against the sky.

The deep-crimson fruits open in great numbers in August; some are taken avidly by wild birds hungry after the moult, but many fall to the ground and lie in profligate abandon. They are in black-berry-like clusters, sweet and sub-acid, and pleasant to eat when well ripened at the end of a hot summer.

At the upper end of this little plantation I would have a few walnuts. These are truly great trees reaching to 60ft or more, and wide-spreading, so they will be planted 40 or 50ft apart. *Juglans regia* is the tree grown for its nuts. It has a strong erect trunk and large pinnate acrid-smelling leaves, which appear in the middle of May.

Except for those intended for pickling, which are taken from the tree in July, walnuts are harvested when fully ripe, that is when they fall to the ground in October. The outer green husk is taken off and the nuts scrubbed to remove lingering fibres which can be pabulum for fungus. They can then be dipped in a bleaching solution and dried before being packed between layers of salt in earthenware crocks, and kept in a cellar until they are needed to accompany a port of sufficient dignity.

All this, of course, is providing that grey squirrels and rooks (my dearest outlaws) have left a gleaning for me. But if not I shall not be unduly concerned because these trees will be growing steadily into money for their timber for my descendants.

To one side of this plot I would plant a brake of nuts, or a nut walk. To produce the largest nuts, hazels are planted 15ft apart, pruned to an open goblet shape and kept down to a height of 6ft with a spread of 12ft or more. But I, not being chiefly concerned with an economic nut-producing unit, would let them grow to their natural height of 18ft, rejoicing in their swinging golden catkins at the time of Candlemas.

The cobnut or hazel is *Corylus avellana*, a possible native, but the Filbert *Corylus maxima* is an introduction from south Europe and west Asia. This nut is longer and in proportion narrower than that of the cobnut, and it is set in a longer husk. *Pace* the squirrels, the nuts are harvested when they are perfectly ripe with their husks brown, which usually means when they fall to the ground in late September. When they are quite dry they are packed like walnuts in alternate layers with salt in earthenware crocks and kept in a cellar.

27 APRIL 1974

Melon lore

By Denis Wood

Melon Frappé, sliced, diced, iced, tarted up with unspeakable maraschino cherries – what a travesty this is of the real thing, and how different when picked from one's own greenhouse and left for a few days in a cool room to come with dignity to its perfect ripening.

A degree of success can be achieved by finishing melons in frames or under cloches in a very warm corner in the south but it is still necessary to have a greenhouse to start the young plants into growth and, in fact, they are at their best grown entirely in a heated greenhouse. To quote from an old classic guide to vegetable growing, *The Culture of Vegetables and Flowers*, by Suttons, published by Simpkin Marshall (my copy is the 10th edition of 1902), 'The melon is grown in much the same way as the cucumber but it differs in requiring a firmer soil, a higher temperature, a much stronger light, less water and more air.'

The authors point out that cucumbers are eaten green and melons are eaten ripe and this makes all the difference.

There is still time to grow melon seeds but the fruits will not be so early as those sown in February or March. Sowing is done in neat pots in a greenhouse in a moist atmosphere and a temperature of 70°F at night. When the roots are well round the pots, the young plants are put in, pot and all, to a bed on the staging of the greenhouse above hot water pipes or electrically heated tubes.

This bed is made up of a few rough crocks on the staging which must have provisions for drainage either through holes in asbestos or corrugated galvanised iron, or through slats in timber. The crocks are covered with grass turves 4in thick which, for this purpose, are all the better for having been stacked for three months beforehand. On to these reversed turves the pots are stood and then surrounded by well-rotted compost of an open texture. It is important that the turves should be in position and the compost stacked inside the greenhouse for three or four days before planting in order that they should take the temperature inside the greenhouse: otherwise there will be a check in the growth.

Syringing the foliage with water at the temperature of the air in the greenhouse will usually provide enough water at the roots for a day or two; but at no time should the plants be allowed to become dry at the roots. Although it should be remembered that the amount of moisture which is necessary for cucumbers would be exceptional for melons, these latter do, nevertheless, need a little extra watering as they come into flower. As the flowers open, watering at the roots should be discontinued and the syringe used in the evenings before the ventilators are shut. It is very important not to apply water round the collar as this may set up canker.

Horizontal wires are fixed to the inside of the greenhouse side-framing and the roof and the plants as they grow are tied to canes secured to these wires. As the fruits begin to develop their weight must be taken off the vine, either by suspending them in special melon nets tied to the wires or by resting them on little wooden platforms hung on to flexible copper or lead wire. Pollination is necessary to set the fruit and to do this male flowers are picked, the petals pulled off, and the pollen on the anthers transferred to the stigmas of the female flowers which can be identified by the immature fruits showing at their bases.

Of the different kinds of melon seeds both Suttons and Thompson & Morgan have the 'Canteloupe Sweetheart', an F1 hybrid with a strong flavour. According to Edward Bunyard in his book – *The Anatomy of Dessert* (Chatto & Windus, 1929) the name Canteloupe came from Canteluppi, a Papal villeggiatura near Rome where this variety arrived in Europe from Armenia in the 15th century. The small 'Ogen' is a type of Canteloupe bred in Israel, only 6in across, with sweet, green aromatic flesh.

'Honeydew' (from Thompson & Morgan) is of the type known as the winter melon which has thick skin and can be kept for a month or more after being picked ripe. For me, the one which I would choose is 'Charantais', grown in enormous quantities near Cavaillon in Provence. It is small, has orange scarlet flesh, is delicious and refreshing and offered by both Thompson & Morgan and Suttons. Most of the greenhouse-grown melons in this country belong to the group variously known as 'Netted', 'Musk' or 'Nutmeg' melons which have a raised network pattern and may be oval and even in outline or segmented. Suttons have the scarlet-fleshed 'Superlative' and 'King George' and the white-fleshed 'Hero of Lockinge', a well-tried variety not difficult to grow.

To us today, certainly to me, melons are one of the great pleasures of summer, but I cannot think that they were Edward Bunyard's favourite fruit. He ends a chapter in his *Anatomy of Desserts* with a recital of the fates of Pope Paul II, Frederick of Germany and his son Maximilian who died after a surfeit of them.

PICNIC TABLES ARE TURNED ON TRIPPERS

A woman got her own back on the family she found picnicking on her land without permission. She went to their home – and had a picnic in their back garden.

It was Mrs Margaret Wright's opening shot in a fight to keep day-trippers off the 17-acre smallholding she and her husband own at Drayton, Worcestershire.

She saw a couple and their two children trespassing on the property, and in conversation with them, discovered where they lived. A fortnight later, a startled housewife looked out of the window of her home in Handsworth, Birmingham, to see Mrs Wright, 51, and her friend sitting on the lawn with sandwiches and a flask of coffee.

Mrs Wright said: 'She came out and asked what we were doing. I told her we were having a picnic on her property in the same way that she had one on ours.

'Her face was a picture. Then she realised who I was and saw the funny side of it.'

5 APRIL 1988

GARDEN WRECKED IN CRASH AFTER HIGH-SPEED CHASE

A computer manager returned home from a night out to find four crashed cars, three of them police vehicles, in his garden.

Mr John Thewlis, 35, of Vesper Gate Drive, Leeds, was told that they had crashed after a 100mph chase that began an hour earlier when police spotted a suspect car four miles away.

Two policemen were injured and a man is being questioned. Mr Thewlis wants compensation for his damaged garden.

4.

'Armed with umbrellas, large straw hats, walking sticks, cigars'

Great, Good and Eccentric Gardeners

✤ 24 SEPTEMBER 1995 ✤

At home with Rosemary Verey

By Elspeth Thompson

'The first thing to realise is that I'm not the best,' Mrs Verey says firmly, bright blue eyes flashing over the top of white-rimmed spectacles. Her voice is clipped and slightly weary. 'I just do pay attention to flowers and I think it's terribly important to remember that you are making a garden for the client, not for yourself. You need an ability to put yourself in the client's shoes without losing sight of your own style.'

Best or not, and much as she professes to hate the title, it is just this ability that has led to Rosemary Verey being revered as the grande dame of British gardening. Seventy-eight this year, and with a kindly but imperious presence that royalty might try to cultivate, she has countless books and television series to her name, has crossed the Atlantic by Concorde to give lectures, numbers the Prince of Wales and Elton John among her famous clients, and is cited as an influence by every other designer worth his or her salt. Her own much-celebrated garden at Barnsley House near Cirencester, draws upwards of 30,000 visitors every year.

Barnsley House garden is open to the public all year round, four days a week. Provided she is at home, Mrs Verey is very much part of the picture, patrolling the lawns with her gardeners – notebook and pencil in hand – or dealing patiently with visitors who corner her with problems with their pelargoniums. In such encounters, she has all the brisk reassurance of a good GP: a few minutes later the complainant is off on his way, with a prescription for treatment and a new plant from the nursery under his arm. This is a good bedside manner in its horticultural sense: one can imagine Mrs Verey soothing the nerves of rich clients as she diagnoses their garden's malaise and comes up with a cure. Polite unflappability may have played almost as great a role as design in her 50-year progress from country housewife to gardening superstar.

Unlike the latest crop of gardening 'personalities', who put in a stint at Kew before securing a television slot or newspaper column, Mrs Verey belongs to the generation of the talented amateur. She came to gardening relatively late, and her fame has grown up alongside the garden she began, more or less from scratch, when she and her husband, David, inherited Barnsley House from his parents nearly 50 years ago. By her own admission, she was a slow starter, her time consumed by children, tennis and horses, her gardening interest confined to reading books and jotting down notes at the Chelsea Flower Show. But as her family grew, so did her horticultural urges, helped by RHS membership (a present from her then teenage son), a gardening notebook from her daughter; and carefully digested words of wisdom from the great and good of gardening.

Gardeners are good at acknowledging debts. Part of this is down to modesty – compared to other branches of the creative arts, they are remarkably well-equipped in this department, and Mrs Verey is no exception. But for her, as for many others, much of the appeal of gardening lies in the hidden layer of personal memories and associations woven among the beds and borders: the cuttings donated by a distant friend, the visit that inspired a parterre or fountain. A walk round Barnsley House gardens in her company turns the familiar landscape into an animated tribute to the people and places that have helped shape the garden – and thereby her career – over the past half century.

The long vistas that sweep the eye down and across the lawn to the

Cotswold countryside beyond, making the garden appear far bigger than its four acres, were born of a suggestion by the late Percy Cane, a friend and adviser in the very early years. The classical temple at one end of the lime walk was erected by her husband, co-creator and constant companion until his death in 1984; he also made the pebble path beneath the famous laburnum tunnel. Other areas bring to mind David Hicks and Sir Roy Strong, while her latest daring colour combinations – shell-pink oenotheras next to flaming Californian poppies – prompt talk of Christopher Lloyd and his dazzlingly unconventional borders at Great Dixter in Sussex. And it is not just the gardening fraternity who get a mention: friends gave cuttings, Nicholas Ridley lent a hand balancing the lime walk, and Hardy Amies taught her discipline, 'the gardening equivalent of dressing, rather than just wearing clothes'.

Discipline is a word that looms large in Rosemary Verey's conversation and writings. Like many of her generation, raised on wartime austerity and a sense of duty, she considers hard work a virtue. Not for her the low-maintenance, casual school of gardening that would have the gardener lazing in a hammock with a book, rather than weeding a herbaceous border. 'I do think it's terribly important to know Latin names, don't you?' she demands, with a gaze like a delphinium-blue searchlight rooting out dissenters. She feels a 'duty to visitors to have something of interest all year round', and her renowned 'planting in layers' system (perennials following several rounds of bulbs, summer bedding dropped diligently in to fill any gaps), is certainly not labour-saving. She gets up at 5.50am, answers letters and writes for an hour before accompanying her staff around the garden, checking on plants to be dealt with and jobs to be done. There may be a group of visitors to show around, a meeting with Prince Charles a few miles down the road at Highgrove, or journeys to other clients the length and breadth of the country. All this, along with the books, the television and the trips to America. How does she do it?

'Well, first and foremost, my husband is no longer alive, so I don't have to make breakfast for him or cook his dinner or be sitting in the drawing room at eight o'clock in the evening looking as if I'd been there all day,' she says. 'Also, I've been doing it so long now that I tend to wake up in the morning knowing that today I've got to talk to Crowthers about the lead urn for a client in America, or that the time has come to plant spring bulbs.' After four decades in the job, she admits to the odd memory lapse, but the notebooks she has kept since the 1950s have never let her down. A cupboard full of them bears testimony to a life of diligence in the garden. Between Florentine-papered covers, in a schoolmistressy hand, are lists of 'grasses recommended by Christopher Lloyd, June'; flowers in bloom when the garden was open to visitors one cold March; of visits made to French and Italian gardens while on holiday in the 1970s.

But it's not all hard work. Just like her garden, which has strong, formal bones but a light touch which beguiles and blurs the edges, Rosemary Verey is not as severe as she at first appears. Ask her what she enjoys most about gardening, and the steely gaze softens: 'I love pruning the trees on wintry days when the sun is shining, or walking through the wilderness area when the spring flowers are coming out.' Best of all, though, she loves people – the reason she became a designer in the first place. As the garden matured, she and David opened it to the public, selling plants in the nursery. Inevitably, she was called upon to give planting advice. 'Visitors would ask who designed the garden, and could I recommend somebody to help them out. I'd say, "Oh, come on, what do you want?" and we'd get a scrap of paper and jot some things down. It grew from there, but only really took off as a business after my husband died.'

These days it is meeting people that she enjoys most – from the young wives who push their offspring in prams up and down the paths on summer days and leave laden with cuttings and ideas ('How do they find the time? When I had two young children I had a nanny and a cook'), to her grandest clients, such as Prince Charles ('He's getting so knowledgeable and full of ideas that I'm sure he wouldn't need an adviser if he only had more time'). Her favourite thing of all is being called back to look at a garden she had a hand in creating years ago. 'It's such a thrill to see how they've turned out, what the owners have contributed to my plans – there's no feeling like it.'

2 NOVEMBER 1991

Roy Lancaster's Bolton beginnings

By Fionnuala McHugh

The first shock for Roy Lancaster had been the lack of pie shops in Bolton. Now he stood in front of his old home in Cameron Street and saw that the front garden had been entirely paved over. For a man who has made a career out of gardening, in television and in print, this was a blow. 'In the old days,' he said sadly, 'the neighbours talked about their dahlias as if they were children and the gardens were tended with religious fervour. Those were the days when the sarsaparilla man came round with a horse and cart and everyone queued up for the manure so that they could spread it round their rose bushes.'

At the back of number 56, things were almost as bad. 'The garden's been shortened,' he began. (The recent owner assured him it was the same size.) 'But I could have sworn there was half as much again. I had my first rock garden in that corner.' It is no longer there.

Lancaster's father was a street sweeper for Bolton Corporation. He talked about his work as if it was an art. 'I can't pick up a stiff brush without thinking of my dad – it was the tool of his trade, like a spade is for me.' His mother worked in Openshaw's cotton mill nearby, breathing in the fibres until they clogged her lungs and she was forced to retire. 'She wasn't that well educated, but she was a smasher. If I was happy, that was fine by her. She didn't have a very happy life. She was in a workhouse at 14 because her father couldn't support her, and it gave me great satisfaction to achieve something in her lifetime. She liked to say, "There's our Roy on the telly."'

Lancaster's early interest in horticulture was not auspicious. When he was five, a policeman hauled him out of a garden where he was systematically destroying all the bedding plants. By 1946, when the family moved to Cameron Street, he was eight and fascinated by birds. His memories, not surprisingly, are of the world beyond the house; of going up to the Pennines to listen to the curlews, of exploring the desolate places which he and his friends called 'The Land of the Lost'.

The other boys liked to collect birds' eggs. 'That was a group activity, until I lost interest in the eggs and just wanted to watch the birds. One day I remember the gang wanted to go nesting and I said I didn't want to come and went off on my own. That was the first time by myself. Much of my plant hunting was done alone, mainly because I couldn't find anyone to share my interest.'

That he became a success was partly due to a failure: because he did not pass the 11-plus he had to go to secondary modern school, and it was on a school walk, when he was 14, that he found a Mexican tobacco plant. 'We were going through some allotments and I looked over a fence at these potato plants and one of them looked different – green with sticky leaves. So I picked it. There was nothing about it in the school library and when I took it to Bolton Museum, they sent it to the botany department at Manchester University and they sent it to the British Museum in London. I couldn't take that in. The furthest I'd ever been was Blackpool. And then one day I got a letter from London telling me the plant was *Nicotiana rustica*, the first recorded in Lancashire and the second ever in the British Isles. For a week I knew what fame was.'

This was the beginning of the bug. Even so, he was thinking of becoming an engine driver until his father died: 'I remember going into the front bedroom when he was dying and I was frightened. I was really scared. He looked very thin, very pale. He could hardly find the energy to speak. He put out his hand for me to go to him – and I panicked, I went out of the room. When I think of that now, I regret it.'

The family needed money immediately; his older brother was in the army, his younger sister at school, so Roy went to work for Bolton Parks Department. At weekends he went on field trips with the Bolton Naturalist Society; at night in his tiny bedroom he pored over a battered copy of *The Flora of Bolton*. 'An amazing world came together in my mind, with those wonderful names Robin-run-up-the-hedge, Devil's-bit scabious, ladies' bedstraw…'

At 17, national service took him to Malaya, which seemed like paradise. 'I had decided on the troopship that I was going to collect everything that there was. I sent more than 1,000 plants to Singapore Botanic Gardens and seven of them had never been found in Malaya before.'

He was 19 when he came home. Almost immediately, he recognised that his life at Cameron Street was over. 'I'd gone back to the park department, but my boss said that it was time I moved, that there was a whole world of gardens out there.' He went to the botanic gardens at Cambridge and then to the Hillier Arboretum near Winchester.

While he was there, he did a few items for BBC South, but it wasn't until *Gardener's World* came to talk to him about his own garden in Hampshire that his television career took off. The producers liked his enthusiasm; he enjoyed imparting knowledge. For the little boy who found the Mexican tobacco plant it was a second taste of fame.

Now, as well as his television appearances on Channel 4's *Garden Club* and his books (his latest, *Shrubs Through the Seasons*, has just been published), he escorts botanical tours to far-flung locations. 'I went to Japan for the first time last year and found that privet, the common hedging of the north of England, is a native. It made me think of my childhood – wherever I go, I'm forever seeing plants and birds that bring back that memory.'

22 MAY 1989

She who has the last laugh

By Audrey le Lièvre

Eccentrics in the garden? Disappointingly, the definition of eccentric offered by my dictionary is 'old, whimsical' – a terrible let-down and far too tame to describe the long line of great gardening amateurs of the Victorian and Edwardian eras.

Individualists is a much more telling term, and individualists they certainly were. Wry, pugnacious, stoutly defending their views, armed with umbrellas, large straw hats, walking sticks, cigars, they seemed to converge on the gardening world as if queuing for entrance at the gate.

Lower in the hierarchy they were paralleled by a battalion of top head gardeners, bearded, bowler-hatted men, all-powerful and as full of foibles as a tipsy cake of almonds.

Every great garden of those days was supported on the twin pillars of wealth and cheap labour. Thus released from every petty worry, the master and mistress did exactly as they pleased – and this factor, missing today, gave them their unique sense of personal worth, importance and inviolability.

From late Victorian times into the 1920s there existed a circle of rich and knowledgeable amateurs who knew each other well, visited each other's gardens, swapped plants, and sometimes tried unashamedly to wheedle from its sponsor a new plant or precious unique bulb before it got into the trade.

Of these, none kept a higher profile than Ellen Willmott. Beautiful in youth, rich and imperious, she was a plantswoman of great skill and intelligence, who later in life developed a sense of persecution and carried a loaded revolver in her handbag, jostling her lunchtime sandwiches.

Once, walking the dark one-and-a-half miles home from Brentwood Station in evening dress after a grand London party, she imagined hearing footsteps following her and stuffed her tiara in a paper bag into the hedgerow for her suffering butler to retrieve the next morning.

Perhaps her finest performance came when, accused of shoplifting at Galeries Lafayette, she confounded the store's manager by telephoning Queen Mary, who sent the King's private secretary over to support her. Declining the settlement offered, she went through a court case whence she emerged victorious.

Ellen Willmott's gardening acquaintances were legion: they included the Hon. Vicary Gibbs, who filled his garden at Aldenham House in Hertfordshire with rarities. A somewhat caustic employer, he remarked to gardener broadcaster Fred Streeter that no one but a gentleman could be expected to pronounce some of the Latin names.

Beckett, his head gardener, bore this sort of treatment with resignation: he had one passion in life – prize vegetables – and knew that he and Vicary Gibbs were at one in considering that it mattered little if the table went short so long as the cabinet were full of trophies.

Beckett thought constantly about peas, carrots and onions, and when a cauliflower revealed itself as a poor doer he destroyed it with his stick.

He was joined in this unpleasing habit by W. E. Gumbleton, who gardened at Belgrove in County Cork and was in the habit of beating inferior ('Tush and Pooh') plants to pieces. Gumbleton's letters, in huge thick-and-thin handwriting full of underlinings, were headed by 'Belgrove' and rendered into French, Italian, Spanish, as took his fancy.

Henry John Elwes, who gardened in the Cotswolds, was a character much larger than life and several times as energetic (he is said to have worn out six motor cars in researching *The Trees of Great Britain and Ireland*).

Plant-hunter, ornithologist, farmer and ceaseless traveller, he was a huge, handsome, sometimes rather terrifying man who thought nothing of asking his wife (through a third party, as they were not on speaking terms at the time) to pack up a ham from the breakfast sideboard because he had decided to leave for China that morning, and wished to take it with him to eat.

Reginald Farrer, a vivid writer and a plant-hunter of distinction in China and Tibet, unwisely took advantage of the preface he was writing for E. A. Bowles's book, *My Garden in Spring*, to make fun of Sir Frank Crisp's garden at Friar Park, near Henley-on-Thames, Oxfordshire, which contained a miniature version of the Matterhorn, with superb alpine plants and tin chamois.

Sir Frank, deeply resentful, rushed into print blaming the innocent Bowles, and Ellen Willmott stood outside the gates of the Chelsea Show distributing his pamphlets from a bookie's leather bag.

So much for outside the gates of Chelsea: inside, among the gardening mighty, speculation always sharpened and rivalry concentrated on who would win a Gold Medal. Whose name would go down in posterity?

Head gardeners were equally intent on what was coming out from under wraps. Chinese plants, perhaps, nurtured in secret?

Ellen Willmott, even now, laughs last. Just a few pinches of seed from the tall silver thistle known as 'Miss Willmott's Ghost', sprinkled in the gardens of her friends, has ensured that her imprint is still everywhere.

8 AUGUST 1990

Peter Coats - obituary

Peter Coats, the garden writer, photographer and designer, who has died aged 80, was a legendary social bachelor, widely known for his long association with the magazine *House & Garden*.

This publication had been incorporated in *Vogue*, but re-emerged in the late 1940s. Coats was appointed gardens editor soon after, and played an influential role in establishing the magazine as an arbiter of taste. He produced a steady flow of amusing and meticulously researched articles, all illustrated with his own photographs, and demonstrated an encyclopaedic knowledge of gardens both in Britain and abroad, as well as a firm grasp of the practicalities of horticulture. These qualities were evident, too, in his many fine gardening books, which included *Roses, Great Gardens of Britain, Flowers in History, Garden Decoration, The Gardens of Buckingham Palace, An A-Z of Plants, Beautiful Gardens Around the World,* and *English Gardens: A Personal Choice*.

A scion of the well-known Scottish cotton dynasty, Peter Daniel Coats was born on 26 June 1910 and brought up at the family home of Sundrum in Ayrshire, where he tended his first garden as a small boy.

He was educated at Eton, where he established many of the friends and contacts who were later to open doors for his garden writing – to which he turned after a brief foray into advertising.

Throughout his life 'Capability' Coats moved assiduously through the aristocracy, weekending at their country houses and, as often as not, advising on the replanting of a border (he had a penchant for silver fern), the design of garden furniture or a swimming pool changing-house.

An irrepressible 'spare man' with a keen appreciation of the social graces, a quick intelligence and a ready wit, Coats jokingly attributed 'any success' he may have had to his 'ability, before most people, to dance the Charleston'.

He formed a lifelong and intimate friendship with 'Chips' Channon, the Conservative politician. The entertaining letters he wrote to Channon became the basis of Coats's first volume of memoirs, *Of Generals and Gardens*, and he played a key role in the preparation for publication of *Chips: The Diaries of Sir Henry Channon*.

During the 1939–45 War he served in the Middle East and India, where he eventually became an ADC, private secretary and comptroller to the penultimate Viceroy, Lord Wavell, a position in which his flair for immaculate organisation found full rein. One greedy general told the hospitable major: 'Coats, I'll get you the Star of India for this salad.'

Coats had the happy knack of reminding his master of the right anecdote for the right occasion. When, for example, a former Mayor of Bombay complained of a rat in his room, Coats observed, 'Ah, a rat, Sir, those are for our most distinguished guests, the others only get mice.'

The Viceroy and the ADC made an unlikely combination – the austere Wykehamist soldier and the gossipy, party-loving sophisticate – but got on famously. It was Coats who helped to persuade Wavell to produce his anthology of poetry, entitled, at Coats's suggestion, *Other Men's Flowers*.

Harold Nicolson painted a memorable pen-portrait of the ADC – 'resplendent in a white and gold uniform, directing with the wave of a trowel, these stupendous creations, stepping gingerly among the cannas and the oriels. Never since the days of Zenophone has a soldier, and aide-de-camp to boot, been so precise and efficient a gardener.'

Such flattery would doubtless have appealed to Coats, whose vanity was occasionally the butt of good-natured ridicule from his wide acquaintance.

He rejoiced in his proud London address, A1 Albany, a 'set' he decorated with an elegance equal to his own sartorial appearance. His tall, distinctive figure, invariably topped by a hat appropriate to the season, could be seen issuing from the Burlington Gardens entrance to Albany as he made the short perambulation to his office at *House & Garden* in Hanover Square.

It would be idle to deny that 'Petticoats' (as he was affectionately known) was a snob and name-dropper. He took an innocent delight, for example, in comparing hospitality with that received at a royal residence ('This is better service than Royal Lodge…'); and of a ball at Windsor he mused, 'I could have asked Mrs Thatcher to dance; I knew her slightly, and to dance with a Prime Minister would have been a novel experience: but I was heavily engaged.'

Coat's many loyal friends spoke warmly of his charm and kindness, and teasingly tolerated his naive social boasting; but he was probably unwise to indulge himself to the extent he did in his memoirs. The pages were larded with Coats's claims of friendship with le beau monde, and the second volume, *Of Kings and Cabbages*, in particular, attracted some sharp criticism. Even so benign a reviewer as the late Arthur Marshall was moved to protest in *The Sunday Telegraph* that the author's ceaseless swanking made the reader 'wince and wince again'.

Peter Coats was among the last of a particular type of urbane bachelor socialite. Although in poor health during the last few years he retained much of his extraordinary energy and enthusiasm for life; he courageously went on working for *House & Garden* to the end.

23 MARCH 1985

E. A. Bowles – one of gardening's great characters

By Fred Whitsey

Although his birth, which is being celebrated with an exhibition of memorabilia at Forty Hall, Forty Hill, Enfield, Middlesex, took place 120 years ago, that venerated gardener E. A. Bowles is as living a figure to many today as his contemporary Gertrude Jekyll. His *My Garden* books written early in the century are in print again, and the garden round the large house near Enfield where he lived for his entire 90 years in splendid Victorian discomfort, is being restored. Efforts are being made by the National Council for the Conservation of Plants and Gardens to regain the 70 plants that were named after him.

More stories are still told and relished about the patriarchal Bowles than any other great gardener. They relate how when he was in his 80s he would be found in a Victorian bathing dress clearing out the pond; how he collected his friends' discarded sponges to make the soil just right for the well-being of one of his special groups of plants; and how he cherished and distributed what he called 'lunatic' plants like the one-leaved strawberry and the twisted hazel and willow. They recall his perceptive descriptions of the scent of flowers: some might smell of coconut or pancakes with plenty of brown sugar, even of a new Mackintosh. But I like best his wounded retort to a colleague on a Royal Horticultural Society committee who happened to remark that a vote against him had been a popular one: 'So was the vote for Barabbas!'

Some of the meticulous flower paintings on which he worked almost all his life are to be seen with the photographs in the exhibition which goes on until May 12.

22 FEBRUARY 2003

Graham Stuart Thomas, aged 93

By Fred Whitsey

Run a finger down the 20-page index to Graham Stuart Thomas's latest book, *The Garden Through The Year*, and you realise that about 2,500 plants are listed – plants you know, plants you know of and many more that you have probably never heard of. Each is given a brief description in the main body of the book and in almost every case there is also some nugget of appraisal – whether of appearance or cultivation needed – to quicken your gardening perceptions.

For each entry reveals Graham Stuart Thomas, now 93, as a plantsman of unparalleled experience and boundless curiosity. His book is a distillation of more than eight decades of gardening. We should listen closely.

The seed of his horticultural enthusiasm was sown at the age of six with the gift of a fuchsia. A half-crown birthday present spent on five rock plants in Cambridge market nourished it. His imagination charged, the young Graham Thomas (it was only later that he took on his middle name) started reading the weekly magazine *Popular Gardening* (which, half a century later, I edited). He studied at the Cambridge Botanic Garden, where he was also inspired by the books of Gertrude Jekyll. It was, he says, 'an enthralling and happy time'.

He began his horticultural career at the famous Six Hills alpine nursery, then entered the nursery trade at Woking. From there he often cycled over to Hascombe, near Godalming, where he met the matriarchal Gertrude Jekyll, by then in her final year. She gave him tea and the run of her garden. 'The memory of her borders, so polished and well ordered, remains with me,' he says.

The influence lasted throughout his decades as a gardener-cum-horticultural-prophet. His disciples would make pilgrimages to the display gardens at Sunningdale Nurseries, which he created with designer James Russell. At Chelsea they introduced his then novel idea of 'three-layer planting', comprising trees, shrubs and an under-storey of herbaceous plants and bulbs. Its influence was profound.

The move in 1955 to Sunningdale – justly tagged 'the most beautiful nursery in the country' – coincided with his appointment as gardens adviser to the National Trust, then the custodian of seven gardens. The number has since grown to more than 100 thanks to his 40-odd years of consultancy.

Recording plants and horticultural experiences has been a major preoccupation since his student days. His study is stuffed with files of his notes, photographs, drawings and watercolours of notable trees or plantings he happened upon. Visiting a garden with Graham is like taking a test – challenging but enlivening. He is an exacting man with an acerbic wit. He invites me to put a name to some obscure plant, praising me if I get it right and expressing horror if I fail the test. He picks up a handful of fallen cercidiphyllum leaves. 'What would you say they smell like? Strawberry jam in the making?' And of course they do. Or, 'What would you say those leaves recall?' Puzzlement. 'A wet dog, of course.'

When I wrote recently of disappointment in old roses over the past two summers, I immediately received a chiding letter: 'You knew you would get my goat ... Of course there's nothing like their fragrance. You should know that,' he wrote. *Old Shrub Roses* was, of course, the book that made his name. He quickly followed it with another on modern roses and a further book on the climbers.

'Sometimes I walk round looking for jobs to do,' he once remarked as he showed me round his earlier garden near Woking. I had no difficulty in believing it, for not a square foot of soil showed through, so densely had he exploited ground-covering plants. It was the garden of an artist, as is his present artfully schemed garden which, like Jekyll's, was a place of pilgrimage until he had to plead for privacy.

He can seem rather highbrow: for instance, each chapter of his books is prefaced with a quotation from a poem. Yet, as is revealed by his *Thoughts from a Garden Seat*, written at the age of 87, he remains a master of gardening technique.

In addition to his OBE there is no horticultural honour he has not received, including having plants bearing his name. I think of the gardening luminaries of the past – from William Robinson to old John Evelyn – and make comparison. No, none can outshine him in the range of his sympathies, the breadth of his knowledge, his study of the history of people, plants and gardens, and his eloquence. He is, I believe, the greatest gardener of all time.

'Come and see me again soon,' he says. 'I can spare you a bit of time from the new book I am writing.' Another? This would be his 20th, if you include the portfolio of his paintings. 'It's about the gardeners I've known.' It will include, I am sure, tales of journeymen and grandees, sons of the soil and ducal proprietors … and it, too, will be essential reading for any who are inspired by the example of a true gardener.

21 JULY 1991

A life in the day of Beth Chatto

I wake at about five; earlier in summer. I'm not good at sleeping; it's the mental stimulus of something always going on. I plan things I know I won't do the moment I step outside. I'm not as fast as I was, but I'm blessed with energy, the joy and sheer vitality of everything I find around me, and also the pleasure of achieving something: a new piece of planting, for instance, or a fax coming through about an article to write.

My days are packed full. I'm 15 years younger than my husband; he's 82 now. We don't have breakfast together because his day goes at a slower pace. He brings me mine in bed; it's important in his life to make this a point of duty. I have a pot of maté tea and muesli, or fruit. My mother had rheumatism in her hands, but she cured herself and was a great one for cutting down on coffee and sugar.

Sometimes I write my diary at breakfast. I'm dressed and out by 8.30am at the latest. The most important thing with clothes is to wear what is comfortable, like double-lined trousers in winter, thermals if necessary, and I even put on two Barbours. What matters is to look neat and tidy because you never know who you are going to meet, but how can you stay tidy in a gale-force wind? One day I had a haircut in the morning, then wore a balaclava during a rainstorm and looked like an urchin by lunchtime.

There are minor domestic things to do before going out. I do a big bake once a month, lots of bread and cookies. On weekdays two girls come in alternately for two hours. I have team leaders. In the propagation house my leader teaches his team where to find cuttings. Rose, my top secretary, is full-time with three part-time helpers. I'm there, next door to the house, by nine and I'll attend to what she calls 'the mulch' that piles up on my desk.

There is hardly a morning when I don't see everyone at the nursery; it's just a little contact to make sure all is well. To me the business is more of a craft or a jeweller's shop than a factory. Then I'm off into the new woodland garden I'm creating. By about 11 I'm back in the office where Barleycup drunk with a teaspoonful of molasses revives me. I'm often running, not walking, in the garden; perhaps next I'll collect plants, which I arrange in the house. The fritillaries, scented skimmia, leaves from different plants to remind me to take cuttings, make bouquets which I use as a notebook. I try to keep a real notebook in my pocket, but this rarely happens; I change my clothes so often, due to the weather.

Andrew and I don't each lunch together either. I find that after a hectic morning I have to flop down and switch off. Lunch for me is a tray with bread, pâté and salad. I'm a fanatic about eating properly and believe, after 40, that you are what you eat. One reason I'm vegetarian is because our grandchildren will have to be, since it takes 10lb of grain to produce 1lb of meat. Gardening is not divorced from food, nor from health, music or painting, nor from people, and I love all these. And I'm fanatical about soil. We are 90 per cent organic here.

On Friday afternoons I do the week's shopping at Wivenhoe, the next-door town. Some afternoons are spent just talking to people – recently, for example, to two coachloads of Americans who were over here on a jamboree about alpines; then I had the negotiations with a neighbouring fruit farmer whose pruners also work for me, and finally a discussion with some film people about a video that may be made.

About every two months I stay for the weekend with Christopher Lloyd, the garden-writer, and there was a crazy month in 1989 when we went to Australia, New Zealand and Toronto on a lecture tour. This year I give a lecture in Dublin.

The way the business is now, I am able to spend much of January to March writing. I do my articles, rewrite my catalogue and work on books at my desk in the window. I am planning another Mediterranean garden with the emphasis on dry summers and lack of rainfall, which in East Anglia we are used to anyway. I was one of the first to write specifically about how to deal with plants in drought conditions. I plan to do this book again on a bigger scale, because since I wrote it in 1978 my palette of plants has greatly extended.

After the mental and physical involvement of outside activities it is a different discipline to create on paper. I enjoy writing, once I get into it, but become withdrawn when there is no flow because there is so much I want to say. It is like a tangled skein of wool, trying to find the free end so the ball will pull and run smoothly.

I return to a proper tea with Andrew at five and we sit by the wood-burning stove or up the book-lined end of the living room. If the French windows are open, we are out on the terrace under the magnolia tree and the ducks come from the pond to join us.

In early evening I'm tempted out again and the vegetable garden is my therapy, crouching down by the earth to thin out onions. I finish in time to make supper at eight. While cooking I'll have music, usually Radio 3. Andrew and I eat together and this is our time for conversation. We've been married for 47 years and he has been the greatest influence from the ecological point of planting. Graham Stuart Thomas is another influence and for me his books are the best, with their intellectual approach. The way a person writes can get to you, put you on their wavelength. My friend Cedric Morris, the artist-gardener, opened my eyes so much.

My husband goes to bed early. I have my own bedroom, so I go to bed at 10 and read for an hour. I like biographies and was very impressed with Berlioz's memoirs. I'll read Freya Stark's travels, cookbooks and sometimes Vilmorin's 19th-century book on the vegetable garden. Many of the salads fashionable now were grown long ago for the Paris market.

After reading, if I'm lucky, I go straight to sleep, but if not, I can lie awake and hear the hours strike. I've learned not to worry. 'Grasp the nettle,' get on with it, was my mother's philosophy, and she was right.

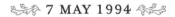

7 MAY 1994

Interview with the master – Sir Geoffrey Jellicoe

By Maureen Cleave

The final part of a new book about the landscape architect Geoffrey Jellicoe is headed: *Full Flowering – The Master Period From 1980*. The significance might not strike you until you learn that Sir Geoffrey is as old as the century and that, between the ages of 80 and 94 he has designed landscapes costing a thousand times more than those of the previous 54 years of extremely successful practice. He has a world reputation and the work pours in: the Moody Gardens in Texas, part of a $150 million project; the Atlanta Historical Gardens in Georgia, to be completed in 1996; a private garden on a massive scale for Mohamed Mansour near Cairo; something else exciting in northern Italy.

Not many people outlive their own 50-year plans: Sir Geoffrey's 50-year plan for Blue Circle Cement in the Peak District was completed this year and the company has asked him for another to take it up to 2044. A second thrilling offer had come that very week.

'A knockout,' he said. 'A real whacker. I can't tell you what it is yet, but they're coming to see me next week. It's all happening since I began to live a life of contemplation. When I was 80, I gave up my office and stopped worrying how I would pay 10 or 15 staff. My mind was free. I really would recommend you retire as soon as possible.'

He is a small man with a completely square head, like a Klee drawing. He wore a cheery pale blue jumper and walked with a stick. Everyone loves him and you can see why: his ideas so exhilarating, his smile so eager, his optimism about what the day may bring so refreshing. 'He's up to very mysterious things,' said an admirer. He is a happy man because, one dares suggest, he thinks things through.

Here is an example of this: 'A year ago last October I took a monk's vow, not to God but to myself. I remember it extremely well. I was preparing to go for my usual walk to Kenwood and I got as far as the front door when I found my legs wouldn't work. I went straight to my bedroom and sat on my bed. I had to work this out. I vowed never to leave this flat again and immediately all sorts of anxieties rolled off my shoulders.' Now everyone comes to him, the executive of the Atlanta Historical Gardens, for instance. They found themselves with 32 acres of woodland, a neo-Italian renaissance building, a quarry, a pre-Civil War village and two modern museums, and were on the plane to London to have him sort it out.

Having spent most of his life in a Georgian gem around the corner, he now lives on the fourth floor of a 1930s block of flats in Highgate designed by Berthold Lubetkin. His small collection of paintings and drawings by his contemporaries, lovingly and inexpensively collected, are along one wall while opposite is the view. In between are the usual tables and chairs and a large red plant, the name of which he doesn't know (*Begonia rex*, in fact). 'I haven't a clue,' he said. 'I don't know about plants. In fact I loathe gardening.' He added that he knew damn-all about trees (though he knew the spirit of trees) and, if I didn't feel I might tumble over, would I like to step out on the balcony and look at the view?

Sir Geoffrey always left the planting in his work to his wife Susan. His gaze is on the horizon and he feasts his eyes on this prospect which stretched that day to Harrow-on-the-Hill. The trees of Hampstead were an early summery green, the rest of London a deep blue.

'Don't you feel you're floating over it?' he said. 'This view, the proportions of the flat itself, my paintings – all keep me in vigorous form, so that I can tackle these thoroughly modern jobs.'

He was born in Chelsea. His father was a publisher, his mother a painter. He remembers her taking him to tea at the Slade when he was five. 'I was stood a tremendous tea by the students and was sick in Gower Street on the way home.' Gower Street was where he later had his office. He had a classical education and a classical training as an architect. Classical buildings, he said, were easy to design. 'Easy as pie. I did a great mansion for some clients in Barbados in the Palladian manner, rather better than Palladio – he always had trouble with junctions – but that's not where the future lies.'

After his training, he took a year off to write a book about Italian renaissance gardens. 'I did the pacing while Jock Shepherd did the drawings. I had concluded I was no good at drawing, I couldn't get the luminosity into it – Corbusier's drawings were pretty awful – and I didn't draw again until I was 80.' His romantic drawings in freehand are now considered so beautiful that he has been made a member of the

Royal Academy; a few are being exhibited in the Friends' Room over the next month. 'We fished out 18 of them,' murmured Sir Geoffrey.

Drawing is vital to his work. 'It's emotional rather than mechanical,' he said. 'It evolves in the head and comes down through the fingers and on to the page.' Pacing was equally important until he had to give it up. He used to pace everything in strides, just over 3ft, and was accurate to five per cent. At the age of 80 he found his pacing was becoming erratic. 'Two years ago I spent five days pacing the Atlanta job and I first tested out my shortened stride in this room. Pacing is valuable because when you're doing it you're wrapped in the landscape, collecting not only the facts but the ethos, the spirit of the place.'

Paul Klee had started him off on what he calls 'this extraordinary sweeping up from the subconscious', and one of the earliest examples in his own work was at Hemel Hempstead, for which he designed a long water park. 'I did the first design, quite harmless, everybody liked it but I wondered why it was so boring. Was it because it was no more than met the eye? Was it possible to plant in it an idea that appealed to the subconscious? London had a Serpentine; I didn't see why Hemel Hempstead shouldn't have a serpent. So I put in a subtle curve which was the underbelly of the monster. The huge head had a foundation for an eye while the tail flipped round an artificial hill.'

He said nothing about the serpent to anyone. The people of Hemel Hempstead enjoyed the water for 40 years until it was decided to adopt a road-widening scheme that would impinge on the monster. 'They were appalled. They came to me and I explained to them why they were so upset. Subconsciously they knew that this scheme would destroy the animal form.'

They lost the case. 'You can't defend the art of the subconscious in a court of law,' Sir Geoffrey said sadly. 'The subconscious bypasses the intellect; it's not rational.' He dislikes having his gardens explained, for example that the serpent in the Garden of Eden at Sutton Place is represented by an ugly rock. 'The guides always tell the secret,' he said.

He began to read Jung in 1963. 'I felt I ought to make serious contact with the subconscious. It is very simple what he said: there are two minds, the conscious and the subconscious, and they are quite separate. When they are in opposition there is chaos. When one operates without the other, it's dreary: when the two go together, you get a work of art. Ever since I did the Kennedy Memorial at Runnymede 30 years ago, I have been putting the subconscious into my work.'

He is at his desk at 9am, in a small green room called the grotto. It contains a telephone, drawing board, chest for drawings and a filing cabinet. There is a view of London to the east. In this little room he did the drawings for Mohamed Mansour's garden, which rests in the shadow of the pyramids, in a mere fortnight – fountains, pavilions, pergolas, a woodland walk, waterfalls everywhere, a sumptuous bathing pool, a Persian garden, an outdoor theatre and a boat trip to the underworld; much to keep the subconscious busy. He breaks for Bovril at 10am, for coffee at 11am and for lunch at 1pm. He spends the afternoon reading and watching television. Students, clients and friends come to visit.

His wife, Susan, the daughter of the historian Bernard Pares and his companion for 50 years, died in 1986. 'Susan and I were a very good pair. She was a scholar and two days before she died the chancellor of Sheffield University gave her an honorary degree. She did all my planting plans, reached a very high standard. You can imagine my loss was very great; I particularly miss going on holiday with her.

'Rather like that Potter on television, I am on the verge of death. I ought to have popped off years ago. I thought I'd reached fulfilment in 1976 with my book *The Landscape of Man*. I imagined it would be my last work ever. Not a bit of it. So, when Susan died, I did recover quite quickly because there is still something I have to give the world which must come out. I'm rather looking forward to death, it may be interesting to explore, but I have a pleasurable life as a nonagenarian. I can toddle about, my housekeeper comes in three days a week and I have serious work to do.'

Why is so much of it abroad? He has created so many beautiful gardens in England – the most famous for Michael and Lady Ann Tree at Shute House in Wiltshire, and one of the smallest and dearest for a friend of mine – but nothing on a heroic scale. The answer lay in the English temperament. 'England is an offshore island. Europe is classical but we are a country folk and we have a domestic, romantic nature in keeping with our very moving landscape, those downs and so on. We don't want straight classical lines running through them. In Europe, gardens are an extension of the formality of the house but we turned away from that with Capability Brown. Because we are romantic we look backwards for strength, the Europeans to the future.' He could have told John Major he would have problems with Europe.

Our surroundings are in the hands of three sets of professionals: the town planner, the architect and the landscape architect – and the greatest of these, in the future, will be the landscape architect. This is why, at the banquet in honour of his 90th birthday, he proposed the Foundation of Landscape Architects to burst upon the world, he said, this summer. He has just finished a paper on the environment of the future for the Council of Europe.

What about England, I wondered. How were all the people and their cars to be fitted in? 'You could fit the entire population of England,' said Sir Geoffrey comfortably, 'eight families to the acre, within a 40-mile radius of Charing Cross. It's a matter of distribution and that depends on people like me.' He wants an emerald necklace of hills around London, joining up the bits of green belt. 'Instead of endless suburbia, we would look at these hills and beyond the hills into the sky.' His plans often involve moving mountains.

The whole of Western civilisation was based on Plato. 'The heavens were geometrical and their proportions were fixed to Mother Earth. But that won't do any more. One day I read an article about Heraclitus in a Sunday newspaper. Heraclitus was a testy old man, very snappy, but he was the father of modern metaphysics and he knew his stuff. Heraclitus said that we were in flux, that history is movement, a continuous sweep, and that the subconscious harmonised the conscious.' Heraclitus helped him solve the problem of Atlanta. 'They fell for it at once,' he said heartily.

I asked what he thought a garden was for. 'I need several days to work this one out. I suppose it's an extension of the ethos of a person or persons into the landscape. When you go into a garden, you enter a place that lifts you out of the everyday world and all its worries into Paradise if you like. I say' – he broke off – 'that needs to be really nicely written.'

He can't visit sites any more. He can't do the pacing, so new work must be on sites he already knows. He can't supervise it in progress. 'And I have no responsibility,' he said blithely, 'if it goes wrong.'

Power without responsibility – a just dessert at 94.

21 JULY 1984

CONFLICT AMONG THE MARROWS

Arguments in the vegetable patch shattered the peace of an English country garden, an industrial tribunal heard yesterday.

Bob the gardener grew too many marrows for the family to eat, it was alleged, and when the mistress of the house asked him to produce fewer, he shouted: 'It's none of your business, go away I'm the gardener here.'

Trouble began when Mrs Cilla Wheatcroft's elderly father-in-law, George, a former university law professor, came to live with her family two years ago, the tribunal at Bloomsbury was told.

Mrs Wheatcroft also allowed her father-in-law's gardener, Mr Bob Clark, 59, to come and help her tend the 1½ acres around the house in Berkhamsted, Herts.

She said: 'I expected to be able to have friendly consultations over how we should plan the garden.

'But Mr Clark and I didn't see eye-to-eye from the word go.

'He wanted to organise the garden in his own way.'

They finally agreed to split the gardening between them but the power struggle continued, she said.

'I took over the majority of the flower beds and he did the lawns, the hedges and the vegetable garden.'

But there was overproduction in the vegetable garden. 'On one occasion we had 70 marrows all at once,' said Mrs Wheatcroft.

The final straw came when she asked him to clear up a rubbish tip. 'He shouted at me "You are one of the nastiest little women I know."'

5.

'At the least, add a few cakestands or lollipops'

Hedges, Shrubs and Bushy Effusions

🌿 21 APRIL 1973 🌿

Who was Hortense?

By Fred Whitsey

W ho was she, this Hortense who is imperishably commemorated in the everyday name of the common or garden mop-headed *Hydrangea hortensis*? In France, the country of the plant's earliest adoption, they even call it familiarly and invariably the 'hortensia'.

At least four ladies dispute with claims for the honour, one a queen, another the girlfriend of a travelling botanist, a third the mathematician wife of a clockmaker and the fourth a Frenchwoman nicely set up in the Bahamas.

I had hoped to run down the rightful heir to the title when the second volume of the monumental *Trees and shrubs Hardy in the British Isles*, by W. J. Bean (Murray), came out in its revised edition. Well, the learned team who have brought this great work of horticultural scholarship up to date knew better than to try to set one woman above the others.

Instead, they content themselves with stating the rival claims and then clearing away the tangle of undergrowth that obscures the true names of the whole genus of hydrangeas as garden plants.

It has taken a lot of detective work to establish a correct family tree, an odd fact when you think how common the plant is. But it is another of those cases where the cultivated plant was known to botanists long before its wild ancestor was ever found.

Apparently the mystery arose because of the secretiveness of the Japanese in whose gardens hydrangeas had bloomed unseen by western eyes for generations. But in the late 18th century someone slipped a head of flowers to a Swedish botanist who was out there studying the Japanese flora by way of the hay they let in every week to feed animals at the one Dutch trading post allowed to exist there.

He immediately thought it must be a guelder rose and named it *Viburnum macrophylla*, a pardonable error because it did look like one and it did have large leaves. The word must have got round that this was some wondrous thing to be brought out of the East, for soon they had it in France and at Kew.

The next to have a hand in making up the tale was the Czar's gardener from Petrograd. He turned up in Japan looking for the treasure for the royal collection and carried home a fine horticultural booty in the way of seeds, bulbs and plants, among them several hydrangeas. The way was then open to wholesale hybridising, thanks to the international camaraderie that has always existed among scientists. But still no one knew the original parents of the hortensia. Not until 1917 did they realise it was a bush that grew wild right on the shores of those islands that pepper the Pacific.

No wonder, then, you see such incomparably fine hydrangeas growing in the wind and rain and sun of Brittany. But the wonder really is that if they are seashore plants they should adapt so readily elsewhere. The answer is that our plants also have in them the blood of another wild hydrangea which is found growing naturally in woodland. And it is a woodland soil that you want to emulate if you want your hydrangeas to flourish.

Look at the roots they make. They're almost as fibrous and intricately interwoven as a rhododendron's. So it's peat they need, back to that ever-present help in trouble. Peat and a bit of shade they like best. Inland, that is. Round the coast they will grow 'as big as a haycock', as an early authority colourfully described one of the first plants here, but that's because of the damp in the air. Without good reserves of moisture in the soil a hydrangea will in summer hang its leaves as dolefully as a spaniel's ears.

They also like the acidity that goes with a woodland soil. Though they will flourish on lime-ridden land, they display their best colourings where the ground is free from it.

Now mysterious in their origins, hydrangeas are also mysterious in their colourings. The plant you admire in some other garden may not prove the same colour when you buy it for your own. Nor are they quite the same colour two days running.

Some varieties otherwise pink will turn naturally blue on acid soil, others resolutely refuse to do so. You can often get the admired blue colouring on neutral or even slightly limy soil by treating them with alum, but unless the plants show a willingness to assume this change they have to be treated afresh every year. Even then you may end up with half measures and a washed-out mauve.

Strangeness again that hydrangeas need to have two types of flower in a single head, small industrious ones for the essential business of fertilisation and seeding and the other kind a sort of public relations organisation to attract the insects that accomplish this consummation.

In the mopheads the two intermingle. In the lacecap type they are segregated. The one is most at home in a rather formal garden setting, the other is seen to greatest effect in the woodsy gardens we make with our rhododendrons, azaleas and our heathers.

Indeed, too often these are spent with the end of spring. Add hydrangeas to them and you have something for your visitors to admire all through summer and autumn, for the hydrangea season does go on that long.

Most of the lacecaps are pink, a few are blue (on really acid soil), but both 'White Wave' and 'Lanarth White' do live up to their names and give variety.

One I specially like for a garden of this kind is the oak-leaved *Hydrangea quercifolia*. The flowers are white or palest pink, but the leaves take on splendid colours when the autumn comes.

Thinking about them as a family, I would say they haven't a rival in length of flowering season or downright garden usefulness.

10 DECEMBER 1961

My roses thrive on a touch of neglect

By Vita Sackville-West

I was surprised (and rather flattered) when someone described a rose in my garden as 'the most photographed rose in England'. I had always taken her for granted, because she does this for me regularly every year, and goodness knows I have never done anything helpful to her in the way of manure at her roots or spraying for greenfly or blackspot or mildew or any of the other horrors from which we ought to protect our roses.

She is called Mme Alfred Carrière, and although she looks white in the photograph she has in fact a shell-pink flush, and a very sweet noisette scent, both adding to her charm.

It sounds as though I behave neglectfully towards my roses. Perhaps I do. One has not the time for everything, and much is left undone. The only thing I can claim for my climbing roses is a certain originality of treatment, to which they seem to respond. I don't prune. Cut out dead or dying wood, yes – but prune as little as possible.

All those long shoots of the summer's growth are tied in, until the leafless branches in winter look like a kind of cat's cradle, tight and flat against the wall, or like a network of crossing and counter-crossing, bending and twisting this way and that. The effect of this bending, furthermore, is to induce fresh shoots to spring from the joints, increasing the thick wealth of bloom.

All the climbers, irrespective of kind, are treated the same way, be they Hybrid Teas, Noisettes, Teas, Wichuraianas, or Multifloras. One must sometimes make an exception, as for Mermaid (*bracteata x tea*) whose long and cruelly armed wands do not lend themselves to bending; being very brittle they are only too apt to snap off even at the junction with the parent branch.

The most one can do is to tie them straight and flat, and the sooner this is done the better, even in mid-summer when they are making tremendous new growth and may be torn away by a sudden gale.

You may say that all this tying-in must take a lot of time. It does. It also takes a lot of string. Rolls and rolls of green twist. But believe me, it pays in the result.

We adopt the same method for a sweet-briar hedge trained on post and wire. Sweet-briar hedges are apt to get thin and straggly at the base, and to grow up towards the light, a very natural thing to want to do, so the only way to correct this propensity is to twiddle the young shoots down towards the base and train them horizontally when the hedge will become as dense at the foot as it is at the top.

Topiary masterclass

By Roy Strong

To misquote the popular song: 'Yew, wonderful yew, it had to be yew.' And who wouldn't, if you are among those who've had to suffer all the scorn of visitors who crow at length on seeing your newly planted hedge: 'You'll never live to see it.' Rubbish. Admittedly, it's not a hedge for those who move house every five years, but if you've put your roots down firmly, so to speak, plant it.

I write this because we're in the month when we cut our hedges, a task at The Laskett divided between our heroic gardener, Robin, and myself. But to start at the beginning. We planted the cheapest and smallest yew, about 2ft high, and you can reckon that with an annual feed it will grow about a foot a year. Don't ever cut the leader until it reaches the height which you require it, but trim the sides. The ideal hedge, the books say, should have a batter, that is the sides should gently slope and narrow to the summit. Ours don't because we didn't learn about that until later and really I quite like them boldly and exactly vertical. My main problem is that in places the foliage isn't thick to the ground. Lawrence Johnston obviously had the same problem at Hidcote, I once noticed, and infilled the gaps with box, which seemed to work perfectly well.

The first few years of growing a hedge are agony. You can count on a few losses but year eight is the dramatic turning point. By then the hedge should be about 4 to 5 feet high and the great thrill, if you are making a green room, is that for the first time you can sit down and not see out of it! I remember being bowled with excitement by this, realising that I'd grown architeture and added mystery. By year 15, your hedge ought to look as though it was planted before 1914.

But to return to cutting. Do, I implore you, think about that from the moment the hedge goes in. Make drawings on a piece of graph paper, one of the elevation and a second of the ground plan. Get inspiration from books or looking at yew hedges in other people's gardens. Cut the bed for the hedge into the ground-plan shape. Articulate the hedge wall with ramparts, pilasters, towers or windows, and crown its summit with an interesting silhouette: crenellations or curlicues, spire or pompons. For cutting the top, keep to hand a copy of your scheme and, with judicious clipping each year, see the hedge fill out into the shape you have planned. In winter, in particular, when the light falls across it, you will be grateful for having conceived it in the shape of a building's facade.

Lucky ones may have a yew hedge already. Spring is the time that you can start reshaping it. Again, draw up a scheme. In the case of the sides all it means is leaving this year's growth where you want a pilaster or bastion. When it comes to the top, wait until the autumn if you wish to cut down into it to form swags or crenellations. If you want to let it go upward again, let it sprout where you need it to. At the least, add a few cakestands or lollipops. In that case, just select the leaders and let them go up. They'll take two or three years but they'll soon be there. I've just done this with a young yew hedge only about 3ft high. My intention is to emulate that wonderful hedge at Knightshayes in Devon where hounds chase a fox along the top of the hedge. In my case it's going to be prancing pussycats all round the little garden!

Here we use hand-shears and petrol-driven cutters. I have avoided the electric ones ever since I severed a cable with a bang. It's amazing how much you can cut in an afternoon. All the twiddly bits are done by hand as works of art and love. On the whole we take care to keep hedges at an easy working height, that is reachable from one of my best garden buys, a set of rolling office steps with a platform balcony at the top and with a brake. It has transformed our annual cutting operation and copes with hedges up to 10ft high. Before that I used to balance on a pair of aluminium steps, one leg of which usually used to sink into a mole channel, keeling me over.

Although Vita Sackville-West and Harold Nicolson fled Sissinghurst for July and August, I regard these as also wonderful garden months. You can stand back and admire your handiwork, happy in having restored your garden's structure. What could be more rewading? And with yew, you can do a good deed. Yew clippings are desperately needed in order to produce the new cancer drug, Taxol. We have sent Yew Clippings Ltd over 30 large sackfuls, but smaller amounts are welcome. The clippings must be clean and fresh and also unadulterated by sticks, stones or leaves. Doing this has sharpened our yew clipping operation and I can't recommend it enough. The demand for successful yew-based drugs, I understand, is still increasing – every reason for planting that hedge this autumn.

1 SEPTEMBER 2012

Grasses – how I got with the programme

By Anne Wareham

Despite expert opinion to the contrary, ornamental grasses have brought me endless grief, expense and hard work.

I had a vision of a small hillside covered in a large parterre, echoing the small fields of the surrounding landscape, edged with box and filled with grasses. I could grow them from seed and plant them in large blocks, their pattern visible from the opposite hillside. There are a great many grass species that are well praised and tough, and they come true from seed.

So I raised a great number, planted them out and the rabbits ate them. I fenced the garden and tried again.

Then – after so many failures, now long forgotten – I eventually bit the bullet and decided that hybrid vigour was needed. Or at least sizeable plants rather than my seedlings. I also concluded that, in a wet climate, it was best to plant in spring to stop the repeated rotting-off from autumn planting.

Now the failures came in variety. Most of the plants still didn't survive the winter – *Panicum virgatum* and 'Hanse Herms' mostly cried off, for example. Or perhaps it was my care of them?

'Pheasant's Tail' grass (*Anemanthele lessoniana*) is one of the most beautiful ornamental grasses, colouring up into a sharp mixture of reds and oranges late in the season. Following the usual guidelines, I cut it down at the end of winter. Do not do this. It will die. I replanted it in the spring. I did not cut it down in winter. It now has some sparse new leaves growing feebly among the faded, discoloured dead leaves.

I grew and lost *Carex buchananii*. Tried again. The problem with this one is that it is almost impossible to tell if it's alive. When a small tug brings it out in handfuls you can conclude it's dead. Currently I think it may still be alive as it appears to have seeds. On some of the plants. The jury's out on the others. When you are planting in generous blocks, random survivals are no joy.

Dutch perennials guru Piet Oudolf visited and looked visibly shocked – he considered that many of my choices would be far too rampant. He was horrified by several, including *Phalaris arundinacea*

'Feesey's Form' which now, several years later, almost fills its space. Most of them feebly fail to ramp, even British natives such as *Carex pendula*. But at least that is one which responds happily to being cut down annually, once established. It also offers year-round (if slightly dull) green. And it seeds itself gently, which delights me.

Our terrace was filled for several years with self-seeded *Stipa tenuissima*, a fountaining grass with soft flowers at just the right height for stroking as you pass. They grew enthusiastically between the paving stones and the effect was well loved. One cold winter they just totally vanished, never yet to return.

Some grasses are so amazingly vigorous that people run away at the sight of them. Lyme grass (*Leymus arenarius*) – about 2ft high in steely grey – is one of these. Or so we thought. A friend, after a discussion about her garden and impressed by my wonderful show of leymus, dreamt of a stunning combination of this with Crocosmia 'Lucifer' for a huge area in front of her house.

It sulked and it rotted, and every time I visited I felt ashamed of my association with it. Eventually, after two or three years, it grew a bit. The scheme is now amazing when the grey and scarlet happen together – but at some price.

Anemanthele lessoniana is not the only grass that presents a management puzzle. There are many which will tolerate cutting down to the ground in late winter with a strimmer … but *Stipa gigantea* is not one of them. Furthermore, this has early, long-lasting, tall airy flowers – beautiful in that situation we all have, of course, where the sun will backlight the flowers. Next spring those flowers are still there, in among the new foliage. You must remove the dead flower stems and leave the foliage. The best way would be to snip off every stem with a pair of scissors – if life has left you wondering how to fill a few weeks.

You may conclude that I am useless at growing things, or have rotten conditions. Clearly I make mistakes, but I have covered two acres of garden quite intensively with a modicum of success.

The other problem besides the cultivation of grasses is – what to plant with them? You don't stick them all together in their own border. They simply don't offer enough contrast of form to complement each other. They work in my parterre because each is in its own space, separated by the box hedges. And, in some desperation, I have added blocks of crocosmia, *Iris sibirica*, together with 'Gardener's Garters' (Phalaris), which is variegated white, and a small running bamboo, *Pleioblastus auricomus*. These offer grassish foliage and some contrasting colour.

A parterre would work on a smaller scale too, so you may wish to know that some of my more reliable grasses have been *Calamagrostis x acutiflora* 'Karl Foerster', 'Overdam' and *Calamagrostis brachytricha*.

Many grasses are too small and, well, grassy, to add much to a border, but some miscanthus, or the aforementioned *Stipa gigantea*, will send their flowers soaring above the surrounding plants from midsummer into winter, adding grace and movement, and in the case of miscanthus, beautiful colour.

Do be aware though – the vigour of miscanthus seems to vary dramatically. I have lost far too many which have failed to establish or, faced with competition from other border inmates, moped. Others will grow huge and happy and irremovable.

Grasses do look wonderful massed, moving poetically in the wind. They look especially good where they can show off the grace of their form – along the foot of a hedge, at the edge of a border or alone in a pot. Try them in ones before dozens, to see whether you can keep them happy. In spite of all the trouble, I do love them. So I persist with my parterre despite 15 years of heartbreak. Oh, and final horror – they change their names every five minutes.

29 OCTOBER 1966

The very best autumn berries

By Gordon Forsyth

What a glorious array of brilliant colouring was provided by trees and shrubs, laden with berries of richly tinted autumn foliage, at the Royal Horticultural Society's Show this week. Some of them, although contributed from famous gardens of considerable magnitude, were certainly worth considering for gardens of average size.

I have never seen more heavily fruited branches of *Pernettya mucronata* alba than those which came from the Exbury estate. It reminded me at once what an excellent evergreen ground cover plant this is, in sun or the light shade of a wild garden or open woodland, provided the soil is lime-free and plenty of peat is mixed with it. Its sex life is, however, a little strange, which is why I occasionally get complaints of bushes failing to bear fruit.

If a plant has a fleshy calyx, it is likely to be hermaphrodite, with both male stamens and female stigma, and so capable of producing a moderate crop of its marble-like fruits without outside interference. If the calyx is dry and membranous, due to this deformity it is likely to be wholly male or female and incapable of producing berries, but in the male form capable of ensuring, by supplying the pollen, a full crop of berries on the hermaphrodites, and the wholly female varieties.

All of which adds to the interest of the plant, but need not worry us unduly, for the nurserymen have selected several good fruiting forms of it, and provide male forms of the type, which if planted in the ratio of one to three or four berry-bearers, will ensure generous crops.

Of the named varieties, their colours referring to their berries (not their small, heather-like flowers), a good selection would be alba or the larger-berried 'Donard White', rosy-lilac lilacina 'Donard Pink', deep-rosy purple *Rubra lilacina*, and crimson 'Bell's Seedling'.

Alternatively, you can plant a selection of 'Bell's Hybrid Pernettyas', which present a lively colour range of large berries. Normally, in sun the bushes grow up to 3ft tall and rather higher in light shade, but spread freely by sucker growths, forming a dense root mass and so capable of choking any weeds that encroach on their domain.

The viburnums are a varied family of shrubs, rich in both flowering and fruiting species, but surely in spectacular effect at this season there is none to compare with the Chinese species *V. betulifolium*. It is a large grower, with the dimensions of our native guelder rose (*V. opulus*), but not averse to restrictive pruning.

Imagine a large bush, heavily laden and bending under the weight of huge clusters 6 or 8in across, of red currant-like fruits, and you have a pretty accurate picture of what *V. betulifolium* looks like. I would suggest it is one of the best of all autumn-fruiting shrubs and well worth a place in any garden that has sufficient space for it.

There must be few gardens that do not boast representatives of the cotoneaster family, possibly the herring-boned red-fruited deciduous *C. horizontalis*, which grows outwards if unrestricted, or upwards to window-ledge height if against a north or east-facing wall; low-growers like the evergreen ground-covering *C. humifusa* (Dammeri), ground and rock contour-hugging *C. microphyllus* in its several forms, or the wide spreading, comparatively dwarf *C. conspicua decora*, the scarlet berries of which, for some unknown reason, the birds leave well alone until winter is far advanced and they are really hard pressed for food.

There are also, of course, plenty of tall-growing cotoneasters, all with the characteristics of the family of fruiting freely and thriving in any average soil, but one which impressed me with its unusual berry colour was Mr L. de Rothchild's tall-growing hybrid *C. exburyensis*. The facts that Hilliers of Winchester list it and regard it as a 'first-class addition to our evergreens', and the birds do not sample its apricot-yellow berries until the new year, are sufficient evidence of its value to the seeker after less common large shrubs for autumn and winter effect.

And what of *Clerodendron trichotomum* as an out-of-the-ordinary fruiting shrub for the connoisseur, provided you have space for a rounded bush that will grow to 10ft or more and as much across? Its flowers in late summer are not very conspicuous, but their rich perfume certainly is, and they are followed in autumn by a generous and colourful crop of light-blue berries, set off effectively by deep-crimson calyces.

It is a curiosity of nature that while the flowers of the clerodendron are so well scented, the leaves have a repulsive smell.

The variety fargesii is I think the best, but it is well to plant it in a position sheltered from cold winds, and to give it winter protection with a screen of sacking in its youth. It is also best to surface mulch it with peat or leaf mould, rather than dig these materials in, for if its roots are damaged it will protest with sucker growths.

For a generous fruiting climber, I know of none more colourful than *Celastrus orbiculatus*, its growths generously clustered with yellow fruits which burst to disclose the vivid scarlet seeds, not a particularly artistic colour combination, but most effective at this season. Alas, it is a very vigorous grower. I have had it to a height of 30ft or so climbing on its own account up the trunk and branches of an ageing ash tree, and have also grown it on a fairly large wooden pergola by pruning its young growths severely each winter.

With its sturdy main branches entwined around the post, it finally supported the pergola when the post rotted at the base, and also had no objection to a Jackmanii clematis using it for support and to relieve its somewhat drab appearance until it was ready to ripen and display its fruits. A climber to consider, but not to be rash about if space is restricted.

DARE YOU LET YOUR PLANTS ANSWER BACK?

By George Plumptre

Over the centuries, gardening history has seen a number of scientific but simple inventions that assist ordinary enthusiasts. In the 1830s there was the Wardian Case. Now there is the Smart Plant Pot, invented by a student of industrial design and technology at Brunel University and the most recent winner of the prestigious Best Invention award on BBC1's *Tomorrow's World*.

Both were invented to help gardeners look after indoor plants, but with the technology of their different periods. Dr Nathaniel Ward was the first to realise that a sealed glass case made a self-sustaining environment for plants, as the water they transpired condensed on the glass to be recycled. The cases named after him were popular with Victorians who were not necessarily expert gardeners but who wanted a fashionable display of houseplants.

The Smart Plant Pot was invented by Rebekka Peterson and inspired by her own love of gardening and from watching her father's houseplants. 'He's always kept them and I've nagged him about looking after them better, so in the end I decided to do something about it myself,' she says. Her research showed that many people who enjoy houseplants don't know how to look after them, and she determined to find a solution.

The critical factors for houseplants have always been moisture and temperature. Dr Ward's case came up with an innovative response for his time and the Smart Plant Pot does the same for the 21st century.

A computer-controlled mechanism constantly monitors moisture and temperature levels. When there is too little moisture, or if it gets too hot or cold, the computer triggers a variety of responses from a sound module. If the owner is away they can telephone in and programme watering from their keypad. Having rung in and heard the monitor sing plaintively 'please can you water me' they then hear the reassuring sound of water being applied before the monitor/plant says 'goodbye' and hangs up.

Alternatively if you're at home, the monitor senses when you're close by and sings out if the plant is in need of change. You can opt for less personal bleeps, but Rebekka knows that the voice bonds plant and owner. It's a bit like being introduced to caring for your first baby: it prompts you to learn how to respond and interact to the plant's simple requirements.

The big question is whether Rebekka's prototype can get sufficient backing to make the leap to commercial production. The idea seems too good not to get picked up by some shrewd investor, so don't be surprised if, when you're next on holiday, a fellow guest gets up and says, 'I'm just going to call home and speak to the ferns.'

6.

'A diet of roast squirrel, squirrel pie and even deep-fried squirrel'

What to do about Wildlife in the Garden

A garden fit for cats

By Brian Harvey

A remark my wife has never been allowed to forget was to the effect that I did not know anything about cats until I married her. Some instinctive understanding of feline nature must nevertheless have lurked within me: for neighbours' cats came to explore and then to colonise the garden I was remaking.

They still visit: even though we now have four of our own – ranging in temperament from Athleticat to Lethargicat. And it is a constant source of delight not merely to observe their wistful but uncooperative curiosity when they see a human being on all fours to do the weeding, but also to share their relish of the habitat created.

They do indeed have their own requirements which go far beyond the obligatory planting of *Nepeta mussinnii* (catmint). That, incidentally, has its dangers. Whether its leaves are medicinal or not, the flowers are a magnet to bees and a kitten engaging in playful remonstrance with the winged intruder can acquire a painful lesson.

Cats need four things from a garden. They need cover; they need runs; they need something to climb. But those three are only physical needs. The fourth is psychological. They also need stability.

It is not that they do not like, say, fuchsias or dogwoods. But those need to be cut back almost to the ground in spring and nobody likes to prune to the accompaniment of a baleful wail. So permanent cover is essential.

Cats support the textbooks about planting shrubs in casual groups (do not go for the symmetry of even numbers). Five of the low-growing *Spiraea japonica* form one favourite hidey-hole. But evergreens are better and the neglected *Sarcococca confusa* in a patch of three gives cool summer shelter. It thrives even in the shade of an overhanging apple tree.

These are individual slumberlands. For a collective playground *Ceanothus thyrsiflorus repens* is unrivalled. Mine has far exceeded the catalogue's predicted maximum growth to stand some 5ft tall with a 12ft spread. By so doing it has encroached over the lawn, the grass of which is there left ragged for inquisitive noses, eyes and whiskers to relish.

For a run down one side (or the end) of the garden a beech hedge offers much more fun than traditional privet, which goes so ragged at the base. Underplant it with ivy as a host to insects.

Down the side especially this will give a kitten its first natural access from the security of the house to the world of adventure awaiting it beyond. There it can scamper, retreat, scratch and explore in safety and without doing damage to more cultivated areas that you have planted with purer horticultural motives. Let it lead if possible to a rough-barked tree or to a dense woody bush such as the evergreen *Garrya elliptica*.

For climbing give any standard tree a stake driven in at an angle – not merely to avoid damaging its roots but to give cats that easier way down which they always seem to leave out of the calculations of their vaulting ambition. And the smaller varieties of weeping tree, such as *Malus* 'Echtermeyer' (which also yields the most delicate of crab apple jellies, both in colour and in flavour), provides a spectacular vantage point from which an adventurous cat can play 'I'm the King of the castle'.

Stumps of old trees should be left anything from 2ft to 6ft high. They are no eyesore to a cat: nor to human sight if bulbs are naturalised around their base. Moreover, since cats can be playfully perverse when it comes to photography, such features provide a natural perch on which they are happy enough to pose.

A last word. Do not be too tidy a gardener. A little corner of wilderness consisting of unkempt grass, rampant rushes, even nettles and thistles, may offend the eye of the perfectionist. But it will bring its own reward when, sickle poised at the ready, you are reproachfully confronted by its sleeping occupant and are given not only an excuse to be lazy but also a lesson in compassion by your master (or mistresses).

Every time you return from work or shopping, your cats should compliment you on your garden by jumping out at your feet from some unexpected quarter and drawing your eye to the beauties you have created.

25 MARCH 2006

Why not make your own wormery?

By Lila Das Gupta

I never cease to be fascinated by the way in which different couples operate. My dear cousin (like his father before him) regularly forgets his wife's birthday: he loves her dearly but she is now so hurt by his negligence that it's a topic they hardly speak of. Like me, she is a very keen allotmenteer, but unlike me, she feels that leaving reminders around the house is unromantic.

Our noticeboard, on the other hand, is a thatch of memory-jogging cuttings, and nestled among them will be a host of gardening goodies that have caught my eye. This week it's my birthday, so there are jagged pictures of wormeries taped to the fridge.

I had always imagined wormeries to be a revolting, seething mass of worms, like maggots writhing in an angler's tin. Then, last year a friend took his apart to show me how they work and I've been smitten ever since. There isn't much to see: a layer of vegetable matter, then the casts, which look like soil, and below that a brown liquid (leachate) which makes an excellent plant feed when diluted.

For those with limited space or who only generate a small amount of kitchen waste, a wormery is an ideal way to make compost (but beware of overfeeding, a common mistake among novice wormers). The bonus is that worm-waste is the El Dorado of the compost world. Not only is it more concentrated than ordinary manure, but because the waste has been digested by the worm and contains an enzyme that helps to break it down, it is easier for plants to access the nutrients in worm compost than in ordinary types of manure.

This means that you can add worm compost to vegetable beds that require manuring and get away with adding it a little later in the season. One of my last permanent raised beds to be filled is an asparagus bed. I've toyed with the idea of including this in my rotation plan, but the truth is I need things to be as low-maintenance as possible, especially since we've now moved grandma into new digs round the corner, so there's her courtyard garden to help with too.

You can imagine my delight when I found VermiSell, a business in Kendal which deals only in worm-related products and asparagus crowns. It strikes me that Greg Holden, who runs the operation, is an ideal sort of dinner guest: 'I'm in the City, what about you?'

'Oh, I'm in worms. And asparagus.'

Greg used to work in marketing for a well-known pizza company. When he was made redundant, he looked around for things to do and decided to take the family chicken farm, which his parents were thinking of selling, in a new direction. He sells worms for fishing and composting, but he also took up growing and selling asparagus crowns, on the following logic: 'Since it's only serious gardeners who tend to have wormeries, I thought they would be more likely than other gardeners to buy a plant that takes time to yield a good harvest.'

I have ordered 10 crowns each of 'Connover's Colossal', traditionally grown in Britain, and 'Mary Washington', common in the US. I like the idea of a 'special relationship' veg bed. It will be interesting to see if the Brits outperform the Yanks.

There is still time to order asparagus crowns, as the cold weather has delayed their lifting (aim for five plants per person in the family). The bed should be well-manured some weeks before planting: this is where worm compost comes in handy. The crowns are then planted on a ridge a few inches high to increase drainage, with rows at least a foot apart. My friend, Jazz, in Ireland, mulches his bed with straw, which goes a long way to suppressing weeds.

Don't expect to get quick results from this nobleman of the vegetable garden. Just remember, good things come to those who wait.

28 JULY 2012

Secrets of the magic mollusc

By Germaine Greer

This is the year of the snail. My one-acre wood is festooned with them: garden snails, banded snails and even, I think, 'Kentish' snails or *Monacha cantiana*. There will be readers of these words whose blood runs cold when they realise that, no matter how many snails they put to death, there are billions more making the best of this summer's dark skies and warm rain.

Every year, as soon as we have a spell of dull, humid weather, we are told that there are unprecedented numbers of snails about. In fact the level of the mollusc population, year by year, is a good deal more constant than that of the insect population.

Snails don't travel far; although I may have seen more snails this year, I probably harbour about the same number as usual. In less sodden years, snails sleep through the summer days and go grazing at night; this year they have been on the move around the clock.

Snails need calcareous soil; some species can even eat limestone. Most of our native species are survivors of the woodlands that once covered these islands. If they are in your garden now, it is because they have no choice. In woodland it is easier to see how necessary they are to the recycling of rotting plant material. Right now, in my wood, snails of all sizes are hauling themselves up the trees. As they climb, the tiny denticles on their radulas, which are rather like powerdriven sanding blocks set in their mouths, are constantly scraping off the algal moulds that have formed on almost every branch.

I wish I could tell you how the snail converts this unpromising material into nutriment; it's just another of the many things we don't know about a fellow Earthling we see every day. Many people find snails repulsive, but to see a big old garden snail hoisting itself up a tree like a Winnebago climbing stairs is oddly moving: and never more so than when a juvenile snail of another species has hitched a ride on its shell. A snail crawling up a window blind has been shown to be able to hoist 51 times its own weight. Snails represent an extraordinary combination of great strength with utter gentleness.

When I gathered a small tub of our native mahogany and cream snails (two species, *Cepaea nemoralis* and *C. hortensis*) and took them into the house to see if I could key them out properly, they motored all over their plastic container, utterly optimistic and trusting. When they extended their delicate antennae and stretched their translucent bodies to travel over my hand, I couldn't imagine smashing them or poisoning them, no matter how many hostas they ate.

Snails are deaf, so you can't train them to carry out orders; but they are capable of associative thinking. They can remember where things are; they know where they sleep; Darwin noticed how one snail discovered how to escape from a tank, and returned the next night to help another snail escape by the same route.

They do not have brains as such. The cell bodies of their nerve cells are concentrated in a set of ganglia. Because mollusc nerves have no insulating myelin sheath, snails have developed long nerve fibres called axons to enable fast transport of impulses. Such snail axons are being used in attempts to make 'semi–alive' microchips for treating problems related to defective brain function in humans, such as some forms of blindness. (The next time you want to stomp on a snail, just fire up your own neurons and go figure.)

Snails can express satisfaction and dejection by the way they move their tentacles: two long ones for seeing, two short ones for smelling. When American author Elisabeth Tova Bailey was paralysed and kept helpless and flat on her back by a mysterious disease, she was greatly aided in fighting off despair by the quiet routines of a snail that had come into her sickroom as a stowaway in a plant pot. In her now famous book, *The Sound of a Wild Snail Eating*, she describes how she got to know and respect her snail.

This was by no means the first time these magical molluscs have teased a writer's curiosity. Shakespeare twice refers to 'the tender horns of cockled snails' and the way a frightened snail 'Shrinks backwards in his shelly cave with pain'. His disciple Keats latched on to the 'tender horn' with the same oxymoronic idea.

When Thom Gunn celebrated a snail moving 'in a wood of desire,/ pale antlers barely stirring/as he hunts … ' he was not thinking of my vegetarian snails. His snail is male and predatory. The image tells us more about the poet than it does about the snail.

The reality is that nothing is more mutual than snail mating: each hermaphrodite snail has to arouse another hermaphrodite snail, and then move in perfect synchrony towards mutual ejaculation. Each snail has a dart that inserts a spermatophore in its sexual partner, and an organ that receives the partner's sperm. Their mating is entirely reciprocal, with intromission occurring simultaneously. So complex are these arrangements that they account for most of the snail's anatomy.

There is a lot of variation from one species to another, but as a general rule this process happens around once a month. But snails are promiscuous, and can store sperm from a number of partners for several years.

After mating, each snail will lay about 100 eggs, supplying each with its own calcium shell which is the beginning of the shell of the born snail. Most of the hatchlings will be eaten by a vast range of predators, including other snails. As creatures near the bottom of the food chain, snails are necessary beings. There is hardly a bird that will not eat a snail; badgers, foxes, snakes, blindworms, hedgehogs, moles, shrews, toads, frogs, ground beetles, fireflies, harvestmen, all willingly eat snails.

Humans eat snails too, which is why we have the brown garden snail which is apparently native to the western Mediterranean. It used to be called *Helix aspersa*, but the gradual realisation that its reproductive apparatus is quite unlike that of other Helix species has caused it to be removed from that genus. It can't be said reliably to have entered any other, so for the time being it is known as *Cornu aspersum*.

Other names have been suggested: Cantareus (the singing snail), maybe; or Cryptomphalos (the hidden navel). But – at least until another member comes along – Cornu remains, quite literally, sui generis.

What to do about squirrels

By Elspeth Thompson

People have been pestering me to write about squirrels. There are those who love them and who put food out for their furry friends, but most gardeners I know are absolutely frustrated by them. One friend spent a recent Sunday planting bulbs; the next day she came home to a scene of such devastation she couldn't believe a small animal could be to blame. All her tubs and planters were ransacked, and some had been overturned. Scattered over the ground were expensive tulip and crocus bulbs, each with one bite taken out. One could imagine the squirrels as miniature Henry VIIIs at a banquet, taking a bite and then throwing the bulbs over their shoulders, as if they were chicken bones.

Another friend bought a 'squirrel-proof' bird table, only to discover that the wily creatures just wait unseen in a nearby tree before pouncing onto the table and scattering all the feeding birds in their wake. And one of my sisters is plagued by an extra-athletic squirrel who runs along the roof of her neighbour's conservatory, shins up several feet of drainpipe and then swings precariously, paw by paw, along the underside of the metal grille beneath her window like the man from the Milk Tray adverts – all because he loves the crocus bulbs in her window box.

I'm pretty sick of the things myself. Our dog has completely failed to deter squirrels from emptying the bird feeders strung around the metal arch outside the French windows – and while I enjoy their antics as they devour their first course, I cannot sit by and watch them help themselves to a 'pudding' of tulip and crocus bulbs. In recent years, I have taken to laying a circle of small-gauge chicken wire over each pot of bulbs, but this can make mincemeat of the emerging leaves if not removed at the right time. Another remedy I've tried with some success is sprinkling dried chilli pepper on the surface of the soil or mixing it with bird feed – it is claimed that this enriches the birds' food with vitamin A, but squirrels, mice and other mammals abhor the taste. It seems to work, but you have to remember to replenish the supplies, especially after rain.

Whenever I complain about the squirrels in our garden, my husband waves his *Elvis Presley Family and Friends Cookbook* at me – apparently, The King's impoverished childhood in Tupelo, Mississippi, featured a diet of roast squirrel, squirrel pie and even deep-fried squirrel. You may squirm, but squirrel has been on the menu of at least one swanky London restaurant in recent years. Few gardeners would want to eat a squirrel, I'm sure. They just want them to leave their trees and bulbs alone. And yet squirrels hardly get a look in on the pages of most gardening reference books. Even the HDRA, the organic gardening organisation, only recommends covering bulbs with netting and wrapping tree bark with protective rings. Squirrels are legally classed as vermin, so if you trap them (and many gardeners resort to rat traps), you are supposed to kill them rather than release them into the wild.

When I touched on the subject of squirrels in a column some years ago, I was shocked by the number of readers who regularly drown or club them to death. It made me determined to find a way of living with the animals in my garden. I have since resorted to using squirrel-proof bird feeders, except for one pot of nuts I keep by the window where I can admire the creatures' gymnastics at close quarters. The bulbs are safe beneath a layer of chicken wire or, in some cases, a mulch of grey beach pebbles. This way, everybody's happy.

Watch the birdies

By Robert Pearson

I wonder how best to describe the average gardener's attitude to birds? To call it a love-hate relationship would be wide of the mark, for the delight we take in their grace and beauty as they quarter the garden far outweighs any annoyance at damage the miscreants may do.

Also, I doubt if any of us put the goodies on one side and the baddies on the other in quite such stark terms.

What complicates matters, too, is that our judgment is often superficial or faulty, or a mixture of the two. It is a fair bet, for example, that the starling is more often condemned for the boorish way it shoulders aside opposition at the bird-table than praised for its diligence in searching for grubs in the lawn. The fact that the starling can be a dreadful nuisance in city centres is a different matter again.

If there is one garden bird with which I thought I was on intimate terms it was the robin, for, like most garden-owners, I have my faithful follower of the spade. Yet recently, to my surprise, I heard somebody on the radio speaking of this bird's pugnacity in dealing with its own kind.

Events soon proved the speaker right. A few days ago my robin, uncharacteristically, brought a companion with which, after a spell of harmony, it proceeded to engage in the most physical of rows. But I would forgive my small friend far more than that minor aberration for the pleasure given me on so many occasions. At least he has none of the anti-social tendencies of the handsome bullfinch which, as my favourite bird book laconically puts it, 'feeds mainly in trees and bushes on berries, buds and seeds'.

The curious thing about bird damage in gardens is its lack of consistency: birds and berries decimated in one district can be ignored in others; and the availability or otherwise of alternative food sources does not appear to offer any cut and dried answer to this.

REVOLUTIONARY IDEA FOR A GARDEN

By Wendy Holden

Towering over the terracotta pots and the garden urns at this year's Chelsea Flower Show are two magnificent statues of revolutionary fighters wrenched from the Communist Party headquarters in Prague. The blackened figures, standing 8ft high, are from a set of six which graced the rooftop of The People's House, formerly the baroque Sporkuv Palace, built in 1651, but renamed by the Communists. Commissioned by the Communist Party in 1950 and carved out of sandstone by three leading Czech sculptors, the six 1½-ton figures – a woman and child with rifle, a Cossack, a flag-bearer, a navy gunner, a rifleman and an infantryman – represent the October 1917 revolution. Doomed to be destroyed with the collapse of Communism, they were rescued by Drummond's of Bramley in Surrey, garden statuary specialists. They are now on sale at Chelsea for £20,000 each or £100,000 for the set.

7.

'Window-box gardening was fashionable during Coronation year'

Gardening in the City

John Brookes and the urban challenge

By Nigel Colborn

W hat does John Brookes make of the urban nightmare garden? Dingy brick walls which wobble and shed mortar; soil impoverished, dehydrated and shaded by next door's monster chestnut; the site's proportions ruined by a tower block which blots out all horizons to the south but seems to funnel the wind straight in through the back door. Depressing? For some perhaps, but John Brookes tackles such daunting problems with aplomb:

'When you look at garden design, the first thing is to know exactly what you want. Far too many people have an over-romanticised view of what their garden should be like, but you have to get away from nebulous ideas and look at specifics. A town garden is a working extension of the home and the smaller the garden, the more it works for its keep.

'First, I believe, it's very important to have an accurate measurement of the plot. Then you can consider practical problems such as rear access, where the oil tank is to be, where the rubbish is stored and where the washing is hung. With these essential requirements in mind, you can then develop a scaled design which will be in proportion to the house.

'Even if you sit in your garden only from time to time in summer, it is still used "visually" for 12 months of the year. It is important to create a structure that is in harmony with the rest of the house and that works with the buildings or landscape beyond. If there is a 20-storey building behind, the garden will be designed on a different scale from one where the background is dominated by nothing more than a neighbour's pear tree.

'The physical problem common to most town gardens is the reduced skyline. Because the sun may not even climb above neighbouring rooftops in the winter months, gardens that are baking hot in summer can have frost lying on the ground all day in winter. The boundary walls may help to deepen the shade and if they are old and crumbling with lime mortar, they intensify drought problems by acting as wicks, soaking up moisture. There is little you can do about shade from neighbouring buildings but effects of moisture loss from soils can be minimised. You need not dig out exhausted soil because you can rejuvenate it with lots of farmyard manure. Organic mulches such as peat or well-wetted compost are beneficial as well, not only to enrich the soil but also to improve its moisture-retaining properties.

'As for planting, the smaller the garden, the more over-scale the planting should be. Go for big plants with huge leaves, such as angelica, acanthus, artichoke (cynara), *Ligularia dentata* 'Desdemona' and the large-leaved ivy *Hedera colchica* 'Dentata', even if it means going over the top. Indoors, you have to live with the décor but outside it can be pure theatre. You can create your own world with different colours, not just of plants but by painting, using statuary, whatever you like. Painted trompe-l'oeil and decorative murals can be extremely effective on the small scale of a town garden. And where the natural light is strong, position plants or architectural features where they will cast dramatic shadows.

'Plants are extremely cheap and, compared to the costs of having interiors designed and decorated, landscaping is not especially costly. You can even get garden design on a mortgage these days and money spent outdoors will always increase the value of the property. So be prepared to spend.

'It's essential to have some plants that look well in winter. *Euphorbia characias wulfenii* is a favourite for its gold-green winter flowers and Loquat, *Eriobotrya japonica*, has huge, leathery leaves which last all winter. It is worth growing just for its foliage, even if few of our summers are long enough to ripen its fruits. The evergreen *Viburnum tinus*, particularly the cultivator 'Eve Price', is useful because its pink-tinged flowers last for months in winter. Hostas tend to get disfigured by slugs but the largest-leaved, *H. sieboldiana* and the summer-flowering *H. plantaginea* are good. I like growing them in pots.

'Bergenias, especially the bronze-leaved *B. cordifolia* 'Purpurea', have excellent winter foliage and for trees I use the huge-leaved *Catalpa bignonioides* 'Aurea' which does not grow to a great size. Lilies and Japanese anemones are useful for bursts of summer colour – the anemones last into early autumn too – and for ground cover, 'Solomon's Seal', geranium species such as Johnson's Blue and *Alchemilla mollis* ('Ladies' Mantle') are splendid.

'Maintenance is a vital element and grass is out. It's far better to use gravel, which can be randomly planted and needs little attention. In my Sussex garden, gravel of different sizes has been laid to give the impression of a stream bed. Water is more trouble than it is worth because fountains keep blocking and ponds need maintaining. Walls painted white turn grey and dreary in the wet but why not try warmer colours like corn or ochre? How fine they'd look in winter with ivies climbing on them!

'What I dislike most of all are "little diddly itsy bits". Cottage gardening on a town scale hasn't come off and I think we've gone through the Laura Ashley Country Kitchen bit. I hope we're actually catching up. I also hate labels such as "Japanese" or "Cottage". A garden should be made for where it is. Now. According to how you live.'

Plants about town

Mahonia bealei is a winter-flowering shrub which provides greenery, colour and scent. It is a native of China and makes a fine, large architectural plant: it can reach a height and spread of 2–2.5m. Useful alternatives are *M. japonica* or, in mild districts, *M. lomariifolia.*

Euphorbia characias wulfenii sports its striking green flowers in February, in sun or shade. It can grow to around 1.2m – cut it back hard if it starts to look tatty. Low-growing euphorbias also make excellent groundcover.

The Loquat, *Eriobotrya japonica*, keeps its bold foliage all year but may succumb to frost in cold areas. The rambling evergreen rose, Mermaid, is armed with 2.5cm stilettos, making it vandal-proof – a valuable property of many roses, such as Bobbie Jones. Thorniest of all is *Rosa sericea pterocantha*, with blood-red thorns.

Solomon's seal or *Polygonatum multiflorum* flowers in late spring but has lush foliage all summer. Japanese anemones brighten September with marshmallow shades – pink or white – and are tough enough to grow through a concrete pavement. *Anemone x hybrida* 'Honorine Jobert' is particularly good. Small trees with big leaves, like *Catalpa bignonioides* 'Aurea', are ideal for urban gardens. If your soil is not limey, camellias are a 'must' unless you live in the north. Their shiny leaves add a luxuriant note to any garden.

✤ 4 JUNE 1938 ✤

Tips for window-boxes

By H. H. Thomas

Although country folk with considerable gardens may not lay much store by window-boxes, these provide the only means of flower growing that is available to many dwellers in towns. Window-box gardening was fashionable during Coronation year and the interest aroused in the subject promises to be maintained.

Those plants that bloom for a long time are obviously the most valuable for setting in window-boxes, but in making a choice it is necessary first of all to know whether the boxes will be in a sunny or a shady place.

Although the window-box of white marguerites and pink ivy-leaf pelargoniums is stereotyped and commonplace it is attractive, and the plants remain bright with flowers for many weeks. Petunias are very showy and free-blooming plants which love the sunshine, those of rose colouring being perhaps the most attractive.

The pink verbena named Miss Willmott is a good window-box plant, and *Phlox drummondii* is a suitable trailing plant to use as an edging.

The orange and yellow marigolds and the golden gleam nasturtiums make a bright furnishing which could be replaced with asters or chrysanthemums for late summer and autumn.

There is no more brilliant summer flower than the scarlet sage, and an edging of dwarf white alyssum sets it off admirably. The fibrous-rooted begonias and the small pentstemon named Newbury Gem are other good window-box plants. All these flowers are for sunny window-boxes.

For boxes in rather shady places a choice may be made from Tuberous begonia, fuchsia, calceolaria, musk and lobelia. Those who delight in the blue and pink hydrangeas may also plant these in the window-boxes on the shady side of the house.

As the quantity of soil contained in a window-box is so small, care should be taken to use the best turf loam. The removal of spent blooms, an occasional sprinkling of fertiliser and watering frequently help to prolong the display of flowers.

Town gardeners derive a good deal of pleasure by cultivating plants in tubs. If the tubs are in a sunny place climbing and rambler roses, the trumpet flower (brugmansia), the lemon-scented verbena (which needs protection in winter), yucca and clematis are suitable plants to choose.

If the tubs are in a shaded place hydrangea, Plantain lily or funkia, the Blue African lily or agapanthus, fuchsia and hardy ferns will thrive.

Although the popular bedding roses do not flower until late June and July there are many that open earlier in the summer, and some are in full bloom in May. My earliest roses this year are the golden yellow climbing 'Lady Hillingdon' and the dark-crimson Australian rose named 'Black Boy'; both are on the house wall. In the open garden generally the first rose to bloom is *Rosa hugonis*, a large bush which bears pale-yellow single flowers.

The Scotch roses (spinosissima), the hybrid Musk roses, *Rosa moyesii*, the thornless rose, and *Rosa altaica* are others that open before the popular varieties are in flower. Most of them grow into big bushes and need very little attention. The best way to manage them is to treat them as shrubs; the only pruning needed is to cut out the oldest branches occasionally.

My town garden fantasy

By Rosemary Verey

My garden at Barnsley House in Gloucestershire is large and well-established, and affords me immense pleasure, but sometimes I imagine what it would be like to design something quite different. How would I design a small town garden or a country cottage garden? My town garden would be strictly formal, with well-tutored box bushes, a patterned path leading symmetrically between the tidy beds of espaliered pear trees. There would be tulips and daffodils in spring and scented white tobacco plants in summer. I would have a tree at the end of the garden – quite a small one, perhaps an apple for bounty as well as shade. And a shallow lily pool for me and the birds – they must always enjoy the garden with me. I must have green to soothe me on difficult days, cool me in hot summer and bring warmth to my life on cold winter mornings, with evergreen hollies, euphorbias, mistletoe, 'Christmas' roses, and, of course, my small lawn.

I would trim my box bushes little but often, so there was never a day when they were not perfect. There would be two special views – one from the sitting-room and the other from the seat by the tree, and from both I would enjoy the symmetry and the simple planting – an oasis of peace where I can forget the pressure of city life.

I would make my country cottage garden quite different, overflowing with plants, every inch of the ground covered in summer and well mulched and full of promise in winter. But I would always find a home for new plants – perhaps to share a seemingly occupied place with a companion: a clematis with a climbing rose, or to add autumn colour to a summer-flowering shrub – clematis *Jackmanii Superba* or *C. viticella* growing through berberis or weigela, perennial sweet peas through a viburnum. An arbour with roses and honeysuckle across the path will give height and an invitation to find the secrets beyond this and my Rugosa rose hedge.

Here lettuce, strawberries, peas and beans will take over from spring bulbs and be followed by Michaelmas daisies, dahlias and phlox. The lavender, ready to gather in July for pot-pourri, will have mint, parsley and chives as companions. And as it is a cottage garden, there will be hollyhock, lilies, bee balm and tobacco plants, with marigolds, rosemary and honeysuckle by my door and an old bay tree.

20 NOVEMBER 2004

Don't blame the poor leylandii

By John Cushnie

I feel sorry for the Leyland cypress. It is certainly ubiquitous and is the cause of much acrimony and worse – but it isn't its fault. It should carry a Government health warning or, better still, a label pointing out that it is fast-growing and that its ultimate height is more than 100ft with a spread exceeding 30ft.

Leylandii are reasonably well behaved when they are regularly trimmed and maintained at a sensible height. The problem lies in their habit of growth. The evergreen foliage is only a shell. Within the green skin the plant is a mass of bare stems that will never in the future have foliage. This means that you can't reduce the width. They may be severely topped, but the growth will quickly be replaced with more of the same.

But without leylandii, what is there to fill the gaps if you are after something quick-growing, evergreen and offering privacy and shelter? The answer is a row of tall mixed shrubs. These would be an asset viewed from either side of the fence. Much of their beauty would be lost if they were constantly cut to a standard height.

There are loads of great varieties suitable for acid soil, including the evergreen camellias that may be purchased as large plants. Avoid east-facing sites where a spring frost, followed by early morning sun, can destroy their flowers. *Camellia x williamsii* varieties, such as 'Donation' (semi-double pink), 'Anticipation' (large, double crimson) and 'St Ewe' (single, rose-pink) are quick-growing and flower well as young plants. Stems that are reaching for the sky may be cut back in early summer. Both *Pieris floribunda* and *Desfontainia spinosa* enjoy an acid soil and are evergreen.

The latter has glossy, dark-green, holly-like leaves with yellow-tipped, red flowers in summer and early autumn.

The leaves of *Pieris floribunda* remain dark green without any colouring but it produces masses of upright panicles of pure white flowers in early spring. Another variety, P. 'Beth Chandler', makes a good display with its pink leaves turning creamy-yellow and then dark green. And it occasionally produces small white flowers in late spring.

You can't be fined for growing spiky plants and a first-class, evergreen barrier is furze (gorse). The secret of success is to grow the non-seeding variety, *Ulex europaeus* 'Flore Pleno'. Its pea-like, coconut-scented, bright-yellow flowers are double, appearing throughout the year. As fellow *Gardeners' Question Time* panellist Bob Flowerdew says: 'When gorse is out of flower, love is out of fashion.' It will seldom grow above 6ft but is tolerant of hard pruning, which will rejuvenate an old plant.

Viburnum japonicum is the only evergreen viburnum that is content to behave itself at about 6ft. Clusters of small, white, fragrant flowers appear in early summer followed by bright-red berries in the autumn.

I can think of no quick-growing conifers that will stop at the 6ft mark. You could invest in specimen plants, such as the golden Irish yew, *Taxus baccata* 'Fastigiata Aureomarginata' with its small, evergreen leaves margined in bright yellow. Being columnar and slow-growing it is easily maintained by clipping at a suitable height, but in my view the practice is nothing short of cruel. The dwarf variety *Taxus baccata* 'Standishii' is a female selection of the Irish yew with golden-yellow foliage, which will slowly reach a height of about 6ft.

Formal hedges may be maintained at an agreeable height and there are many desirable plants to provide an aesthetically attractive screen. For instance, beech with its retained brown winter leaves and new, light-green foliage has many admirers. Others prefer variegated holly, which forms a dense green and gold screen but requires twice yearly clipping.

Informal, flowering hedges are good value for money. Escallonia has attractive, glossy, evergreen leaves and panicles of flowers all summer. There are white, pink, red and crimson-flowered varieties. *Evergreen berberis* include *B. x stenophylla* with tiny, dark-green, spine-tipped leaves, and lemon-yellow spring flowers on long arching branches. In late summer these branches are laden with blue-black fruit.

How to plant

These long-term shrubs deserve the best of attention at planting time. Where they are replacing large plants that have had to be removed the soil will be exhausted of nutrients. Enrich it with the main elements of nitrogen, phosphate and potash. Digging in lots of old, well-rotted farmyard manure and compost will bulk up the humus content, making the soil more moisture retentive.

Remove as many of the previous occupant's roots as possible. They are difficult to work around and may encourage diseases such as honey fungus. Large, container-grown specimens may require a stake, especially if they are providing shelter by filling a windy gap.

A deep mulch of compost or shredded bark will finish the job.

6 APRIL 2002

Ten ways to make shade cool

By Anthony Noel

There is no urban retreat more appealing in the summer heat than a cool and private outside space. Town gardens that are both small and shady are often considered the ultimate green-fingered challenge but you would be amazed at just how attractive you can make them. I certainly was when I lived in Dulwich, south-east London.

The 'problems' vary. Is your garden shady all day or does it get shafts of sunlight at certain times? Or perhaps it is only shady in the winter? Maybe it is in the lee of the house, or is the shade made by a tree that cannot or should not be removed? Whatever the conditions, there is always a solution. All you need is confidence and the most rudimentary knowledge of what will survive.

Here are 10 pointers that worked in my L-shaped, 37ft by 15ft town garden.

1. Scale

The low light-levels in shady gardens make things appear smaller. Boldness in everything from layout to planting and ornament redresses the balance. So, make borders deep, paved areas generous and containers as big as space will allow – planted boldly with one or, at most, two varieties. In the ground, vary things a little, with one weird or wonderful plant occasionally taking the spotlight. Shady gardens, especially, need character as well as beauty.

2. Boundaries

If you have brick walls, power-jet or paint them (see no. 4). Otherwise, consider covering fences with panels of split bamboo, woven reeds or the endlessly versatile trellis. Stylishly modern or grandly traditional, easy to install and inexpensive, trellis is the answer to an urban gardener's prayer. I like to use the plain squared variety as exterior wallpaper, floor to ceiling, to disguise ugly walls and fences, and transform sunless places that the rain never reaches.

As a real boundary or a disguise, trellis gives a feeling of space beyond. Grey and cream marbled ivy, interspersed with different types of clematis (nearly all are shade-tolerant), soon creates a beautiful evergreen barrier. Top the supporting posts with ornamental balls, acorns or turned wooden pineapples.

3. Tree control

Never get rid of a tree unless absolutely necessary; once gone, all that beauty and maturity will take another 100 years to replace.

Under a deciduous tree, you can grow the choicest bulbs that thrive on spring sunshine and summer shade. Dry shade from a beech tree – the one really dense, deciduous tree – or an evergreen is more restrictive but there are still solutions. You could grow different varieties of wild cyclamen all year round or carpet the ground with variegated ivy. In the worst case, gravel the area and bring different pots to it to liven things up.

It is amazing how you can improve light levels by carefully pruning trees and shrubs that have grown too large or tangled into a more elegant, open shape. The great garden designer Russell Page called this 'carving with air'.

I once turned a collapsed white willow into a huge bonsai tree by thinning out the branches. The tree did not seem to mind and underneath I created a raised bed, full of good soil, where smaller plants did not have to compete with the tree's roots. If you do this, be sure not to bury the trunk.

4. Paint colour

Unless you live by the sea, white-washed walls look cold and gloomy – they seem to green up more quickly too. Instead, I find that Fowler Pink, a shell-pink/pale terracotta paint, manufactured by Farrow & Ball, brings the warmth and light of the Mediterranean to the gloomiest outlook.

In the man-made environment of a roof or courtyard, rich warm colours, like bright red, raspberry pink and Chinese yellow, can glow like embers on Bonfire Night if used boldly.

5. Sparkle and glamour

White flowers and silver foliage bring a unique sparkle and glamour to a garden. Many such plants will thrive with little or no sun, as do variegated varieties – too much sun on their delicate leaves can burn, bleach or fade them.

Urban gardens, even shady ones, are always a few degrees warmer than their country cousins, so take advantage of this protected micro-climate. Quite a few exotic-looking, architectural plants will be perfectly happy in the shade: cordylines (Torbay palms), Trachycarpus

(Chusan palm), and *Fatsia japonica* (Castor-oil fig), to name but three. More glamorous still are those with grey and silver leaves: stunning *Melianthus major* (cut it to the ground each Easter), *Astelia nervosa* (soft, sword-like leaves, 2 or 3ft long), *Santolina pinnata subsp. neapolitana* (clip into huge globes each spring for a change in texture and shape).

All silvers need sharp drainage, so mix in a couple of generous spadefuls of grit or gravel with the soil at planting time.

Just as a checkerboard marble floor brings life to a Georgian hall, painting an aggregate one black and white will do the same for a roof. As it weathers, the texture of the slabs will show through, creating a delightfully ancient, seedy and exotic look.

Gravel also gives sparkle to a shady place. Pea shingle is kindest to shoes, but there is a coarser one called Cotswold buff. Paving stones laid by the door into the house will prevent half the gravel ending up on the kitchen or sitting-room floor.

6. Planting

The legendary American fashion editor Diana Vreeland suggested decorating a room in nothing but different shades of green. Try this in your garden by mixing different leaf textures and shapes with some opulent white flowers – perhaps hydrangeas or tobacco flowers – and chic touches of black, silver and lime.

Viola 'Molly Sanderson' has jet-black flowers, as does Viola 'Bowles' Black' which seeds freely but never becomes a nuisance. Giant mopheads of bay look wonderful in squares of easy-going black ophiopogon, underplanted with baby-pink and white cyclamen, set in old flag-stones. And glamorous hostas are never so happy as when they are grown in a shady place. You will not do much better than *H. sieboldiana var. elegans* with its huge blue/green quilted leaves. Insist on elegans – the regular *H. sieboldiana* is not worth having. Hostas are very happy in pots and a ring of Vaseline around the rim will protect them from their arch-enemies, slugs and snails.

Talking of hostas, which are moisture-lovers too, do have an outside tap fitted or install a watering system, as shady gardens tend to be on the dry side.

7. Climbers

In my view, all houses should be softened with climbing plants, but avoid sun-lovers which strive upwards towards the light, leaving their feet bare. Instead, concentrate on varieties that are happy in shade, such as *Hydrangea anomala subsp. petiolaris*, *Akebia quinata*, clematis and camellias.

Add height with trellis pyramids, wreathed in climbers. I also use large urns planted with low-maintenance architectural plants; often light levels are better 6 or 7ft up, and sometimes it is actually quite sunny. Another way of adding height, with space at a premium, is with large standards such as bay (*Laurus nobilis*).

8. Containers

Always go for the largest containers possible. They will need watering less often, besides looking good. Square, wooden, Versailles tubs with mirrored panels bring another dimension to a small area – the reflections make a strongly patterned floor appear to go on forever.

Not only do plants grow well in naturally porous terracotta, but this takes the patina of age well and adds warmth. Terracotta is also a particularly effective foil for architectural box-wood shapes – globes, squares, pyramids and mopheads – and for yew, which is best trained as a cone or pyramid. Bay, box, holly and yew will all be happy in shade, as long as they are not underneath dripping branches.

Ban plastic containers unless they are black and shiny; if used with confidence, these make a sophisticated foil for plants. For spring, cram them with white hyacinths. For the summer, raspberry and black pelargonium 'Lord Bute'. And, for the autumn, pink, green and cream ornamental cabbages. Lilies look elegant in galvanized florist's buckets.

With all garden containers, make sure you provide adequate drainage holes. Generally, John Innes No 2 is a safe bet for planting up. Do not economise by using garden soil: you will get worms, usually a gardener's best friend but very disruptive in the confined space of a pot.

9. Ornament and vistas

The smaller the space, the more important it is to place things well.

In a shady garden, try to site benches, ornamental urns or wall-fountains in the light, so that they can be seen through the gloom. Think about the different views, not just from your window to the end of the garden, but also across the space and looking back at the house.

Nothing brings a garden to life like moving water: a wall fountain opposite a bench, for instance, or at the far end of a vista. There are some excellent ready-made fountains, both traditional and ultra-modern, which run on a concealed re-circulating pump, so all they require is a safe electrical connection (do consult a qualified electrician over this). Or you could go for a white seat or pale-stone ornament surrounded by ferns, hellebores and moss.

10. Atmosphere

Apart from weekends, you probably use your garden most at night – to relax after a busy day or to entertain friends.

Do not be afraid of lighting your outside space. Uplighting is as effective in the garden as it is inside, so keep everything low down, and many small sources of light are much more atmospheric than a few large ones. Consider flares, strings of fairy-lights and thick candles in hurricane jars. And white flowers and heady scents should be added for maximum evening romance.

The correspondence reproduced below resulted from a letter of complaint – printed in *The Times* – from Enid Bagnold, the novelist and playwright, and author of *National Velvet*. The impetus was the perceived disparaging attitude of the RHS towards women, illustrated by remarks made by RHS president Lord Aberconway about the desirability of allowing female members to join its council.

25 APRIL 1967

ALAS, MISS JEKYLL

Sir, – The letter from Miss Enid Bagnold (21 April) is a prime example of the device of damning a speaker not by misquotation but by incomplete quotation. Readers of her letter who were unaware of the full reply of the president of the Royal Horticultural Society to his questioner would naturally conclude that Lord Aberconway had been both curt and arrogant, for the implication was that his sole reply had been the single quoted sentence, giving in fact no reply at all to the question.

The following extract from the report of the proceedings of the 163rd Annual Meeting of the Fellows of the Society (Journal, RHS (1967) 92, 147) shows that a full, courteous, and reasoned answer was given:

Question 1: I should like to join with others to enquire why it has not been possible to include a few ladies on the council.

The president: We have never had ladies on the council. We

appoint to the council people who we believe can best serve the interests of the society. It so happens that at present there are no ladies who, we think, have as useful experience as the men available. Our council members are required to work extremely hard and have to be specialists in particular fields, and while we have considered the names of particular ladies in this context, we have always come to choose people who happen to be men.

The cause of feminism is done a disservice by letters of the type under discussion. Lord Aberconway's reply, quoted in full above, shows that women have indeed been considered for the council, but so far none has been found to be suitably experienced. Militant feminists always insist that they only claim equality of opportunity with men, but it would appear from Miss Bagnold's letter that the real intention is that privilege should be given, and women chosen not because they are better suited for a given position than rival men, but simply because they are women.

I have the honour to be, Sir,
Yours faithfully,
D. Irwin Stock
43 The Woodlands, Esher, Surrey

1 MAY 1967

Sir, – The treasurer of the Royal Horticultural Society made it plain at the annual general meeting that all is not well with the society. There is a falling off in the number of visitors to both the Chelsea Flower Show and the Great Autumn Show; hall lettings have dropped by about £5,000, and the minimum annual subscription rate has had to be increased by more than 40 per cent.

However hard Dr Stock may attempt to defend the president, the fact remains that Lord Aberconway's immediate reaction to the question about the inclusion of ladies on the council was: 'We have never had ladies on the council.' It would seem, however, that change of some kind is desirable in the management of the society, and the inclusion of one or two ladies on the council is surely an experiment work making.

'Our council members are required to work extremely hard,' the president informs us, thereby implying that this is something of which women are incapable! They are also required to be 'specialists in particular fields'. A little research and a little goodwill would undoubtedly discover one or two ladies who would not, on either score, be debarred from serving on the council.

I am, Sir, yours faithfully,
Madeline Spitta
Badgers Rake, Winkworth Arboretum, Godalming, Surrey

2 MAY 1967

Sir, – While Dr Irwin Stock (25 April) quotes correctly the published views of the Royal Horticultural Society's Council on women councillors, he has failed to grasp what the bother is about.

It is that many Fellows with considerable experience and knowledge disagree with and dislike these opinions. As but a small proportion of Fellows attends the meeting and few read accounts of such boring affairs, we are therefore being noisy.

The RHS now exists primarily for amateurs. The other aspects of horticulture are represented by specialised organisations. A visit to Chelsea Flower Show suggests that a majority of the Fellows are women, to whom gardening is a pleasure. Surely at least they should be represented on the council.

In several comparable bodies, carrying greater responsibilities, women are on the controlling bodies. Such are the National Trust and the Royal Forestry Society of England, Wales and Northern Ireland, while a woman is the vice-president of the Royal Scottish Forestry Society.

Yours faithfully,
Miles Hadfield
Dillon's Orchard, Wellington Heath, Ledbury, Hertfordshire

8 MAY 1967

Sir, – The Royal Horticultural Society is the premier horticultural society of the principal gardening country of the world. We are now in the 67th year of the 20th century. The RHS refuses to disclose a membership list but must have some 40,000 women fellows. It is run by a self-perpetuating council of 16 men the majority of whom are distinguished nurserymen or exceptionally wealthy landowners with big gardens. The rest have a lifelong professional connexion with horticulture.

One does not have to be a feminist to see that in this narrow company a woman may never emerge who is undeniably superior to all others.

There is, however, no good reason why a horticultural society should in perpetuity be run in this particular way. Amateur gardeners who practise horticulture with their own hands form the bulk of the membership and women presumably form half of it. Neither are represented on the council at all. This fact is painfully evident in the decisions taken by the council and the attitude of mind which permeates its every word.

It is time a wind of change blew through this evergreen thicket of reaction.

Yours faithfully,
Deenagh Goold-Adams
Colliers Farm, Frieth, Henley-on-Thames

9 MAY 1967

Sir, – Enclosed with the May issue of the Journal of the Royal Horticultural Society was a draft of the bye-laws of the society including the amendments to be submitted at a special meeting next 13 June.

On page 12, chapter 10, no. 63 deals with the election of council. It appears that women have equal rights to be members of council.

The next annual general meeting is their opportunity.

Who will be the first woman to storm the ramparts and enter the citadel so long occupied by man?

Yours faithfully,
Harry Wheatcroft
Harry Wheatcroft & Sons Ltd., Edwalton, Nottingham

1 JUNE 1967

Sir, – The various letters which you have recently published criticising the supposed attitude of the Council of the Royal Horticultural Society to the election of women to its ranks, were so misconceived as not to warrant an answer. But when you choose to dignify the matter by an equally misconceived leading article, as you did on 23 May, I think that I should, in fairness to my colleagues, put the record straight.

At the Society's Annual General Meeting last February I was asked (by a man) why it had not been possible to include a few ladies on the Council. It occurred to me that before I answered I should, in courtesy, make the facts clear to the 500 or so Fellows present (a normal gathering for this occasion); accordingly I prefaced my answer by saying that we had never had a lady on the Council. Obviously, and contrary to your misconception of the position, this was not 'one of the arguments used against ladies'. Indeed that was evident from the account of the proceedings published in the RHS Journal for April, and was made even more clear by Dr Stock, who came to my defence in your columns on 25 April (and who I may say was unknown to me).

This little storm in ladies' teacups would never have arisen had not the lady, who started the correspondence in your paper and who showed less fairmindedness than her accomplishments would have led one to expect, taken deliberately from its context this preliminary statement, and quoted it and it alone in her letter, as if it were my whole reply; your readers were thus left inevitably to infer that my colleagues and I were crusty die-hard misogynists who were not prepared to have women on the Council, because women never had sat there, and because we were against it on principle.

Nothing could be further from the truth. I went on in my answer to say that we appoint to Council those people who can contribute most to our affairs; and that they had in fact always happened to be men.

We have nothing against the ladies. As soon as a lady comes to our mind or is suggested informally (or proposed formally, as under our domestic constitution she can be by two other Fellows – of either sex!) who can contribute in our view as much to our multifarious activities as any man available, we shall support her appointment. Equally however we shall resist any candidate of either sex who is proposed by Fellows and seems to us less suitable in the above sense than our own candidate; and I am sure Fellows generally will support us in this.

Council is a working body, managing in detail the many facets of the Society's work. Council members are called upon to play their part not only on the Council but also in many other ways, such as being chairmen of various committees, linking them to Council. We have no room on Council for passengers or for people who are there to 'represent' any body or any class of Fellow. It is no more logical to say that because (I would guess) at least half our Fellows are women, we should have a proportion of our Council members women, than it would be to say that because at least as many women as men travel in trains, a proportion of ticket inspectors should be women.

Unfortunately it appears to be the case in the gardening world, that fewer ladies than men appear to have the time available as well as suitable experience of organisation, administration, finance, and business generally, in addition to specialised knowledge of some facet of the activities that we pursue. Several names of ladies have been in our minds in this connection and I personally (and I can speak with confidence for my colleagues) would be more than happy to welcome a lady member to Council.

But she must be there not just because she is a lady, nor to represent any class of Fellow, but because she is the best qualified person for the purpose, and with time to spare for our affairs.

Yours faithfully,
Lord Aberconway, President, Royal Horticultural Society
Vincent Square, SW1

21 FEBRUARY 1968

MRS FRANCES PERRY ON RHS COUNCIL

By Roy Hay

Mrs Frances Perry was elected to the council of the Royal Horticultural Society yesterday, the first time a woman has been proposed for the Council. Her election followed considerable pressure in the society and in the press.

Mrs Perry was formerly chief horticultural officer for Middlesex and is a well-known author on horticultural subjects. Her election was enthusiastically received by the Fellows of the society.

8.

'These plants present an aspect so fantastic and so bizarre that one's thoughts are carried away'

Plants and Gardens in Faraway Places

On discovering the flora of New Zealand

By Dan Pearson

L ast autumn I visited South Island, New Zealand. At times I found the sheer beauty of it incredibly moving: mile upon mile of unspoilt landscape with no signs – or only very small ones – of man's impact. At other points I became unnerved by the sheer magnitude of it – a feeling I have experienced only once before, while flying over the endless, relentless Australian desert. Here, in the vast gorges of the west coast, with waterfalls pulsing from mountains that dropped into a rough and untrustworthy sea, one felt humbled.

I was in my element with the plants and saw enough to inspire my own designs for several years. The contrast between different environments was one of the most exciting aspects of the trip – from the reduced, dry tussock lands to the complex and multi-layered life in the wet temperate forests of Nothofagus or Southern Beech. There the trees hung with lichen, mosses and epiphytic plants, creepers straddled ravines and cartwheel tree-ferns were suspended above the still moss-covered clearings. What each environment had in common, however, was that the foliage was so much more interesting than the flowers, and the greater majority of the plants were evergreen.

I was curious to see that few designers there use native flora. 'Traditional' garden plants with showy flowers are the norm and vast tracts of cultivated land are bereft of indigenous plants. But there is a slow and progessive native plant movement and the nurseries had some incredible specimens and ornamental selections on offer – hebe and phormium cultivars, for instance, a whole range of bronze-tinted astelias, and red and pewter corokias.

As for using New Zealand's native plants here, our climates in many respects are similar: cool but not overly cold winters and damp, not overly hot summers. Ornamentals – for great texture, structure and evergreen appeal – might include *Astelia chathamica*, with its silvery strap-shaped foliage, the colour of which does almost better in the shade. The plants I have against our east-facing wall are now 1m high and wide and, save the occasional clean-up to remove the oldest foliage, they're incredibly low-maintenance.

I saw astelias growing in the wild, up trees in the moist clefts of branches where the rainfall was high. A. nervosa is the smaller-growing form and can be a wonderful plant for containers. Watch out for the coppery selections in British nurseries – they're sure to become popular as they were on the New Zealand stand at Chelsea 2004.

Look for smaller varieties of plants, which are easier to use in a garden setting. I rarely use phormiums because they grow so vast and look best on a grand scale, but *P. cookianum* is a lovely thing, half the size and with pleasant arching foliage. Phormiums are nectar-rich and almost indestructibly resilient. They're one of the best plants for the seaside garden, for instance, and in the wild, phormiums are used as sand-dune stabilisers. The rusty-coloured tussock grass, *Chionochloa rubra*, loved it on the dry side, too, and I saw mile upon mile of it shifting in the breeze. I loved it teamed with olive aciphyllas, which have domed mounds of the most wicked foliage I have encountered in a long time. When they flower, it is with a dramatically armoured spike that is sent up several feet. Wonderfully dangerous.

Many of the plants in New Zealand have an otherness about them, such as copper and silver-toned creeping acaena, and felted silver

Brachyglottis repanda or 'Bushman's Friend' (so named because it can be used as loo paper if you get caught out). I saw groves of lancewood, *Pseudopanax crassifolius*, in leafmould-rich clearings. Its foot-long dark-red leaves look just like the legs of a locust until the plant reaches a height of 10 to 13ft, when it has the curious habit of changing to round inconspicuous foliage.

The list of new things is too long to mention but check out the corokias, which form a low shrub of divaricating growth like balls of wire. The shrubby *Muehlenbeckia simmondsii* is of similar habit, a shrubby form of its climbing, more easily obtainable cousin. The pseudopanax are great plants for a shady position but they are best grouped together for real drama. Just the tip of a glorious iceberg of garden plants.

25 SEPTEMBER 2010

The new perennials movement: how it all started

By Noël Kingsbury

In 1994, British garden design was in the doldrums. I remember a run of Chelsea Flower Shows where the dominant theme in show gardens was ruins: houses, castles, gardens (of course) and even a mine. Britain's garden heritage was certainly being mined for inspiration – I recall a stream of books with 'period' and 'traditional' in the titles. It seemed as if no one was capable of looking forward or thinking up new ideas.

'Time to look abroad,' I thought.

Others were thinking along similar lines. Many of us in the garden business remember a conference at Kew Gardens to introduce the work of German garden designers in May 1994; this was a watershed occasion where you could almost feel the ground moving.

Since my partner had just moved to a job in Bratislava, I had an excuse to drive across the continent and visit some of the parks and gardens that had been mentioned; to meet designers and to bring plants home.

So, during the summer of 1994, I made two trips. In June, I discovered the extraordinary Westpark in Munich, where familiar garden plants were used in spectacularly expansive drifts, and a suburb of Amsterdam, Amstelveen, where wild-flower plantings were not just in the parks, but integrated into the city infrastructure, alongside roads and tramways. Later in the summer, I decided to follow up reports of a nurseryman who also designed gardens – Piet Oudolf. Arriving at the nursery I met a Swedish academic, Eva Gustavsson, who wanted to interview Piet about his design work, and another Dutchman, Henk Gerritsen.

One of the first things I learnt was that Piet was first and foremost a designer, but had set up his own nursery to grow the plants he needed for his design work that were difficult to find commercially.

Piet's wife, Anja, ran the nursery. Her outgoing personality and incredible memory for people made her ideal for the job. Piet made few appearances in the garden when it was full of nursery visitors. I suspect he was glad that Anja was so happy to deal with the public. I think a lot of his time was spent looking at his plant combinations, working out what species looked good together.

The Oudolf garden made an immediate impact on me, not just for its perennials and grasses, but for its formal touches – such as the layered yew hedges with wavy tops, and a series of yew columns and borders arranged along a central axis, but staggered rather than opposite each other. I was struck by how this garden evoked traditional European formality, but with a twist.

Later that first day, we went to visit Henk's garden, about 90 minutes away, known as the Priona Garden. Again, there was the combination of wildness and formality, except the wild bits here were even wilder. There was humour, too, in the form of an enormous fibreglass sculpture of a baby, a nest of giant eggs and topiary chickens on the lawn.

I continued to visit Piet and Henk. They and other gardeners I met here were quietly evangelical about wanting to change gardening, to introduce a new spirit, and, in particular, more nature into the garden. Piet's way of doing this was within an architectural framework; he had been a garden designer most of his working life and much influenced by Mien Ruys, the grand old lady of Dutch landscape design, whose modernist style dominated post-war Holland.

Most of the other people I met were more influenced by the counter-culture of the 1960s. Of these, the most remarkable was Rob Leopold. His great inspiration had been to take the common hardy annuals that so many people grew and make them into seed mixtures, themed by colour – you could sow a packet of mixture and watch as different species performed from early summer to mid-autumn.

This idea, which he launched commercially in 1990, was taken up by Nigel Dunnett at the University of Sheffield, who developed a similar set of mixtures for use by local authorities in Britain.

Henk Gerritsen, too, had been a creature of the counter-culture and the environmentalist movement of the 1970s. When I met him, he had recently lost his partner, Anton, with whom he had created Priona. Until he died last year, Henk had lived with HIV, which gave a poignancy to a very central principle of his gardening – an acceptance of death. 'Once upon a time,' he told me, 'a leaf going yellow was seen as something going wrong – now we know that death in the garden can be beautiful.'

He was referring mainly to the discovery he and Anton made that seed heads, of garden flowers, wild flowers and even vegetables, can contribute to the garden in autumn and winter. Piet had made the same discovery, even saying that 'a plant isn't worth growing unless it looks good when it's dead'.

Piet spends a lot of time with a camera. Shots of perennial and grass seed heads sparkling in frost, looming in mist, or looking dank, gave us a new way of looking at the garden. They stimulated a new genre of photography, much of it celebrating a more emotional way of looking at gardens rather than the purely visual.

The use of herbaceous plants in our gardens has hugely increased over the past 30 years. While this would have happened without input from the Dutch, there is little doubt that photographs of Piet's work, his work here (which includes borders at RHS Wisley and three other major public projects) and of other Dutch gardeners has had a big influence on how this herbaceous revolution has developed.

The widespread use of grasses is perhaps the most obvious sign; I can remember the very idea of ornamental grasses being mocked in the 1980s. But there has been another development – a greater willingness among British gardeners to look at the gardening cultures of other countries and learn from them.

Flowering of market values

By Trevor Fishlock

A lexei is rather surprised to find himself, at the age of 66, in a small way of business. It is very small indeed, he says, and he reaches into his worn old leather jacket and pulls out his wallet to show me his morning's takings. A few crumpled rouble notes. 'I'm such a little fish,' he says, 'that the crooks and the racketeers wouldn't give me a second glance.'

Alexei is a fairly distinctive figure. His white hair is covered with a flat cap made of brown fur and he has bright blue eyes, a ready smile revealing a few surviving teeth which stand up like bollards, and a white mandarin beard 9in long. You can see from his face that he lives in the country. He does not have the end-of-winter Moscow pallor.

Alexei has a gardener's hands. He is a grower and seller of tulip and gladioli bulbs and the seeds of other flowers. That makes him a smart fellow, because he can bring his produce to market in his battered suitcase – 'and I couldn't do that if I grew potatoes, could I?'

He lives a dozen miles from Moscow, in Romashkovo, a village typical of rural Russian settlements – wooden, tin-roofed houses with carved and painted window frames and green wooden fences, ducks waddling in streets of thick mud and headscarved women at the well. They are timeless and traditional and young people are leaving them in droves for the cities.

These days Alexei rises at 5am. His wife packs some bread and butter and a flask of tea and he catches the electric train to Moscow. He is in position early, just after six, to get his favourite section of the central market, which is a few minutes' walk up the muddy, rutted road from our office.

His pitch, a white-tiled counter, costs him £1.70 a day. He lays out his small tray of seeds and bulbs in small punnets with cards giving their names – 'Polar Bear', 'Daughter of Europe', 'First Love', 'Amber Baltic', 'Ballet on Ice', 'Saxophone Sounds', 'Homeland', 'Best Girl'. He is proud of some American seeds called 'Big Apple'. Alexei's pitch is between a swarthy man selling carnations who assiduously teases and primps each bloom and a brace of plump ladies, as bright as robins, who also sell seeds and bulbs. But as Alexei says, they are not all the same sort of bulbs and anyway a bit of competition is a good thing. The plump ladies smile assent.

The flower section of the market is large and crowded because Russians adore flowers and give them as presents for the slightest reason. Alexei sees himself as a specialist. 'I sell to people who love seeds and know about them,' he says.

It was only two years ago that he became a tiny particle of the free-enterprise economy that President Gorbachev is trying to implant within the massive and petrified Soviet system. He worked for 32 years as an engineer in a factory making parts for aircraft. Today, he says, under the programme to convert part of the defence industry to production of badly needed consumer goods, the factory makes children's bicycles and ski poles.

Alexei retired on the maximum pension, £132 a month. Many people get a lot less, but £132 does not go far. Alexei says it is not enough. So he has turned his love for gardening to some modest profit. His patch of land is 1,000m² and he works it with the occasional assistance of his seven grandchildren and a great-grandson. They help him harvest blackcurrants, strawberries and plums, shared among the family.

Alexei used a gardening metaphor, saying Gorbachev had planted a lot of hope. In the bad old Brezhnevian days, he said, he was not even allowed to repair his own home. If you painted your house and made it look pretty people it would have marked you down as a kulak. Kulak, a scrooge, was the Communist term of abuse for the peasant farmers destroyed by Stalin as class enemies.

The good thing about Gorbachev, Alexei says, continuing his unsolicited testimonial, is that he is encouraging people to live like human beings. These days you don't have investigators sniffing about as you used to and you can actually begin to believe in something again. He is sad about the mess the country is in, particularly about the food shortages. 'To think we have to buy grain,' he said.

Alexei comes to the market to sell his bulbs for about three weeks and he will finish early in April. He says if he makes £30–£40 a day during this period he is happy. His wife wants to spend some of the money on repairing the roof and floor of his wooden house, and on paint and wallpaper.

He will prudently plough back much of his profit to produce better and more fashionable seeds and he plans to branch out into roses. He will come back to the market in August to sell his cut flowers.

Private growers are an increasingly important part of the economy. They occupy a tiny proportion of the land but produce, for example, 29 per cent of the vegetables. For a people brought up on cheap subsidised food, the markets where hundreds of Alexeis sell their fruit, vegetables and chickens are expensive.

There is much grumbling about profiteering and, of course, party diehards disapprove of the growth of private trade licensed by Gorbachev.

But Alexei won't have it. He makes a few roubles and buys his grandson a new bonnet, but best of all he gains a lot in self-respect.

Cézanne's garden

By Elspeth Thompson

Artists' gardens are fascinating places, especially where there is a strong connection between the garden and the art. William Morris, Emil Nolde and Patrick Heron are among the many artists who drew on their gardens for inspiration; for Barbara Hepworth and Henry Moore the garden was both workplace and gallery; while Claude Monet created the glorious garden at Giverny expressly in order to paint it.

For Paul Cézanne, whose paintings bridged the gap between Impressionism and the abstract advance into Cubism, gardens were a recurring theme, leading him to create a studio in the garden at Les Lauves, the Provençal property in which he was to paint every day for the final four years of his life. On the centenary of his death, the National Gallery is staging Cézanne in Britain, an exhibition of his works held in UK collections which includes several with a garden theme.

It is for vast monumental landscapes such as those of the iconic Mont Sainte-Victoire, rather than intimate garden scenes, that Cézanne is best known, but he found endless inspiration in the grounds of the houses he grew up in. Indeed, some of his most enduring motifs – tunnels of trees, paths through woodland, views through a cross-hatching of branches or hazy backlit flowers and foliage – have their roots in these gardens, which were atmospheric and often overgrown places as opposed to the formal, flower-filled borders that were the fashion of the day.

Cézanne's family home, the Jas de Bouffan, with its melancholic mature garden of ancient trees and a dark, formal pool with mesmerising reflections, was important from the start of the artist's career. No fewer than 39 oil paintings and 17 watercolours were produced here, including the almost impressionistic *Pool at the Jas de Bouffan*, and countless views of the red-roofed house seen across a sunlit lawn or through a tracery of chestnut tree branches, some of which are featured in the exhibition.

The equally gloomy grounds at the neighbouring neo-gothic Château Noir, which Cézanne tried to buy when forced out of the Jas de Bouffan following his mother's death, were also a great inspiration. He loved its gnarled, ivy-clad trees and crumbling terraces, and was still painting it when he moved to Les Lauves, the property he bought himself in 1901, just five years before his untimely death at the age of 67. It was here – a sloping half-acre plot with views over Aix and the Mont Sainte-Victoire – that Cézanne's great love of gardens could really take root.

For him this was an unspoiled, unsuburbanised corner in which he could create a sanctuary from the world and from his frequent dark depressive moods. Though the house he built there was certainly big enough, Cézanne chose not to live at Les Lauves, but walked up the hill every day from the flat he shared with his wife and either painted in the studio (with its 3m slit in the wall for passing out paintings) or shady terrace, or made excursions out into the surrounding countryside to draw or paint direct from nature.

The garden itself, with its shaggy shrubs, flowering trees, labyrinthine paths and frequent resting places made from rough-hewn blocks of stone, was a favourite place to walk and paint – and he often included fruit and potted pelargoniums from the terrace in still lifes. Vallier, his trusted gardener, was instructed not to tidy up too much in the wilder reaches of the garden, but to maintain the preferred air of poetic neglect. It is fitting that one of Cézanne's best-loved paintings, *Portrait of Gardener Vallier*, shown in the National Gallery's exhibition, was his final work.

Les Lauves and Jas de Bouffan opened to the public this spring, so you can see for yourself the strong correlations between Cézanne's gardens and his art. Walking in a painter's footsteps and appreciating the effort to which he went to compose particular effects can help when we come to designing our own spaces. No one knew better the importance of well-constructed views, whether at the end of an avenue or across the surrounding landscape; and in his use of plants as a frame or veil in the foreground one could even say he pioneered the current fashion for gauzy or 'see-through' plants.

It can also help us to a deeper understanding of the natural world, cultivated and wild. As Cézanne put it: 'Nature is not on the surface; it is in the depths. Colours are the surface expression of the depth. They grow up from the roots of the world.'

New ascent of Ruwenzori
Grotesque and Gigantic Plants on Africa's high Mountains of the Moon

By Patrick M. Synge

R ight on the Equator lies Ruwenzori, almost in the centre of Africa; yet on its higher peaks there is perpetual ice and snow. Ruwenzori is only its modern name. Here has been placed the 'Mountains of the Moon' referred to by Ptolemy and so many other classical writers.

Two valleys, hitherto largely unknown, were explored by the recent expedition organised in connection with the British Museum (Natural History) to study the most peculiar flora and fauna of the higher Equatorial mountains of East Africa.

There are three groundsels up to 30ft, and giant lobelias 15ft high, which one inspired traveller has aptly compared with the obelisks in a Turkish cemetery. When seen against a background of swirling mist, these plants present an aspect so fantastic and so bizarre that one's thoughts are carried away from this world to imaginary reconstructions of landscapes in other geological ages.

Indeed, it is possible that they are remnants of a flora which was formerly much more extensive, and now survives only on these mountain tops, which stand out as biological islands in the surrounding plains.

Dr F. W. Edwards and Dr George Taylor, both of the Natural History Museum, cut a path up the Namwamba valley and reached the snows at Observation Peak. A second party, consisting of Mr D. R. Buxton as entomologist, Mr Stuart Somerville, the artist, and myself as botanist, ascended the Nyamgasani valley, visited the eight lakes at the head of that valley, and climbed Weismann Peak, 15,163ft, the highest point of Mount Luigi. Only once before had this peak been climbed.

It is only with the experience of this second party that the present article attempts to deal.

Everywhere we went it was necessary to cut a path through the dense growth; consequently progress was very slow. After much discussion and haggling we gathered together a force of 40 porters and set off into the dark forest above us. Each porter was given a blanket and a sweater; higher up, each man got a second extra garment. Every sack that the expedition had was in demand for extra clothing as soon as it was emptied. Very neat tunics the sacks made, too, with slits cut for the head and arms.

The porters were mostly pleasant and jolly fellows, and had not the extreme sophistication of so many of the Uganda natives. Old customs and legends had survived to some extent with them, and these played an interesting part in our expedition. Among them was a rain man. He had a magic whistle. Every morning he would wave his whistle in the air and look up to the sky, murmuring a few words of prayer. Then he would blow a blast on the whistle. His efforts were attended with almost uncanny success. The mountain positively beamed on us, while many former travellers had not been able to find words strong enough to express the cold and continual dampness which they had experienced.

We were unable to learn very much of the ideas underlying the power of the whistle. We gathered that it had been purchased from a witch doctor for two goats some time previously.

We passed first through a zone of luxuriant forest, glorified with the most magnificent tree ferns and great wild bananas. At 7,500ft we emerged into a zone of giant bamboos. Many were over 50ft in height, and formed arches over our heads. Only a dim and fitful light penetrated into this curious green world below, where our figures moved like gnomes in a fairy pantomime.

There was little life, but we were rewarded by the sight of a herd of the beautiful Colobus monkey. He is a magnificent beast, and from close up looks like an old man, with his superb white whiskers and face framed with white fringe. Behind hangs down a long white tail.

We also saw the rarer blue monkey, a big grey beast, which appears to be solitary in its habits. Once, when collecting alone, I spent several minutes watching an unusually large one, which sat on a branch only a few yards away and delicately devoured a fruit. After every bite he would look up at me and shake his head, as if to say, 'All right, Guv'nor', almost smiling with a cockney impudence. Finally he finished the fruit, threw the skin in my direction, and vanished into the forest.

From our camp among the bamboos we caught our first glimpse of the snow, just a sprinkling, obviously fresh. Progress was still slow, but after some days we suddenly emerged at 10,000ft from the bamboos into a zone of gigantic and monstrous tree heathers. They were twisted into fantastic forms, and from their branches dangled long streamers of sulphurous-yellow lichen.

Here we found the first giant groundsels, and the stiff spikes of the lobelias barred our way like figures with upraised lances. Against a background of eddying mists, it seemed a landscape peopled with vegetable ghosts, a place of mystery, haunting and antagonistic to man.

Here we had our first and only hailstorm. Our rain man became so agitated that I feared he might suddenly burst. However, it did not last long.

At night the valley resounded with gruesome shrieks and screechings. For a long time we could not discover where they came from. They seemed so uncanny that I at least felt momentarily cold and shivery. We found out that they were made by the rock hyrax, a small and rather harmless-looking beast, something between a rabbit and a beaver in appearance. He is closely related to the cony of the Bible.

One day a young one was brought in to us, and we kept it for several days as a pet. It was a charming little beast, and gave no signs of screeching in captivity. Still there was no sign of the lakes, and we had not seen snow a second time.

Our fifth camp we named 'Speculation Camp', since we all indulged in much idle speculation as to what we might see when we crossed the next ridge. The next morning our hopes were rewarded, and we saw away in the distance a jet-black lake nestling at the foot of Mt. Watamagufu, and beyond it the snow ridge of Mt. Luigi.

From this ridge we climbed a peak to which my aneroid gave a height to 13,800ft, although no such high peaks had previously been recorded in the vicinity.

A week later we stood at the top of another pass and looked down on the water, now close by but still black and mysterious. We gazed dreamily for a few moments until the spell was broken by voices behind us: 'Bakshish, Bwana, bakshish.' It was an odious reminder of the advance of civilisation, which we wanted at that moment to forget.

Nor had we thought such a word known to our rather uncivilised porters. I fear they got no money. That night they all had an extra ration to celebrate the accomplishment of the first part of the journey.

Bring the Italian Riviera home

By Fred Whitsey

Sauntering round gardens in northern Italy the other day – though failing to find any weather any more congenial to the craft than at home – I was struck again by the fact that it is the abundance of the climbing plants there that helps to give these places their characteristic air of richness. As well as embellishing walls, the climbers entwine pillars, snag balustrades and railings and cascade from balconies with a looseness that is half controlled but hardly looks it.

Pity, I thought, that in our gardens, where the variety is so much greater, the lack of architecture prevents us from exploiting climbers more. These plants are without rivals for producing quantities of blossom and for wearing it elegantly. Pity, too, that this range of clematis offered us in garden centres should be so enticingly great now and the opportunities for growing them so slender in our gardens.

Perhaps we should revive the Edwardian garden cliché of the rose arch. Certainly when there is no more room for gardening laterally due to the over-planting that afflicts most keen gardeners' plots all the vertical possibilities should be explored.

For several seasons now I have been meeting the problem by growing climbers on tripods made with 7ft. bamboo canes thrust into the ground and drawn together at the top. I prefer these to the square red cedar posts available in garden shops today as they quickly become less conspicuous. When the climbers reach the top, they either stop growing or hang down, which is an advantage in itself.

I find clematis, for one, take to this treatment very well, while occupying very little room, since the canes are put only a foot and a half apart at the bottom.

The new plantings consist of the winsome *Clematis alpina*, in its white and ruby forms, for the late spring, in company with some of the smaller flowered summer clematis whose nature it is to die away almost to the ground during the winter so that they grow up afresh each year. This should take care of the problem of sorting out whose shoots are whose.

But it is not only clematis by any means that lend themselves to this treatment. Take honeysuckle. This shares with ivy a tendency to become arborescent, as they say, when it has nothing more to cling to, making twiggy growth instead of reaching out further. Wisteria lends itself to close spurring like a cordon fruit tree, while the up-to-date varieties of climbing roses have none of that wild abandon of the Albertines of this world but ask for no more than a few canes for the main growths to be tied to.

Climbers trained in this fashion need not be in the open ground. This elementary bit of technique makes it possible for people with no more than little patios or even balconies to grow climbers in pots that need little lateral space, only about 6ft above them.

It is a very good way of growing morning glory, in particular, for with their roots restricted by the pot the plants have a greater inclination to flower than in the ground where they can feast on the fat of the land. The same goes for cobaea.

Passion flowers suffer from the same reluctance. If the plants are grown in a big pot they seem to realise that something awful could happen to them if they don't open their flowers and get them fertilised to produce seed. It's really like growing them on poor soil, where they are always so much better. Other climbers, however, do need feeding when they are grown in pots in this way to keep up their strength.

America's wild bunch

By Dan Pearson

In November last year I went on a lecture tour of the US with the Royal Oak Foundation, an American organisation affiliated to the National Trust. The lectures took me across a whole continent, from New York to Chicago and on to Los Angeles. It was fascinating to see how differently the people there looked at the world through their gardens. Examining how a culture responds to its environment is one of the most interesting ways of getting to grips with a people, and there is no better place to do that than in the garden.

The last time I visited Chicago was in 1997, when I went to see a group of activists called The Wild Ones Natural Landscapers. America is famous for its rolling front lawns but, as Michael Pollan argues in his book *Second Nature*, the obsession with the perfect lawn could be a representation of the American fear of nature.

In a part of America where you could be fined for letting your front lawn grow long, the Wild Ones were making some controversial moves. The group started more than 30 years ago, when Lorrie Otto dug up her lawn and replaced it with 'American prairie'. The prairies used to be the natural state in this part of the world; now, as little as one per cent of the native prairie remains.

By ripping up their lawns and replanting them with prairie plants grown from wild seed, the Wild Ones instigated a radical change. When I met them, I could see immediately that the prairie 'lawns' were an inspiration. Filled with familiar garden plants such as echinacea, rudbeckia, aster, bergamot and solidago, they were a reminder that a garden need not be about control and convention, but a sanctuary to wild plants, insects and animals.

Returning eight years later I was interested to see whether the movement had gathered pace. The neatly clipped lawns were still there, but there was a new development among the high rises in downtown Chicago. The Lurie Gardens, attached to the new Frank Gehry concert hall at Millennium Park, were designed by landscape designers Gustafson Guthrie Nichol and Robert Israel and planted by Piet Oudolf. It was exciting to see this combination of talents; the powerful building, the sophisticated lines of the landscaping and its juxtaposition with Oudolf's naturalistic planting. I was fascinated to see that it had taken an outsider to take the movement further and to put native plants together in a way that caught the imagination of the US public.

One reason for the garden's success is that it gives a nod to the American need for order; it is less radical than the environmentalists but more communicative, and so brings more people along with it. Unlike the prairie lawns of the Wild Ones, the plants that Oudolf has used are ordered and organised into groups. I suspect that they are more palatable like this. Although the look is less anarchic, it still has the feeling of a wild planting, as it is an ornamental and romantic interpretation of a meadow.

It would have been hard to do this planting in Britain using our limited palette of natives, not least for the comparative lack of choice but also for the fact that the flowering season would have been considerably shorter, with most of our plants blooming in the first half of the summer. Though the planting in the Lurie Garden uses many forms and varieties, I was amazed by the sheer range of American natives that pass muster as good, long-flowering border perennials.

Here was a list as long as your arm of tried-and-tested, fully hardy plants: black-eyed Susan (*Rudbeckia hirta*); Culver's root (*Veronicastrum virginicum*); prairie blazing star (*Liatris pycnostachya*); queen-of-the-prairie (*Filipendula rubra*); and a host of others.

It was good to be reminded of the provenance of many of the plants that I use quite regularly, and to think about them growing in the deep plains where the winds blow, the sun bakes in the summer and the winter freezes hard. It made sense that the towering Joe Pye weed (*Eupatorium purpureum*) grew beside Jerusalem artichokes, lofty plants that have to be placed with care in the garden.

I enjoyed seeing other wonderful outsized American natives that we do grow here, but which are still rare because they can be difficult to accommodate. The cup plant (*Silphium perfoliatum*), which grows to more than 2.4m (8ft) tall, has a fascinating cup formed between the leaf and the flower. Like its cousins helenium and coreopsis, the daisy flowers splash gold into the garden in late summer.

It was an education to see where some of the newer introductions to our shores come from: the switch grass (*Panicum virgatum*) and the sweetly scented prairie dropseed (*Sporobolus heterolepis*). The latter is a delightful gauzy grass which Oudolf has teamed with rattlesnake-master (*Eryngium yuccifolium*) in his borders at RHS Wisley.

In the spirit of all good gardening trips, I was inspired to try a few more things myself at home; sea oats (*Chasmanthium latifolium*) were one experiment. This delightful grass has charisma and the most delightful fish-shaped seedheads. Grow it where its feet can draw moisture from cool but not overly wet ground.

Where the Countess of Zeppelin fits in

By Noël Kingsbury

I remember very clearly my first encounter with what makes the German gardening scene so different. One afternoon in early June 1994 I parked my car on a suburban street in Munich and walked up a grassy incline into the Westpark (a huge public park). At the top of a small hillock, a shallow amphitheatre-shaped area was planted with perennials and grasses. All of them were familiar species: bearded irises, red valerian, hardy geraniums, but used in a way I had never seen before.

The effect was stunning – midway between a wildflower meadow and an overflowing herbaceous border. There were little paths running through the planting, with people on them, looking at the plants, photographing them or just wandering. Beyond was a wide grass area, with more people – it was a public holiday (on a Thursday – can you imagine that in Britain? No one would go into work on Friday) and big Turkish family groups were grilling smoky meals around purpose-built barbecue griddles.

The Munich Westpark typifies what is so good, but also so different about gardening in Germany. In Britain, the exciting stuff in gardening happens in private; in Germany it happens in public spaces, like parks and botanical gardens.

What is really exciting though is to go to a Gartenschau (I probably don't need to translate), which is a big summer-long event where all aspects of gardening – public and private – are represented. They are an opportunity for landscape architects to show off their skills, nurseries to flaunt their plants, and visitors to pick up tips on everything from vegetable growing to how to make a green roof on the summerhouse (green roofs were invented here). At the end of the year, the temporary installations are taken out, and a high-quality public park is left behind, maintained by the local council. The Gartenschau system is a way of regenerating old industrial or military sites; it continually creates exciting new public spaces.

After this rather Damascene moment in Munich, I keep coming back. The quality of public horticulture in Germany is incredibly good, and often daringly experimental. I was struck initially by the use of perennial combinations, but there are wonderfully inventive annual plantings too, often combining grasses, wild flowers and vegetables with summer bedding.

Key to German public gardening is thinking about plants not so much as individuals but as components of communities. This reflects an important strength of plant sciences in Germany – *pflanzensoziologie* (I think we can all manage to translate this too).

The early part of the 20th century was an incredibly fertile time for gardening in Germany, as it was in Britain, and there was much exchanging of plants and ideas, although names tended to get changed along the way: we couldn't cope with Penstemon 'Andenken an Friedrich Hahn' – 'Garnet' is so much easier, and Aster 'Kaiser Wilhelm II' didn't survive the First World War without becoming 'King George'. Many British varieties were widely grown in Germany too. Much of this closeness has now been lost, although Beth Chatto was friendly with the late Countess von Zeppelin, a leading grower of perennials; Beth used to visit the nursery regularly and learn about propagation.

On this question of history, a very interesting and beautiful book has just landed on my desk, *Neue Pflanzen, Neue Gärten* (German is so easy to understand, isn't it?). The thesis of Swantje Duthweiler, a Professor of *pflanzenverwendung* (oh dear, this is difficult, one of the famous untranslatable words I love about the language – 'plant usage' I suppose), it looks at the connections between nurseries, the plants they produced, garden designers and colour theory during the early years of the 20th century. Lavishly illustrated with contemporary photographs and paintings of plants and gardens, and designers' plans, it shows the sophistication with which perennials and bulbs were used in gardens in this period.

A key post-war development has been the Sichtungsgarten (literally 'viewing garden') as a place where amateur gardeners and garden designers can go and see a wide range of plants and plant combinations. Most are attached to teaching institutions, but my favourite, Hermannshof, is owned by a corporation (Freudenberg, which makes flooring for airports), which is itself partly owned by the town council. Hermannshof, in the middle of Weinheim in the Rhineland, is open as a public park, with around 30 varied habitat-themed plantings. It is a paradise for anyone who is interested in new garden plants and novel ways of using them.

The gardeners here log their time, so that at the end of the year the director can tell you how many manhours per square metre each planting has required. 'How German' hoot the Brits when I tell them this. 'How sensible' is my response – as the figures are crucial to improving our understanding of how to make lower-maintenance but attractive plant combinations. This love of technical detail is something which has rubbed off on me, and I think I am a better gardener and journalist because of it.

What about 'ordinary' gardens in Germany? For the most part I find them very old fashioned in a pleasantly nostalgic way: fruit trees, vegetables and strips of flowers, all very unsophisticated by British standards, a world of gardening unaffected by the garden design revolution. Much gardening happens in *kleingärten* – allotment-like colonies where each plot has a little cabin, and there are flower borders, ponds and children's play equipment, not just vegetables. Such places are the natural habitat of the dark secret of what really lies at the heart of German gardening.

Once, on a trip to Berlin, I came across a book entitled *The German Soul*. The mind's eye instantly pictures a Wagnerian scene of forest and brooding mountain. Open book. A picture of a gnome. Turn page. A group of gnomes.

Turn another page. Elderly couple dressed as gnomes. Turn to introduction for an explanation, where I discover that a Japanese photojournalist was dispatched to Germany with a brief to discover 'The German Soul'. On day two of his trip he decided that garden gnomes expressed the national soul and proceeded from there. Apparently, there are 50 million of them for a population of 80 million.

From the sublime to the ridiculous maybe, Germany is a fantastic country for garden visiting. My favourite places are the public parks, but there are also some world-class and very visitor-friendly botanic gardens and many extensive historic gardens, often lavishly and lovingly restored. Just watch out for the gnomes.

On the trail of the plants of the gulag

By Charles Lyte

The history of plant collecting in remote places is rich with remarkable tales, but Ray Brown has probably scored a first by riding the wilderness trail in search of new and exciting species on top of a Russian amphibious tank.

Ray, who owns a botanic garden and nursery, Plant World at Newton Abbot in Devon, spent August on Sakhalin Island, one of the remotest spots in the Russian far east, collecting seeds of remarkable plants from a remarkable flora.

Eight years ago he spent a month collecting in Chile, and since then he had been searching for another place in the world with a climate like ours, yet one that no British collector had visited for years. Sakhalin Island, on the same latitude as Britain, was perfect. Under the old Soviet regime it had become a notorious Gulag, the largest prison camp in the world, and has been out of bounds to plant collectors for many decades.

With the Sea of Japan on one side and the Sea of Okhotsk on the other, Sakhalin is the remnant of a land bridge between Japan and the rest of Asia. It has a remarkably mixed flora growing in a wide range of terrain, from coastal plains to mountains.

Although the expedition had been set up with the help of a Russian botanist, Vladimir Safanov, it soon became the target of a mini crime-wave and Ray had to call on the Russian army for help. His Visa card was stolen in Moscow. At Yuzhno-Sakalisk, the capital of the island, where they made their main base in a health farm, burglars stole their clothes off a washing line; three plastic sacks of seeds were stolen, not for the seeds, which were dumped in the woods, but for the sacks. Luckily, they managed to find the contents of one. And, just when they thought things could not get worse, a maid threw bundles of seed heads into a waste disposal unit thinking they were dead flowers – even though they were in buckets labelled 'Please do not touch' in Russian.

On a salmon-fishing trip they were confronted by two men armed with Kalashnikov rifles and a Dobermann pinscher. 'They said the president had banned fishing during the salmon run, and told us to "Reverse away, fast",' said Ray.

Despite these early setbacks the team managed to collect seed from 70 different species, some of them new to cultivation. Although they were collecting on the same latitude as Torquay, the sea freezes in winter and plants are protected by a thick blanket of snow. When this melts the weather warms, creating the damp environment in which many of them thrive. Some of the most spectacular plants will be ideal for bog gardens and soggy spots.

'Sakhalin is a treasure trove of plants and a great many of them are giants,' says Ray Brown. 'It has cow parsley that grows up to 6m tall and coltsfoot with leaves that measure 1m across.'

He found *Senecio cannabifolius* in full golden flower. It grows to 8ft tall and has palmate leaves like cannabis, but is not a narcotic. He also found avenues of the world's biggest umbellifer, *Heracleum sosnovski*, growing to 20ft.

The Russian soldiers, who laid on four-wheel-drive vehicles as well as the tank, took them to a spit of land where the magnificent bear angelica (*Angelica ursina*) towered above the undergrowth, its layers of white flowers making it look like a cross between a wedding cake and a firework display, and the coastal meadows were alight with golden *Arnica sachalinensis*.

Herbaceous perennial dog wood (*Cornus canadensis*) carpeted meadows. They found the beautiful *Geranium erianthum*, *Iris setosa*, the water iris, the day lily (*Hemerocallis middendorffii*), a form of *H. esculenta*, the pink flowering oyster plant (*Mertensia asiatica*), a dwarf linaria, the sea pea (*Lathyrus japonicus*) and *Aconitum sachalinense*.

One of the most spectacular plants they discovered in fruit was an elderberry (*Sambucus sachalinense*) with brilliant scarlet berries. 'It is the most incredible plant. It lit up woodland clearings like a red searchlight.' The shrubby tree is new to cultivation but, like all the plants he has collected here, it should prove hardy in Britain (except in areas of extreme weather).

Among their finds were some lovely roses including *Rosa acicularis* with fragrant rose-pink flowers and pear-shaped red hips, *R. amblyotis*, and a dwarf form of *R. rugosa. R. rugosa ssp. sakhalinensis*, which is unique to the island, has enormous flowers.

Also discovered were false spirea (*Sorbaria sorbifolia*), a shrub with huge panicles of white flowers, a mountain ash (*Sorbus sambucifolia*), now known as *S. decora*, and a graceful wake-robin (*Trillium kamtschaticum*) whose white flowers fade to purple.

They did not touch anything in the *Red Data Book*, which lists endangered plants, and Ray was licensed by DEFRA to bring seeds back. He also went to great lengths to obtain permission from the Russian authorities to bring seeds out of the country.

The expedition was a great success, 'But we barely scratched the surface,' says Ray. 'There are countless new plants to be collected on the island, and I would like to go back and explore the mountains.'

As a memento of the trip, Ray is going to plant a Sakhalin Garden at Plant World, which should be mature in five or six years.

After the subscribers to the expedition have received their allocation of seeds any surplus may be included in the 2004 *Plant World Seed Catalogue*.

RED RUSSIA'S GLADIOLI: ENVOYS OF THE COLD WAR

Sir, – I hate to be a spoil-sport over Fred Whitsey's charming story 'Perestroika in full flower' (15 August), but the truth will out.

The opening paragraph about the arrival of the first flowers from Russia 'since Tsarist days' is just too colourful.

In 1960-1961 I imported many new Soviet gladiolus varieties from my colleagues in Russian botanic gardens and grew them under trial in Sussex.

Several were quite good so, in the 1962 growing season, large importations were made for the August Royal Horticultural Society show in London, and a display put up.

It caused great interest, coming as it did at the height of the Cold War, and was covered extensively by the media.

The most noticeable difference in the 30 years since they were first introduced in England is the change of names given. My plants were burdened with names such as 'Cosmonaut', 'Youth', 'Congo Patriot' (after Patrice Lumumba) and 'Pionerski Galatuh' ('Young Pioneer's Tie') and so on.

At one point a party of gentlemen from Whitehall – unable to tell me their names, they said, 'because of our work' – arrived at the display stand that I was manning and showed great interest in how I'd got them into the country (a mole?).

Obviously MI5 was worried about just what sort of Russian bug these flowers were carrying.

So, 'Gladiolus Glasnost' (not 'perestroika' by the way), occurred in 1960 in the good old days of shoe-thumping Nikita Khrushchev.

A. P. Hamilton

London E15

9.

'When poking stems into the globe, always aim for the centre of the sphere'

Houseplants; and the Mysteries of Flower Arranging Divulged

Cool houseplants

By Robert Pearson

If you think you've got heating problems – and don't we all – let me tell you about Rochfords, the house plant specialists, whose nurseries at Broxbourne, Hertfordshire, I visited the other day. They have 50 acres of glasshouses to heat and, in normal times, use four million gallons of oil a year.

As Mr Thomas Rochford said: 'We are faced with a serious problem which we are tackling logically, and we are confining our worrying to the things we can do something about.' Those stoical words from the chairman of a notably efficient company put things in perspective, for me at any rate.

Of one thing we can be sure, and that is that the more temperature-sensitive house plants are not going to take kindly to reductions in room temperatures we are all willingly enduring at the present time, and it was on just this matter that I put a leading question to Mr William Davidson, Rochford's show manager, who, for 25 years, has lived and breathed house plants. What can we do to alleviate the shock?

His answer was short and to the point. 'Keep your plants drier than you normally would.' Then he went on to talk of the two 'killer combinations' which house-plant enthusiasts should avoid at all times: cold conditions with too much moisture, and hot conditions with too little moisture. The most reliable way you can tell whether a plant needs water is to lift the plot and judge by its weight. That takes a little experience, but you can soon learn to tell the difference between a dry and a wet plant.

What you must be aware of too, though, is the wide disparity in moisture needs of individual types of plant. If you are given one of those marvellous forms of *Azalea indica* this Christmas you must keep it really moist – a daily soaking is what it needs, combined with a spraying over of the leaves.

If it is a florist's cyclamen you are given then you should almost let the leaves flag before you give water, while with those ever-popular Christmas flowers, the poinsettias, with their vividly coloured bracts, it is important never to let them get dry or, for that matter, too wet. All these plants are happy, incidentally, with a farenheit temperature in the low 50s.

Then there is that other excellent plant for a cool room, the easily grown *Sanseveira trifasciala laurentii*, rather unkindly called mother-in-law's tongue, which will cheerfully go through from November to mid-February without any watering – just living on the reserves in its leaves, for its needs are so small.

What other plants, I asked Mr Davidson, would you especially recommend for cooler rooms? Well, the plants mentioned above, of course, and quite a wide selection of really first-class material. The ivies (hederas), naturally, of which *Hedera canariensis*, the Canary Island ivy, is a notably fine example, and *Cissus Antarctica*, the kangaroo vine, which, with its rich green, shiny, toothed leaves, is, I think, one of the best of all house plants. This last will not tolerate hot conditions.

Then there is the bold-leaved *Falsia japonica* (syn. *Aralia japonica*), which in any case is hardy enough to grow out of doors in a sheltered part of the garden, preferably in some degree of shade.

Not surprisingly, that tolerant climber *Rhoicissus rhomboidea* is also included, and the tough and showy – when well-grown – *Chlorophytum elatum variegatum*, with its white and green-striped, narrow leaves.

Araucaria excelsa, the handsome Norfolk Island pine, too, so attractive for a nicely lighted position with its tiered branches and airy appearance, as well as that pretty succulent plant, the crown of thorns (*Euphorbia splendens*), so cheery at this time of year with its bright-red flowers.

Others are the hardy variegated euonymus, *E. japonicus aureus*, a shrub now grown as a room plant; primulas, chrysanthemums and hydrangeas; and many cacti and succulents, if they are kept dry in winter, in addition to the crown of thorns just mentioned.

If you keep it fairly dry, too, you can expect that striking dracaena, *D. marginata*, to be happy in a coolish room, its red-margined, sword-like leaves, some upright, some arched, adding lustre to the scene. Much better, though, is its variety tricolor, the aptly named rainbow plant, which will also withstand cool condition – a minimum temperature of 55°F – if not over-watered. This compact, lovely plant has spear-like leaves striped in pink, green and white, and was introduced by Mr Rochford from Japan.

On that same visit, too, in the spring of 1972, he also spotted a delightful foliage plant, like a schefflera in appearance, in a hotel at Bepu in the south of that country. Its name is *Heptapleurum arboricola*, its leaves, like those of the scheffleras, divided into many leaflets – up to nine or 10 in this case – with pointed ends. Cuttings were sent here from Japan, at Mr Rochford's request, and I understand that plants, now in limited supply, will be freely available from next spring. You can also grow this in coolish rooms.

10 AUGUST 1954

How to make the perfect 1950s pot-pourri

By Constance Spry

The simplest pot-pourri is a mixture of dried, scented rose petals to which a little bay salt is added, and possibly a spice such as grated nutmeg. Dried lavender is a favourite addition. Crushed in the fingers this will smell sweet and remind one of summer. But this dry mixture of petals will not perfume the air for long, and if you want a pot-pourri which will impart a subtle fragrance to the room, then you must do more.

I have an old-fashioned recipe for pot-pourri which lasts for years. It contains some flower oils. For a long time these were hard to get and expensive but they are again available and I found that this pot-pourri could be made at a reasonable cost. I can of course, keep the cost down by using very few of these essential oils. Later on, perhaps next year, I can add more and so vary the fragrance.

Drying the flowers.

It is important at the outset to dry the fresh flowers and petals by spreading them out thinly on paper in a cool, dry place. Later, when you have a good bunch of pot-pourri it does no harm to add a handful or so of freshly gathered petals. While your petals and flowers are drying, make the base of the pot-pourri as follows:

Mixing the base

Mix together:
220g (½lb) bay salt
30g (1oz) saltpetre
15g (½oz) ground cloves
15g (½oz) allspice
115g (4oz) powdered orris root
30g (1oz) powdered gum of benzoin

To this mixture add such flower oils as you wish — I suggest a drachm each of sweet orange oil and oil of bergamot. This will give you a start and if you like to spend a shilling or two more, add also a drachm each of oil of lavender and sweet geranium.

Put this mixture in a capacious jar and cover it tightly. Add, to begin with, a few of the dried flowers, stir well, press down tightly and cover. Do this until all the flowers are used and keep covered for a week or two, so that the flowers are well impregnated.

Other additions.

Now the pot-pourri may be put into a bowl, and the following additions are all good:

Thinly pared lemon rind, cut in small slivers; lemon thyme; rosemary; sweet mints; verbena; all dried and crumbled.

If the mixture is too damp it should be dried by the addition of more orris root, if too dry, more salt may be added. Make further additions of flowers in small quantities at a time and NEVER add large quantities of moist petals.

Wedding flowers à la mode

By Sarah Raven

O ur niece was married last weekend, and we grew and arranged all the flowers. The party took place in the most incredible tent I've ever seen – a huge, wood-frame, cream canvas yurt, large enough to fit 200 people, with a bicycle wheel of trestle tables arranged around a dance floor.

This simple, yet magnificent, thing sat in the middle of a meadow on the South Downs, where the smart flowers of this time of year – lilies, roses and eremurus – would have felt all wrong. We went for larkspur, delphinium, foxglove and peonies to fill a circle of hanging globes, but most of the flowers were simple – cornflowers, poppies, love-in-a-mist, even docks, grasses and oats picked from the fields of a friendly neighbouring farmer.

A corn stook of these sat in the middle of every table, like one sweep of a scythe from an arable field studded with cornfield weeds – that's what we wanted these bunches of flowers to feel like.

Small stooks

We made a series of small corn stooks that we used as table centres at the beginning of the evening and then – when the food arrived – they were placed in buckets around the edge of the dance floor to encircle it in a field of flowers. We also used the small stooks to line the aisle of the church, tied with hop bine to the end of every pew.

That's a good money- and time-saving system, to make double or triple use of the flowers, in the church and for the reception. There was an opportunity, while the guests had a drink after the service, to move the stooks from the church to the marquee.

You will need:

Grasses, oats, barley, large handful of each

Dock seed heads, 5 stems

Alchemilla mollis, 10 stems

Cornflowers, blue, 15 stems

Nigella (love-in-a-mist), blue and white, 15 stems

Single opium poppies, 10 stems

Step 1

Sear the stem ends of the poppies in boiling water for 30 seconds. This enables even the most delicate poppies to hold their petals for at least a day or two. (Tip: If there are more buds than flowers on a stem of poppies, peel off the outer layer (calyx) and the petals will unfurl gradually over the next couple of hours. Do this carefully, separating the sections of the calyx gently with your thumbs and then peel them back.)

Step 2

Arrange each small stook in your hand, starting with the barley and wild grasses, filling out with *Alchemilla mollis* and dock to give the bunch some bulk. Then add flowers, threading them through the foliage – larkspur, love-in-a-mist, cornflowers and opium poppies, whatever you fancy, a random sprinkling of each .

Step 3

Tie the bunch with a double length of twine, looping the two cut ends through the loop. Then take each end in opposite directions, twist it around the bunch a couple of times and tie it off. Cut the stem ends to the same length so the bunch has a flat base. This is key, so the stook will stand up easily.

Step 4

Cover the green twine with hop bine using the same knot and twisting system. This gives a chunky, straight-from-the-field look. (Tip: If conditioned well and given a good drink for at least a day after picking, the small stooks should last fine for a few hours, just standing on the table. However, our bunches had to last a whole day, so they needed to be in water. We secured them into the base of shallow glass bowls using pin-holders and Oasis fix. In the case of larger, heavier ones, we wedged them in with stones covered in hessian.

If you don't have trays, lean them at an angle in a bucket so they look as if they've just been dropped in.

Large stooks

These are glorified versions of the smaller stooks, with more flowers which are bigger and more glamorous – delphiniums, white foxgloves, larkspur, dill and ammi (bishop's flower). We stood these at the entrance to the church and then moved them to the marquee, so that people had to brush past them as they came in.

You will need:

Bupleurum, 30 stems

Dill, 30 stems

Moluccella, 30 stems

Grasses and docks, huge armful

Delphinium, blue, 15 stems

Larkspur, blue, 30 stems

Foxglove, white, long, 20 stems

Ammi, 30 stems

Oats, 80 stems

Step 1

Start in the same way as for the small stooks, creating a bunch as big as you can, holding it in your hands, but mix the flowers and foliage as you go.

Step 2

Once the bunch gets too big and heavy to hold, lay it on the table and continue adding to it, lying it flat, tying it once or twice as you go, and then adding more around it. You create an inner bunch and carry on adding around the outside.

Step 3

Lift up the large stook and stand it on the ground. Check from a distance that the overall flower balance is random, not clumped. Then tie it off with twine using the same knot as you did for the smaller stooks and finish it again with hop bine .

Hanging globe

A hanging globe is perfect for a party, with flowers coming at you from every direction, hovering above your head like a star burst. They always create quite a stir and are much easier to make than they look.

You will need:

Oasis globe, 8in in diameter

Chicken wire about 2 ½ ft long and wide, to wrap around the Oasis globe

Florists' wire

Stronger wire (or rope), to hang the globe

Hellebore leaves, 20 stems

Euphorbia oblongata, 30 stems

Alchemilla mollis, 30 stems

Moluccella laevis, 15 stems

Peony 'Sarah Bernhardt' 20 stems

Larkspur, pink, 30 stems

Foxgloves, white, 20 stems

Ammi majus, 15 stems

Oats, 40 stems

Step 1

Soak the Oasis globe for a few minutes in the bath. It will end up weighing about 9lb. Wrap the chicken wire around the globe as if you are wrapping a present. At each end, fold in the flaps of wire neatly. Don't use too much, as when it is doubled over it is difficult to insert stems. Sew wire together, using florists' wire, making sure it's secure. At the top, attach a loop of strong wire. You'll use this to hang the globe. Attach a good length of rope or strong wire to the loop and hoist the globe up to a convenient working height. Attach the end of the wire to a temporary anchor out of the way, ensuring that the knot is secure.

Step 2

Start adding foliage. Cut it all to about the same length – about 1ft long – or else your globe won't be round. When poking stems into the globe, always aim for the centre of the sphere.

Step 3

Add the flowers. Cut the stems to 12–14in, with a few shorter stems, so that some hide in the foliage and some stand out a bit. Scatter them in a balanced but not totally symmetrical way. Pick the biggest and most beautiful for the middle, equatorial zone. Few people will stand under the globe and look straight up at the flowers, and you'll hardly see those at the top.

Step 4

Hoist the globe to its final position, high above people's heads, but not so high that they won't notice it.

Step 5

If you want this to last several days, water the Oasis globe twice a day with a watering can with a wheelbarrow below to catch the water.

14 OCTOBER 1959

We Hate to Remind You …

…but Christmas is only 72 days away.

Originality in Christmas decorations is something one always envies. It is one of the things at which Constance Spry is outstanding. Never let Christmas decorations be expensive; it is against the Christmas spirit, she insists. They should be gay, light, cheap.

The ideal material for festive tablecloths and mats is tarletan in white or a pastel colour. She buys lots of bright Christmassy motifs, tarletan and adhesive and sets to work.

Her Christmas tree tablecloth is stuck round with bright green trees in little red tubs with gold bugle candles and red pear-shaped stones for flames.

Pink sequin swans with silver wings were stuck on blue tarletan. And for church decorations she sticks berries and silver leaves on to broad white satin ribbons to fasten round altar vases of flowers.

To make bases for little silver trees she winds 4½d egg poachers with silver tinsel; the trees are made of straight pieces of wire wound with tinsel and are cemented in the silvery poachers.

MAKE YOUR GARDEN INTO A POP-UP COCKTAIL VENUE

By Elspeth Thompson

Looking at the cocktail list in a trendy London bar the other evening, it struck me that I was paying through the nose for drinks made largely from ingredients that were growing for free in my garden. As well as the mint and borage that feature in classics such as Mojitos and Pimm's No 1, there were all manner of fruit purées – rhubarb, raspberry and passion fruit, to name but three – mixed with Prosecco to make new variations on the famous Bellini.

Elderflower cordials and liqueurs cropped up with great frequency – such as in the Hedgerow, which partners elderflower cordial with gin, sloe gin and pressed apple juice, all of which (bar the Gordon's) I produce at home. We gardeners are sitting on an unexploited asset, I began thinking. And so, in the spirit of our current enthusiasm for home-grown produce, may I guide you down a new avenue of horti-culinary delight: the home-grown cocktail.

If you grow nothing else for making cocktails, it should be mint. Apart from being a prime ingredient in Mint Juleps and Ernest Hemingway's favourite tipple, the Mojito (see below), it practically grows itself. Choose a classic spearmint variety (*Mentha spicata*) and give it damp, moist soil, ideally with shade at the roots and sun on the leaves. Mint is invasive, so, to prevent it taking over, plant in a large container, buried in the border if you wish. Keep well watered and protect from snails, which will strip the leaves before you can say 'Jack Daniel's'.

To make a Mojito, place six to eight mint leaves in the bottom of a tumbler together with a tablespoon of freshly squeezed lime juice and a teaspoon of white sugar. Crush with a pestle to release the mint's flavour and taste. Then fill the glass with ice, add a good slosh (2oz approx) of white rum and top with sparkling mineral water and a sprig of mint to decorate.

For a Mint Julep, follow the same instructions but start with five to six mint leaves, one teaspoon of sugar and one teaspoon of water, then pour 2oz of Kentucky Bourbon over the ice and garnish with mint.

For Pimm's, borage flowers are a must – and they also look lovely frozen into ice cubes. Borage will seed itself once you have it; if you did not grow any this spring, buy a plant in full flower from the garden centre and place it in well-drained, light soil in a sunny position. It is a good companion for strawberry plants and its capacity to attract bees also helps in the pollination of runner beans. To make Pimm's, place plenty of ice in a jug, adding two parts lemonade to one part Pimm's No 1. Thinly slice an orange, a lemon, half a cucumber and a few strawberries (the latter two coming from the garden if possible) and add to the mix, along with the leaves from a small bunch of mint and a sprinkling of borage flowers. Mix well and serve in tall glasses.

Bellinis are a doddle: just purée two cups of fruit (strawberries, raspberries, cooked rhubarb or blackberries are favourites), strain and stir in a bottle of chilled Prosecco. Serve in Champagne flutes, chilled in the freezer for 20 minutes if possible. If you're short on time, placing one strawberry or raspberry in the bottom of each glass and using pink Champagne is a good second best.

For non-alcoholic drinks, one of the nicest things to have on the summer lunch table is a jug of still water with ice cubes, sprigs of mint and a squeeze or slice or two of lemon, all of which add a note of real luxury. Or make fruity and herby ice cubes to have in water or the drinks of your choice. Children love making them – and waiting for the ice to melt and release the fruit and flowers into their drinks. Just place a small piece of fruit – a single raspberry, or segment of strawberry or watermelon – and a sprig of mint or a borage flower into each section of an ice cube tray, fill with water and freeze. Using filtered water ensures the ice cubes are clear.

With fruity, herby concoctions like these, it seems to me you have the hangover and the cure together in the same glass. So, next Saturday night, instead of going out for a drink, it's going to be home-made, home-grown cocktails in the garden. Here's to the rest of the summer.

10.
'It was like a galleon under siege'

Where Trees Stand in the Garden

Blossom in the sky

By Denis Wood

M aud burst in the other day with her latest theory on garden design. 'All you want,' she said, 'are things in the air and things on the ground, nothing in between, no bushes to spoil the contrast between height and space, just flowers in the grass – aconites and cyclamen, nothing taller – and blossom up in the sky.'

I have some sympathy with this, but I thought it rather sweeping for her and wondered how happy she would be without her roses, to mention only one of the despised bushes.

It was such a fine day that we resolved not to argue but to pursue only her point about blossom in the sky, and cherry blossom in particular. It is easy to be scornful about the Japanese cherries and call them ornamental and suburban, but they are perfectly suited to the gardens of small houses in housing estates in which a good proportion of our population lives, and it would seem sensible, therefore, to choose for these gardens trees of the correct scale. Also, many of these Japanese cherries when they get old with thick stems are very fine indeed and splendid near water.

One of the earliest is *Prunus yedoensis*, known in Japan as Yoshino; a vigorous tree reaching to 20ft, having a graceful arching growth, its branches in spring covered with single blush white flowers and a faint almond smell and appearing before the leaves. This is the chief cherry in America's Potomac Park in Washington. A much later one is *P. serrulata longipes* known also as Oku Miyako, flat topped and semi-weeping, its branches are loaded with long, large double flowers pink in bud but opening to a dense pure white on long stalks. The foliage appears at the same time, or very soon after, the flowers.

Between these are some very good garden varieties, such as Pandora, a hybrid raised by Waterers, with white flowers flushed with pink, and Hillierii raised at Hilliers of Winchester about 30 years ago, with soft pink flowers. Ukon, *P. Lannesiana grandiflora* has flowers of an interesting and unusual pale lemon colour. The autumn cherry, *P. Subhirtella autumnalis*, has an open-branched structure, and flowers twice in the year, on the bare branches in November and on through the winter to a main flowering in March.

A real monster in every sense is Kanzan, *P. Serrulata sekiyama*, until recently known as Hiskura. It has, at any rate until its late middle age, an aggressive upright growth, its branches reaching upwards like outstretched arms inviting retribution for its creation. Its flowers are particularly aggressive, violet-pink, dreadful on the tree, but curiously beautiful when lying on the ground, as I once saw them at Frogmore many years ago, a transient effect which could not have been contrived.

The fortunate countryman has no need to concern himself with these ornamental trees; he has at his disposal two of the most beautiful of all flowering trees. The native single white flowering cherry and its double form *P. Avium plena*.

The single one is the Gean or Mazzard – in Gean incidentally, the 'g' is hard – it may have come from the French 'guigne' which means 'a black-heart cherry'. Mazard (spelt with one 'z' in the OED) was apparently a dialect word occurring in 1577 simply meaning 'a small black cherry'. This is the tree responsible for those miraculous towering clouds of foam which you see in the spring on the outskirts of beech woods still dark from winter and it must be the one which in Housman's poem '...stands about the woodland ride'. Loveliest of trees he called it and I think he was about right.

The double-flowered one may be better for gardens; it holds its flowers longer and its white colour is denser. It, too, is a large tree 60ft or more, and could overpower a small garden; therefore, it needs a fair amount of space around it.

In the prunus family we have such a wide choice of cherries that I do not feel the need of any of the plums. But I respect the peach for its long association with Persian and Moorish gardens and I like its rather weeping, often pliant outline.

The variety Klara Meyer is the one I have seen the most. The pink of its blossom is far from cool, a hot, almost hectic, colour. I deplore the so-called double almond produced no doubt with laborious, but mistaken, good intent in Australia in 1904 and now called *P. amygdalo-persica Pollardii*. It is usually described as having double, richer pink flowers larger than the classic common almond, part of whose charm lies in its rather smaller flowers in scale with the branches of the tree and their indescribably beautiful cold paleness when seen against a blue sky in spring. When will they ever learn?

8 JANUARY 1977

Planting for posterity

By Fred Whitsey

This year, my friend was saying, really would be the year when he would at last plant his avenue of trees across the paddock to which

I had been exhorting him for so long. The field would become a park.

It must be the sort of resolution made in many a breast under the stimulus of the Jubilee celebrations. Fortunately, we can hope to see many trees planted to mark it. They will help to heal the ravages of the elm disease.

What kind, though? What makes a true commemorative tree, worthy of being set upon so important a stage?

I would have said, first, nobility – if you are prepared to classify trees so arbitrarily. A lime qualifies, but not a laburnum. I would apply the term sentimental to the latter. In between comes charm, a quality – winning none the less – that might be perceived in the maples, even in the birch.

Doubtless majesty must always remain in the eye of the beholder. Another friend of mine who likens people to plants, as some do to breeds of dogs, holds that trees are like women – ceaselessly changeable but dependable just the same. Perhaps, I wonder, is this what the botanists had in mind when they decreed that, in their codified version of Latin, all trees should take the feminine gender?

Anyway, a noble tree need not have flowers of any consequence. The oak hasn't but leads them all. If it was a stout-hearted oak I was planting commemoratively it would either be the Turkey kind, which goes such a fine colour in autumn, or the equally fast-growing red oak, again for autumn colouring, or perhaps the so-called cypress kind, because it has a narrow silhouette rather than a bounteous one.

Chestnuts qualify, both the edible one and the conker tree, and here my choice among the latter would be the red-flowered kind, *Aesculus carnea briottii*. So does the ash, and here it might be the flowering Manna ash, which has white flowers in late spring and purplish leaves in autumn.

Beeches? Not terribly distinguished in small numbers, or singly until they get really old, but the closely related hornbeam is splendid if one or other of its narrow-growing forms is chosen. They manage to combine elegance with robustness.

If the avenue or single tree is to be of lime, then it had better be of the hybrid *Tillia euchlora*, which neither suckers like the ordinary kind does nor sprays the unwary below with the honeydew secreted by greenflies.

I have never heard of an avenue being planted with davidia, the handkerchief tree, but someone ought to make the attempt. It has nobility all right, but verges on the charming when in bloom and hung with its ivory bracts.

One other thing all these have in common is that they grow slowly. Which justifies them for gardens if you buy ready-grown standards, and provided you choose the site well, seeing something from them in your own lifetime. And it justifies them for public planting where it is posterity that is to be taken by the lapel and reminded of some historic moment past.

From the charm school you can get something for your effort by buying smaller and less expensive trees and watching them reveal themselves gradually. This you can do with any of the snake-barked maples and the brownish-barked *Acer griseum*. Also with the Chinese mountain ash trees that give autumn berries and rich leaf colour. However, if it was an avenue I was planting I might settle for the wild *Acer campestre* which grows elegantly, has rich gold autumn colouring and is gravely undervalued.

Have you yet met the variegated-leaved poplar, *Populus candicans Aurora*? It manages to combine in its leaf tints bright green, silver and pink, all shimmering in the summer breeze. A delectable tree and a convenient upright grower, to judge by those I have seen.

How often have you smelt a balsam poplar? This would be a felicity for which posterity would be grateful.

Both are charmers. So, as I say, is the birch, particularly in its whitest-stem species – see them in the bark first, before ordering. Sometimes the wild one is almost as good as the esoteric kinds. And another charmer is the weeping willow-leaved pear, *Pyrus salicifolia pedula*, whose leaves are silver right to the end of the season and whose outline has the right degree of decorous grief but never becomes an embarrassing flood, like the willow itself.

The sentimental breed? All flowering cherries and all flowering crabs. And, I submit, the ornamental thorn trees and the whitebeam that carries its berries ready prepared with foliage for harvest festivals. One of their great merits is no waiting. You can buy, plant and watch for the results in the very first season. And you don't have to remove the flowers or fruits in that year as you do from true fruit trees.

As for the technique by which you can declare a tree well and truly planted, I would say a hole big enough to take the roots at full stretch – peat over them before the soil to promote the feeding fibres – a stake to train it up in the way it should go, and a bare patch of soil kept weeded or mulched for the first season at least so that no competition for nitrogen comes from grass or other weeds growing round it.

When? Don't wait for the Jubilee day. It falls too late for dependable results to flower. Eschew the ceremony and get it done before the end of March while there is still plenty of prospect of rain to water the tree in well and get it established. Then all will be all right on the night.

Get cracking

By Ursula Buchan

I have a young plantation of hazelnuts, both cobnuts and filberts, that I planted almost three years ago because I love the look of nutteries – or 'plats', as they are known in Kent. I especially like the idea of them in spring, when the hazels are in fresh leaf and chime brilliantly with yellow primroses and bluebells. There is also something deeply satisfying about growing one's own food for the table, especially at this time of year. And the hazelnut – with its ancient history and association with Christmas – comes close to the top of my list.

Cultivated hazelnuts come in two forms: the cob, which has a husk shorter than the nut, and the filbert (or full-beard), with a fringed husk that extends beyond the nut. Cob nuts are forms of *Corylus avellana*, the native hazel, while filberts descend from the Turkish *Corylus maxima*. There are about eight available cultivated varieties: 'Cosford Cob'; 'Pearson's Prolific', which is sometimes listed as 'Nottingham'; 'Webb's Prize Cob'; 'Kentish Cob', which is, in fact, a filbert; 'Gunslebert'; 'Red Filbert'; 'White Filbert'; and the impossibly named 'Halle'sche Riessennuss' or 'Merveille de Bollwyller' (also known as 'Halle Giant').

In my nuttery the shrubs are planted in two staggered rows, with 12ft intervals between the plants. Hazels are largely self-sterile and may need to be fertilised by another variety to set fruit, so I have planted three kinds: 'Cosford Cob', a vigorous, upright-growing variety that produces large, oval, thin-shelled nuts and is a good pollinator;

'Pearson's Prolific', which has a more compact habit and rounded nuts; and the filbert 'Kentish Cob', another vigorous, upright grower with larger, longer nuts. These differ in size and shape rather more than in taste.

Before planting up the nuttery I prepared the soil really well by digging it over and incorporating a little well-rotted manure into the planting hole. I also mulched generously with compost, since the stuff I have is too heavy to be ideal for nuts, particularly cobnuts.

I bought my shrubs as two-year-old bare-rooted plants. Initially I cut back each one's stems to roughly 12in from the ground, cutting to outward-facing buds in order to promote the growth of a strong framework with an open centre. But I doubt I will have to prune them as hard in future years as commercial nut-growers would, since I want them to look good and to grow tall enough to provide effective shelter. I may, however, be tempted to 'brut' them in summer if leaves are growing at the expense of female flowers, which can be a problem on heavy soil. This charming term means snapping – but not quite breaking off – leafy young shoots halfway along their length, which encourages flower-bud formation and also ripens the nuts. The broken shoots are then cut back hard in winter.

Whether these shrubs eventually produce masses of nuts will depend on the climate as much as anything else. In mild winters the long, yellow, male catkins tend to flower earlier than the separately borne, tiny red female flowers, so pollination may not always be successful. However, hazel pollen is carried on the wind, so I am hoping that the nearby native hedge with plenty of ordinary hazel in it will help matters.

I do know that I haven't a chance of getting any nuts before next year at the earliest – hazelnuts need to be at least four years old to fruit – and then only if I can deal successfully with the grey squirrel that appears each autumn. Unfortunately, since this pest can eat nuts before they are fully ripe, I anticipate a right royal tussle with it. (That is the reason, incidentally, why grey squirrels are chasing out red squirrels, for the latter wait until nuts are ripe and starve as a result.) I suspect that I will have to learn to eat the nuts when the husks are still green and before the full flavour has developed if I am to taste them at all. Though even if I never get huge crops of nuts I shan't be too sorry, for the hazels themselves are handsome, especially in autumn when the leaves turn a russety yellow.

Once the shrubs are really well-established and beginning to shade out the coarse grasses I shall plant masses of wild primrose, grown in plugs from seed, beneath them. To these I'll add the many bluebell bulbs that appear unbidden in my borders each year. My hope is that, one day, the nuttery will be virtually self-sustaining, requiring little work on my part – then I will be proud to say that I am completely nutty.

21 JANUARY 2006

Trees for your dream orchard

By Dan Pearson

I have planted three new orchards in clients' gardens this winter, going as strongly against the flow of current farming policy as possible. The removal of long-established orchards over the past few years is a tragedy, and landscapes have changed dramatically in Kent, Somerset and other apple-growing counties. I was brought up with a big, old orchard at the bottom of the garden and have a particular fondness for them. Our trees were gnarled and heavy with age and lichen, but come spring, the flowers were one of the most wonderful things in the garden and in the autumn, the clearing in which the trees grew was filled with the smell of fruit.

All three orchards were planted mainly with apples, which were chosen to reflect the area, so local varieties would continue to grow where they had for centuries. This took some research, but there is something satisfying about a little history in a garden. We also took great care to match the rootstocks to the site. M25, the largest and most vigorous stock from which you would expect to rear decent-sized trees in reasonable time, was planted on the wetter heavier clays (in general, apples do not like it wet and are more prone to canker in these conditions). On the drier soils and where we wanted bush or half standard trees, the MM106 stock was used.

I prefer to plant fruit trees that will reach a decent size because they are such good value, given blossom, fruit and a fine outline. I would use a smaller stock, such as M9, if space were an issue but the soil must be in good condition, as dwarfing rootstocks need better conditions. A dwarfing stock will, however, allow you to grow cordons, fans and step-overs and offer a great way to have fruit without committing to a tree.

Medlars, mulberries and quince fit less well into an orchard setting and I tend to keep these as isolated specimen trees. In truth, I have never really understood the obsession with the medlar. This curious tree is very popular again today, but I have never met anyone who has said they were really looking forward to biting into a medlar. They are an acquired taste. The fruit should be harvested late in the autumn and kept on a shelf until they are rotten or 'bletted'. The russety skin, which remains strong enough to contain the fermented fruit, can then be broken open and the sweet paste eaten with a spoon. Mrs Beeton has a recipe for a medlar jelly that can be eaten with cold meat. As the pretty flowers are its main attraction, I would recommend the larger-flowered variety, 'Large Russian', and try it grafted onto quince rootstock, as this is less prone to revert than hawthorn.

I would much rather grow a quince. These are great for adding a culinary atmosphere to a garden and I use them in herb gardens or within a potager setting as there is a timelessness about them and their fruit never fails to conjure up images of glowing fruitbowls painted by the old masters. They are easy to grow as long as they get plenty of sunshine, and they seem to do better in a damp position, which is unusual among fruit trees. Here they will form a dome as much as 13ft across.

The large, fairly sparse flowers appear, like the medlar flowers, well after the tree is in leaf in May, and they are lovely to chance upon. The heavy fruits that ripen to a powerful gold are wonderful, and you will enjoy them even more if you can smell them when warmed in sunshine. This potent perfume gives no clue as to the nature of the fruit, which is astringent and needs to be cooked to be enjoyed. As an addition to apple crumble, however, quince is excellent and it also makes a delicious jelly or paste.

My favourite fruit tree, of those that sit better outside an orchard setting, is the black mulberry, *Morus nigra*. This has the ability to assume character and a feeling of age within just a few years of planting, and many trees that are thought to be hundreds of years old are not, even though it has been cultivated here for centuries. The black mulberry likes the warmth and will grow fast and fruit young in the south. It should be given a sheltered, free-draining site against a warm wall further north. Make sure you ask for the black mulberry, and the form called 'Chelsea'.

Morus alba, the white mulberry, is a disappointment, useful for feeding silkworms but, in comparison with the luscious tanginess of *M. nigra*, its small fruit are barely worth the effort. It is inferior if you want character in the garden. In time, the black mulberry will arch to the ground and stain your paths with its rich dark fruits. It is almost impossible to pick the fruit without the tangy juice running down your arms and staining your fingers red but this is, in my book, not a problem.

28 MARCH 1982

All spruced up

By Robert Pearson

As a small child I remember being somewhat in awe of a huge elm tree that dominated the middle distance from my bedroom window. In blustery winter weather, with grey clouds scudding over its gaunt head, it was like a galleon under siege.

But even that patriarchal tree took second place, at that impressionable age, to the conifers – sometimes brooding and perhaps sombre, but often with beautiful shapes, and, as I came to understand later, with many variations in leaf texture and colour, especially the latter.

How much of our appreciation of plants must stem from such half-forgotten memories. Apropos conifers, too, how long it takes any gardening enthusiast with broad (rather than specialised) interests to gain a full understanding of the remarkable range of species, varieties and hybrids within the different genera – if, indeed, it is ever achieved. But that is why gardening is a lifetime's adventure.

Like many other people, I find conifers continually fascinating: lovely at all times of year (think back to this past winter) and adding so much to gardens of widely disparate character and size. It has been good to see the great advance in interest in recent years in the dwarf and slower-growing conifers, so marvellously ornamental when well displayed in smaller gardens; but what of the larger kinds that can be made a focal point of a vista in a garden of reasonable but not over-large size?

My thoughts turn immediately to the handsome Serbian spruce, *Picea omorika*, which, with an eventual height from about 60 to 70ft and a spread of perhaps 15ft, makes a narrow column of dark-green foliage that is very easy on the eye. Its silhouette is pyramidal, with the longest branches near the base curving gently downwards before rising again at the tips. Culturally, too, it has considerable virtue, for it will do well on most soils, including those of an alkaline nature, in sunshine or light shade, and it will withstand more air pollution than most conifers without distress. Air pollution is far less of a problem than it used to be, but the Serbian spruce's ability to cope with this hazard must explain why one can see it breaking the skyline, on occasion, in residential areas around large towns and cities.

If the Serbian spruce is handsome, then *Picea breweriana* is beautiful. This native of the Siskiyou Mountains of California and Oregon makes a tree in cultivation up to 40ft or so in height (although it is much taller in its native habitat), with rank on rank of near-horizontal branches bearing masses of slim, dark-green pendulous shoots up to 10ft long. The effect is of a series of curtains forming a kind of waterfall – truly memorable. The snag, for the not-so-young, is that its rate of growth is somewhat slow and the branchlets which are its crowning glory do not begin to form until it is well established. Many of us may move home more frequently than used to be the case, but then many trees of great worth have always been planted with the enjoyment of others much in mind.

This spruce needs a neutral-to-acid soil in which to grow and will not take kindly to over-dry root conditions. A degree of shelter from cold winds is also necessary, and that you will find has always been provided in those rather grander gardens where it can be seen when garden visiting. I look on it as one of nature's marvels.

It would be impossible to leave the spruces without touching on those splendid forms of *Picea pungens*, the Colorado spruce, with silvery-blue foliage – ones like Koster, for instance, which will in time make a tree of 25 to 30ft in height with a spread of perhaps 15ft. This is the best known of the blue spruces, as they are called, and it makes a dramatic plant in many different garden settings and notably where it can be associated with low-growing heathers or other ground-cover plants. Others of similar appearance to Koster are the varieties Hoopsii and Erich Frahm, the latter of a rather deeper shade of blue. The pungens varieties also need to be grown in a soil on the acid side. They also need exposure to sunshine and shelter from cold winds.

To talk of deciduous conifers sounds like a contradiction in terms, but, of course, that is what the graceful larches (or larix) are and the noble swamp cypress, *Taxodium distichum*. Also, of course, the now-popular dawn redwood, *Metasequoia glyptostroboides*, which is a tall conical tree and has a fast rate of growth. Its main attraction is its pretty foliage; such a bright, light green early in the season and, in autumn, of almost pinkish hue. This seems to grow well in varied conditions, but is undoubtedly happiest where a moist but well-drained soil can be provided. Another deciduous conifer that can be pleasing is *Ginkgo biloba*, the maidenhair tree, which has highly distinctive fan-like leaves that turn to butter-yellow in autumn. Like the dawn redwood, it has a history that goes back to the fossil age. In size it can be classed as of medium height (perhaps 10m to 12m), but it is slow to get into its stride. Its width can be variable, but 4.5m or a little more would be about average. It is another conifer best given a sunny, sheltered position and it needs a well-drained soil of average quality.

Lemon trees with zest

By Fred Whitsey

The long tradition of growing lemon trees in pots has received a fillip from the arrival in garden centres of so many young plants. These offer exciting possibilities to conservatory and patio gardeners. Specialist growers are now offering as many as they do in Mediterranean nurseries. Often the plants are already in flower or fruit.

Lemon trees are determined plants. They begin to flower very early in life and, with a little coaxing under glass, will bloom almost all year round. The delicious scent that greets you whenever you open a greenhouse door is a luxury, even if you have only a single lemon tree growing there. It can also turn a conservatory into what was once known as a 'winter garden'.

To refer to them as trees is misleading, however, for lemons grown in pots are chubby little bushes – evergreen and, with pinching and gentle pruning, as neat in form as if they had been cultivated as bonsai. What is more, they are very long-lived.

In Italy I've seen bushes, only 3ft across, which were reputed to have been cared for by three generations of gardeners. And at a nursery near Rome recently, there were plants for sale that were said to be 100 years old.

The ultimate achievement is training lemon trees into the shape of ice-cream cones. Half-a-dozen canes are pushed into the soil round the rim of the pot, sloping outwards. The plants are then given a high-nitrogen diet to make them produce plenty of soft growth. This is tied to the canes in tiers like a peach on a wall. Eventually, after the feed has been changed to one high in potash, the lemons hang from the outside of the 'basket' formed by the technique.

The variety most readily available is named 'Meyer Lemon'. It is said to be of hybrid origin and to have been brought from China early in the century. This is the one I have grown for a good many years. It has proved itself tough in the face of winter chill, even in an unheated greenhouse, though one would try to give it a night temperature a few degrees above freezing. So it is safe in the average conservatory, provided you are mean with the watering during the winter. Those whose only growing place is a shed or garage should be able to keep it safely if the plant is swaddled in horticultural fleece.

However, I learn from Amanda Dennis who, with her husband, Chris, runs The Citrus Centre near Pulborough, West Sussex, that the 'Meyer Lemon' is far surpassed in ease of growth and abundance of flower by 'Four Seasons'. This is, however, more difficult to get hold of and more expensive.

It is one of about 10 varieties available these days. I'm intrigued by the variegated ones: not only are the leaves marked with cream on the fresh green, but the fruits are striped too.

From the way our plants respond to a summer outing, I would say they really get a boost from being stood out of doors for about three months, whether it is a good season or a rainy one. Of course, they must be given a position where they get all the sun going. It is also important to put some ant powder under the pots. Ants are inquisitive creatures and will quickly colonise any newly arrived container, entering through the drainage holes.

Moving the pots around twice a year can be troublesome. Lemon plants are not very happy in soil-less compost and thrive best in loam-based John Innes II compost, which, in a pot of fair size, can be very heavy. So a trolley or two pairs of hands are needed.

I was once at Versailles when they were packing away the ancient citrus trees into the orangery. The occasion seemed to be something of a festival. There were many cries of excitement as they used old carts specially built for the job, but which are now hauled by tractor instead of horses. The plants were growing in the traditional timber caisses de Versailles, but I'm sure lemon trees look best in highly decorated terracotta pots with steeply sloping sides to a narrow base, for preference each resting on its own matching plinth, as you see them still in historic Italian gardens.

If real lemons are too much, there is a nice cheat. Stand on your terrace or beside a flight of steps, as we have, a row of the Chinese privet *Ligustrum lucidum*. Their leaf is exactly like those of the lemon and you can leave them there all the year. The impersonation is hard on the lemon but is uncannily effective.

28 APRIL 1973

In a poet's orchard

By Denis Wood

Some day I will make a poet's orchard where one may lie in long grass and read Marvell. It would be surrounded by a hawthorn hedge for song-birds to make their nests in and could be as small as half an acre, into which 14 standard trees can be planted in a quincuncial pattern.

Now, it is not economic to plant standard trees because they take a long time to come into bearing and, worse, when mature become so tall as to be difficult to spray against the embattled forces of 'pests-and-diseases' which haunt the dreams of sound practical growers and horticulturists, and for which poisonous remedies fill half the shelves of garden supermarkets. But this is an undertaking to be carried out in wanton disregard of sensible up-to-date advice – even the trees themselves are chosen for the beauty of their blossom, their attractive names, their history and lineage.

First, three for the blossom. One is James Grieve (Edinburgh 1890), an eating apple ready in September and having, besides its lovely flowers, curiously yellow fruits hanging on its branches. The next two are both cooking apples: Arthur Turner (1914), whose blossom is bright pink and white, the fruit green with a pale pink flush, the flesh white and slightly acid bakes well. October and November. The third is Annie Elizabeth (Leicester 1857), brilliant red and yellow when ripe, the flesh crisp and acid. January and February. One which cooks to a froth, the Rev. W. Wilks, a large cream-coloured fruit streaked with deep pink. September to November.

For the rest we shall be guided by Edward Bunyard, who died in 1940 and is still sadly missed. His *Handbook of Fruits, Apples and Pears*, was published by Murray in 1920. The second volume, *Stone and Bush Fruits, Nuts, etc.*, followed in 1925; and his entertaining, humorous and instructive *Anatomy of Dessert* was published by Chatto & Windus in 1929 and 1933.

For an eating apple in October, I will have Gravenstein (from Schleswig-Holstein in 1760). Of medium size, pale yellow with red stripes, crisp, juicy flesh – what Bunyard called 'the very attar of apple'. October to December.

Although I shall disregard most of the precepts, I shall try to follow the fertility rules. Gravenstein, owing to the curious arrangement of its chromosomes, is a triploid needing at least two other varieties with the more usual diploid arrangement of chromosomes and flowering at the same time to ensure its polygamous satisfaction, which will be accomplished by Sturmer Pippin, Margil and the Rev. W. Wilks, all diploids and all flowering at the same time as Gravenstein. Margil (raised before Cox and Ribston and possibly one of their ancestors) stands on the threshold of high apple festival time. Bunyard wrote of its flesh as 'delightfully fondant and marrowy ... flavour of great price ... to be placed among the Old Masters'.

Blenheim Orange (Woodstock c. 1818) is a dual-purpose fruit. Cooking excellently and of fine quality, also for dessert, crisp, yellow and refreshingly sub-acid. Bunyard wrote of its 'nutty warm aroma ... the real apple gust'. He went on to say, 'I take the Blenheim as a test case, the man who cannot appreciate a Blenheim has not come to years of gustatory discretion...' November to January. This is another of the dreaded triploids, but will be pollinated by James Grieve, Arthur Turner and Rosemary Russet.

Ribston Pippin, if only because of Belloc's

'I said to Heart, "How goes it?"

Heart replied: "Right as a Ribstone Pippin!" But it lied.'

Raised at Ribston Hall, Knaresborough, about 1709, from seed sent from Rouen, a highly spiced aromatic apple keeping to January. Another triploid pollinated by Sturmer, Margil and The Rev. W. Wilks.

Orlean's Reinette (before 1776) was Bunyard's favourite apple. He wrote of it: 'For those who incline to the dry in food and drink, Orlean's Reinette is an apple made for their purpose, rich and mellow, and as a background for old port it stands solitary and unapproachable ... it stands of all apples highest in my esteem.' Until February.

Rosemary and Russet (c. 1831), yellow fleshed, brisk and crisp with a characteristic russet tang of fennel. One of the best late winter apples. Until February.

Cornish Aromatic (17th-century Cornwall), small, light olive-green, bright-crimson flush. Yellow, crisp aromatic flesh. Bunyard considered it to be the highest quality and appearance. December to February.

To round off a dozen apples, Sturmer Pippin (c. 1843), greenish crisp flesh. Should not be picked until November or December. February to May.

To make up the 14, I would have two pears, Doyenné du Comice (Angers 1849). Unsurpassed and unsurpassable. November. And to pollinate it, Beurre Hardy (c. 1840) of tender flesh with rosewater flavour.

I have left out Cox's Orange Pippin and Bramleys Seedling and also that interloper, Golden Delicious which, for its name alone would never be admitted. These three can be bought to excess in the shops, but unless a few like me, while there is still time, preserve some of the classic apples and pears, they will go down to oblivion.

PUBLIC GARDENS LOSE HUNDREDS OF RARE TREES

By Fred Whitsey

Hundreds of rare and prized trees in some of Britain's important public gardens were uprooted and destroyed during Thursday's ferocious storm and their custodians spent yesterday assessing damage before attempting any first-aid measures.

A survey in Kew Gardens showed that some of the most prized trees had been lost. They included the only cork oak, planted in 1840, and the first *Eucalyptus gunnii* planted from the original collection of seed in Tasmania around the same time, a 200-year-old Caucasian zelkova, a Chilean yew from the Andes and several of the Southern Hemisphere beech trees.

These were among 100 trees that fell almost simultaneously in a gust at 2.10pm. Another 50 were so badly loosened at the root that they may have to be felled.

Mr John Simmons, curator of the gardens, said yesterday the strongest gust recorded in the 1987 storm had been 50 knots; on Thursday 70 knots had been reached.

As the storm eased in the late afternoon, staff who had been evacuated from the greenhouses earlier in the day returned and worked until midnight replacing large areas of glass with sheets of hardboard to save some of Kew's rarest plants from night chill.

At Kew's country annex, Wakehurst Place in Sussex, where 20,000 trees were blown down in 1987, Mr Tony Schilling, deputy curator, said they escaped with the loss of about 90.

Sheltering belts of trees at the Royal Horticultural Society's Wisley Gardens in Surrey suffered badly and nearly half the remaining pines and fir trees that gave shade cover to rhododendrons and camellias were brought down.

Mr Jim Gardener, the Wisley curator, said several of the Garden's important conifers had gone or been severely damaged. They included the incense cedar of south-western United States origin, Himalayan deodar, and Mediterranean maritime pine, the source of turpentine. Many mature oaks had also fallen.

Very large trees that had fallen in the Valley Gardens in Windsor Great Park had seriously damaged the exotic plantings underneath. But Mr John Bond, keeper of the Windsor gardens, said many were old trees close to the end of their lives and 'waiting for help to come down'.

In the nearby Savill Garden, one of the most notable trees of the whole collection, the large-leafed *Magnolia macrophylla*, which originates in the south-eastern United States and which has leaves 18in long, had been blown down.

Among the 50 trees down at Shield Park Gardens, Sussex, was a Chinese coffin juniper grown from the original seed collection when it was discovered by Reginald Farrer in 1920.

At Sandling Park, Kent, the country's worst devastated garden in 1987, Mr Alan Hardy, the owner, found the last of his large rhododendrons had been blown out of the ground.

11.

'You do not expect to find innocence by the end of summer'

Weeds and Their Unexpected Qualities

Divine hogweed

By David Hicks

Hogweed is a horrible name for a truly majestic plant. In autumn the bare flowerheads have an architectural grandeur, outlined in a white rim of frost, and the stems are almost monumental, fluted like classical columns. I have always loved cow parsley, its more delicate relation, which transforms the hedgerows at the beginning of summer. Some of my earliest memories are of English country lanes with the May trees in blossom and underneath them a frothing, drifting sea of white. Hogweed was a slightly later discovery – it inhabits rougher, damper grassy areas like the banks of rivers – but I have loved both these plants since boyhood. Apart from their magical effect on the landscape, I associate them with Cecil Beaton and those very romantic photographs he took at his country house, Ashcombe, in the 1930s and early 1940s. I bought a book of these photographs aged 16 and almost all of them have these wonderful backgrounds of cow parsley, hogweed and other wild flowers.

In my own garden, I encourage cow parsley on either side of the drive and the giant hogweed, *Heracleum mantegazzianum*, around my pond in the wild part of the garden. The hogweed is particularly dramatic and I never cut it down – I want it to grow more and more. I started by collecting seeds from the wild – one of the best sources is the Great West Road at Ealing. But hogweed is terribly invasive. Occasionally I allow a stray seedling to grow up in the middle of a bed of roses, hostas, lilies and peonies as an exciting sort of punctuation mark. But when the umbel has reached maturity and the seed is ready to ripen I make sure I cut it off, otherwise it would soon be everywhere.

Hogweed dries very well, and can look very effective indoors. I find the best method for drying it is to leave the stalks upright in an outhouse and let the water evaporate – it's smelly, but the plant retains its form much better when allowed to dry out slowly. The trick with dried flowers is not to keep them for too long, because once they get dusty they look sad. Keep arrangements simple; too many different things can look a bit 'tea-shoppe'. A single stem of dried hogweed can look stunning – it throws the most dramatic shadows.

20 SEPTEMBER 1997

How I gave up and learned to love the bindweed

By Mirabel Osler

I am a contriver, not a gardener, and I find it not a bad method. More than at any other time of the year, this behaviour parades itself now – in the season of blowsy tawdriness – when I surrender to pots of white petunias in the foreground reflecting back the elegant strands of bindweed twining through the holly and dogwood.

Bindweed! You do not expect to find innocence by the end of summer, but these flowers epitomise purity. Their fragility is as good as anything I have grown all the year. The fact that in early spring it was war between us, as I got down on my knees in an attempt to dig up every single thread of their intrusive roots, is forgotten. Long ago I surrendered. By August I knew the plants had got the better of me. My vitality is dispersed; my pride is non-existent and havoc reigns.

But it is now that I discover one of the great miracles of gardening; what happens to be a disaster can, when looked at with other eyes, be a celebration. The radiance and grace of these flowers, smothering even my clematis Montana until it appears to have a second flowering, leaves me sighing with gratitude amid the black spot bedevilling the roses.

At the start of the year, like my plants, I feel vigorous, determined to be in control. But by late summer I have acquiesced; my contriving has permutated into slothfulness. Only when I see the convolvulus throttling a meconopsis do I gird my loins enough to tear the stems out of the baked earth. But I am not fooled; this is no way to go about annihilation. I know that underground there is a tangled web of invaders preparing for next year's annexation.

It is all a matter of philosophy (an underestimated concept when tackling a garden). For those setting out this autumn to make a garden for the first time, take heart. Remember that there are no right ways of doing it – only alternatives. You must not let yourselves be browbeaten or intimidated. Do not feel put down by the inches of expertise appearing in print, or let television programmes rattle you with their pictures of harmonious colours and 'good taste'. To hell with good taste. Forget what the neighbours will say as you go in for a bit of deviant planting.

Be unashamed when the cognoscenti ask you the name of a plant and you have forgotten it. I love it when this sort of person visits my garden and says: 'What a lovely *Dimorphotheca barberiae* you have.' Have I? Do show me where. Oh, that? I always thought of it as a pretty pink daisy thing.'

To be a gardener we do not all need to be grounded in Latin. I began to garden too late in life to sharpen my wits. I no longer remember anything except for the poems I learnt in my youth and that I still have an unappeased longing for wildness.

Few gardeners exult. We meet, commiserate and complain. Slugs, moles, rust, frost, weeds or weather. Look back on the year and think how many of us you meet who are in despair. Only in June, and possibly March, do I encounter people who talk with rapturous buoyancy about the beauty of their gardens. For the other 10 or 11 months we are forever apologising. Cooks hold their tongues; they never admit that the sauce should not be like this or that the soup is really from Neal's Yard.

Notice gardeners need convincing that plants are survivors and that it is not the end of the world if something is planted in the wrong place. Many things can be moved with what appears as reckless folly. Roses that I have cut to the ground in order to transplant them have flowered prodigiously in a new site. Trees, even quite large ones, withstand this kind of upheaval, too. Take courage, the garden can be transformed by this method.

If you want to make a garden but feel overwhelmed by shiny picture books offering an unobtainable nirvana, start off by putting in a few bulbs, a tree, one or two roses, a pretty painted bench with pots of unsophisticated flowers at your feet, and I promise your spirits will soar, your confidence burgeon. Forget about design, balance, herbaceous borders, 'flowers for the house' and 'colour in winter' – in fact, the plethora of advice thrown at you – and start with a modest number of sights, smells and shapes. You will be in heaven.

Whatever you do, forget about lawns. They are bullies. More time is spent fussing over greensward than on any other garden activity. All those sprinklers. Think of them. All that scarifying. Imagine it. And all that mowing. Avoid it. No garden should tyrannise you like this.

Rather, it should be your personal escape, your country for friendship and a harbour for contemplation. Never forget: easeful moments are intrinsic to gardens as mulching a rose.

24 APRIL 2005

You call it cow parsley, I call it *Cenolophium denudatum*

By Elspeth Thompson

One of the first plants I ever fell in love with was cow parsley. I remember standing in an orchard, aged about 10, with snowy-white cherry blossom above me and a foaming sea of cow parsley all around. The cow parsley came up to my shoulders, leaving a 'breathing space' of only 12in or so between it and the blossom overhead. It felt as though I was swimming in springtime.

Since that early epiphany, I have looked forward every year to late spring, when the hedgerows froth with these delicate white flowers – not for nothing is *Anthriscus sylvestris* also known as Queen Anne's lace. It grows along the layered hedge that borders my allotment, and I love to gather it in generous armfuls to arrange about the house. Some people hate the smell, but not me. Forget expensive wedding flowers; if I were getting married in May, I'd deck the church in blossom and cow parsley.

Cow parsley in the hedgerows is one thing; in the garden, though, it is another. It spreads like wildfire, so unless you are lucky enough to have large wooded areas where wild, woolly planting is in order, it is best left by the roadside. Luckily, its lovely black-leafed cultivar, *Athriscus sylvestris* 'Ravenswing', is better behaved. Rightly fashionable in recent years, its finely cut chocolate-purple leaves are attractive in themselves, and the perfect backdrop for the lacy white flowerheads. Beth Chatto grows it in her woodland garden, with the fresh lime-green fronds of ferns such as *Dryopteris erythrosora*, purple and white Martagon lilies and *Actaea simplex* 'Atropurpurea'. I've also seen it looking lovely in long grass studded with purple alliums and nectaroscordums.

Another attractive relation of cow parsley, *Chaerophyllum hirsutum* 'Roseum' (pink hairy chervil) has tiny pink-to-lilac flowers – like cow parsley in miniature, dipped in pink dye – that appear to float above the feathery, apple-scented leaves. This self-seeds happily, but not indiscriminately – try studding it with the bright blue stars of brunnera, or letting it weave in and out of honesty or the creamy spires of tellima. In a wilder setting, where native cow parsley will smother smaller plants, try *Pimpinella major* 'Rosea' – the richest pink flower of all the umbellifers – or tiny *Meum athamanticum*, just 75cm high, with fine filigree foliage and tiny pure-white flower heads. There is also a handsome lime-green version of cow parsley. *Smyrnium olusatrum* – or Alexanders, as it is often known – has umbels of chartreuse yellow which are opening in the hedgerows and beach-side shingle near our seaside house right now. The first year I saw it, in a patch of scrubland by our drive, I gathered it greedily to stand in large jugs around the house. It looked lovely … but it smelled so appalling I had to throw it on the compost heap after a few hours. More desirable in a garden is *Smyrnium perfoliatum* (Perfoliate Alexanders), which has bright yellow euphorbia-like leaves – plant with bluebells, and white and purple honesty (*Lunaria annua*) for a pretty, naturalistic effect.

For something a little more robust, the rarely seen Russian species, *Cenolophium denudatum*, grows to 1.5m tall and has fern-like leaves and full heads of creamy-white umbels late into summer. Or, for a spectacular show in July on sturdy stems of a similar height, try *Selinum wallichianum*, crowned 'the Queen of Umbellifers' by the plantsman E. A. Bowles. These look fantastic threaded through the back of a long border, and shouldn't prove too invasive, provided you keep an eye out for the seed.

Most splendid of all the family are the angelicas – often grown in herb gardens as the leaves can be used for tea and the stems chopped in salads, or candied for cake decorations. I grow *Angelica archangelica* every year from seed, and am astonished by the 6ft of growth it puts on in a single summer. One year I pushed a spare seedling into a gap in my front garden, and passers-by told me they'd taken detours to watch the buds unfurl into milky-green flowers 8 or 9in across. More spectacular still is *Angelica gigas*, whose stem, leaf-veins and flowers are infused with crimson red. Largest of all is the giant hogweed, *Heracleum mantegazzianum*, whose heads of flowers sit like upturned umbrellas on stems more than 9ft high. It's another of those plants that people fall in love with – but beware: it's also poisonous, and so invasive that it's an offence to plant it or allow it to seed in the wild.

Most of the umbellifers are native to dry, sunny climates and are therefore reasonably drought-tolerant. The exceptions are sweet cicely and its pink form, *Chaerophyllum hirsutum* 'Roseum', which likes moist soil in dappled shade, *Selinum wallichianum*, and the angelicas, which will thrive only in rich, moist soil. *Anthriscus sylvestris* seems to do best in conditions that mimic a hedgerow – dappled shade will suit it well, along with moist but well-drained soil. Few umbellifers can grow in heavy, wet soils. Angelicas and other plants that die down in high summer after flowering should be planted at the back of the border, where their dead foliage will be hidden by late tall perennials and shrubs. To avoid inundation with seedlings, remove the seed heads before they ripen, or tie a paper bag over the flower to catch the seeds. Fresh seed germinates best – sow in situ or in deep pots or root trainers.

There is more to nettle than meets the eye

By Charles Elliott

'Long live the weeds,' wrote the poet Gerard Manley Hopkins, whose romantic nature led him up more than one leafy blind alley. Possibly he had dandelions or corn poppies in mind, maybe – at a stretch – a thistle. But one thing's certain: he must have overlooked *Urtica dioica*, better known as the stinging nettle.

According to the books, stinging nettles are common in the United States where I was born, having been imported (presumably accidentally) by early settlers, but I can honestly say that I never ran across them in any memorable way until I moved to Wales.

My wife, Carol, is convinced that my remarkable susceptibility to nettle stings is due to the fact that I didn't grow up with them as she did in Ireland. She's practically immune, whereas if I merely brush against a nettle leaf I can still feel the painful prickles 12 to 15 hours later. According to *The Flora of Monmouthshire*, a fascinating compilation largely composed of records made by local amateurs with a taste for botany, the normal habitat for stinging nettles is 'roadsides, hedgerows, wood borders and waste places', in other words: everywhere.

One problem seems to be that they have no competent antagonists. Most animals won't eat them, for obvious reasons (though my farmer neighbour claims that sheep will eat them after they're cut), and apart from the caterpillars of a few kinds of butterfly (the comma is one), insects don't pay much attention to them either. Normal plants, needing insect contact to pollinate them, might find this lack of interest awkward, but not nettles: they boast an ingenious self-pollinating system involving spring-loaded anthers that simply toss the pollen into the air, whereupon the wind carries it where nature intends it to go. It is said that on a calm morning you can sometimes see nettle pollen puffing out like tiny fountains.

There was a time when mankind regarded nettles more positively than we (or at least I) are inclined to do today. Fibres from the lanky stems were twisted into rope and woven into cloth, especially in northern Europe, until surprisingly recently; before the First World War the Germans were harvesting up to 60,000 tons of nettles a year to make soldiers' uniforms. In the early 1940s, as part of the war effort, County Herb Committees in England called for 100 tons of nettles to be gathered. Mystified local collectors obliged, discovering only later that the leaves would be used for green camouflage dyes and chlorophyll extracts.

Nettle soup, which calls for the earliest tender tops of the plants to be plucked and boiled in stock or other liquid, has always had a following. When the diarist Samuel Pepys stopped in to see his friend William Symons one cold winter day in 1661, Symons' wife thoughtfully served him a dish of freshly made 'nettle porridge', which Pepys – who fancied himself a connoisseur – thought 'very good'.

The doctrine of plant 'signatures' – which held that every plant had some human use, and that its shape, colour or other characteristic would tell you what that use was – suggested that nettles were just the thing for skin ailments, and probably wouldn't do rheumatism any harm. The treatment was flogging with a bunch of nettles. Nettle seeds mixed with wine (how much wine?) were supposed to treat impotence, and nettle ale was taken to be a cure for jaundice. A gypsy prescription even employed nettles as a contraceptive. The man was supposed to line his socks with nettle leaves and wear them for 24 hours before engaging in sex. If this worked, it may have been for the wrong reasons.

The nettle leaf and stem are covered with microscopic stiff hairs that can puncture skin at a touch. Until recently, they were thought to do their painful dirty work by injecting formic acid (the same stuff that red ants and bees employ), but research has now revealed that a multiple whammy of at least three chemicals is involved – a histamine to irritate the skin, acetylcholine to bring on a burning sensation, and hydroxytryptamine to encourage the other two.

Various folk remedies for soothing nettle stings exist, but so far I have not found one that works for me. The classic is probably juice from a dock leaf, for which Paul Simons in *The Action Plant* (Blackwell) offers a bit of scientific evidence: dock apparently contains chemicals that inhibit the action of hydroxytryptamine. Another putative remedy I have read about is the juice of jewelweed. I haven't seen a jewelweed since I left New England. Possibly another impatiens, say a nice *I. niamniamensis* 'Congo Cockatoo' – might do just as well. The most radical proposal, I've come across suggests applying nettle juice to the nettle sting. By the time you got the juice, you'd need it.

There seems to be a belief that approaching a nettle in a calm and fearless manner, as if it were an unfriendly dog, can save you from the prickles. 'He which toucheth a nettle tenderly is soonest stung,' observed John Lyly 400 years ago. I shall leave the proof of this to others more leather-skinned than I. After all, these things demand prudence. A keeper at the Natural History Museum in London is supposed to have been stung by a nettle that had been pressed and mounted by Linnaeus two centuries before.

At Towerhill Cottage, where we live, forests of nettles are flourishing, particularly along the route of an old overgrown track that used to carry wagon traffic up to Coedangred Common. This is only to be expected; nettles demand phosphates, and phosphates accumulate in the soil where humans and animals deposit them over a long period of time – in gardens and churchyards, along roads, in places where creatures have lived and (especially) died and been buried. So in a way nettles are more domesticated than most wild plants, and bound to be our companions whether we like it or not. They make terrific compost, and nothing is better than an old nettlebed as a place to put a new raspberry patch.

This said, I have still got a lot of nettles that I would like to get rid of. Back in 1878, a gentleman wrote a plaintive note to the RHS magazine, *The Garden*, explaining that he had a vast patch of nettles growing under trees on his property and asked for suggestions about eradicating them. One respondent argued that if you mowed them to the ground five or six times during the growing season, 'this wears them out'. Another claimed that all you needed to do was to cut them down and dig over them shallowly. But why worry? 'All who have plenty of luxuriant nettles may rest satisfied that they have some good land.'

It was left to the well-known Victorian gardener, the Rev. Charles Wolley-Dod, to come up with a really constructive solution. This solution was to plant an interesting new polygonum in the midst of the nettles, thus overpowering them. It was called, he thought, *Polygonum sieboldii* (though he bought it under the name of *P. japonicum*) and he reported it 'rejoicing in the cool, damp, open soil in which nettles generally grow'. Facing up to the native inhabitants, 'it quite holds its own, and gradually beats them. It grows seven or eight feet high … '

Now *Polygonum seiboldii*, otherwise known as *P. cuspidatum* (or, more recently, *Fallopia japonica*) is none other than the noted aggressor Japanese knotweed, which – we now know – spreads like wildfire and is almost impossible to eradicate. There is an old saw: 'Better stung by a nettle than prickt by a rose.' Or strangled by a knotweed, I'd say.

ᘒᘒ 19 MARCH 1977 ᘒᘒ

Beware: Britain's most poisonous plants

By Denis Wood

Poisoning of human beings by plants is mercifully, perhaps surprisingly, uncommon. However accidents do happen and I have been prompted to write this after reading the Ministry of Agriculture bulletin *British Poisonous Plants*, by A. A. Forsyth.

In this space it is only possible to mention some of the most dangerous plants (excluding fungi), and to indicate symptoms and first-aid measures. In all cases of suspected poisoning a doctor should be consulted immediately, because the action of some poisons is rapid. Parents and others who are concerned at the risk should read Mr Forsyth's book, which has illustrations of some of the plants; drawings of others can be found in *The Oxford Book of Wild Flowers*.

With children first in mind, the chief danger arises from plants bearing conspicuous, attractive berries or small fruits. One of these is yew, *Taxus baccata*, whose red, fleshy fruit encloses the seed. The pulp of the fruit is sweet and comparatively harmless, but the seed is deadly. Therefore children should never be allowed to put the fruits into their mouths, even if they protest their intentions of spitting out the seed.

The poison is taxine, rapidly causing vomiting, diarrhoea, severe abdominal pain, convulsions, coma and death. A doctor may carry out gastric lavage and inject pethidine for the pain; if before he arrives breathing is affected, artificial respiration should be carried out at once. Yew foliage is notoriously poisonous to horses and cattle.

Deadly nightshade, *Altropa belladonna*, is a wild plant about 3ft high, with bell-shaped purplish-blue flowers about an inch long. The berries in August and September are purplish-black and could be mistaken by children for black cherries. The poison is hyoscyamine and the symptoms dilation of pupils, loud heartbeats, delirium and coma. The method of first aid is to give an emetic (but no attempt must ever be made to give an emetic to an unconscious person) such as mustard and water, followed by stimulants – coffee or tea.

Two other nightshades are dangerous, woody nightshade, *Solanum dulcamara*, and black nightshade, *S. nigrum*. These contain solinine, which causes prostration and drowsiness. First-aid treatment is sweet, strong tea.

Daphne mezereum, the scented garden shrub, has berries a little like redcurrants in size and colour. These contain mezerinic acid, which causes burning sensations in the mouth and stomach, vomiting and prostration. First aid is to give an emetic salt and water, followed by a soothing mixture of milk, eggs and sugar. The black fruits of the spurge laurel *Daphne laureola*, are also poisonous and first-aid treatment is the same.

The deep-pink fruits of the spindle tree, *Euonymus europaeus*, are also toxic and the symptom, which may not occur for 10 or 12 hours, is acute purgation. First aid is to give astringents, milk which has been boiled and allowed to cool, or eggs followed by stimulants.

Lords and ladies or cuckoo pint (*Arum maculatum*) has spearhead-shaped leaves and when ripe, red berries on the spadix (flower spike) which may be purplish or yellow, surrounded at first by the yellowish-green leaf-like spathe. The berries contain a dangerous, irritant poison, against which treatment consists of giving an emetic following by soothing mixtures of egg, milk and sugar.

Plants without attractive berries include *Laburnum anagriodes*, the familiar ornamental tree, whose drooping clusters of yellow flowers are followed by pods containing the seeds. The poison is the alkaloid cytisine, which causes dilation of pupils, stomach pain, vomiting and convulsions. An emetic must be given and artificial respiration if breathing is affected. Hand bowls and water should be on hand for the doctor to use a stomach pump or give an enema.

Hemlock, *Conium maculatum*, is a wild plant up to 6ft high, with hollow, purple-spotted stems and cow-parsley-like umbelliferous flower heads. Symptoms are dilation of pupils, rapid respiration and stupor. Stimulants – coffee, tea, even spirits – should be given and artificial respiration applied, if necessary. The poison is coniine. Hemlock constituted the poisoned cup given to Socrates in 339BC.

Henbane, *Hyoscyamus niger*, grows 2 to 4ft high and has flowers about an inch in size, lurid yellow and veined with purple and with a purple eye. The poison is hyoscyamine and the symptoms and first aid treatment are the same as those for deadly nightshade. Hyoscyamine was used by Dr Crippen to murder his wife in 1910.

Children should not be allowed to pick and play with flowers of meadow saffron, *Colchicum autumnale*, sometimes wrongly called autumn crocus, nor of foxgloves, *Digitalis purpurea*, which contains digitoxin. Digitalis was the bane in the bitter brew which Gideon Sam caused to be given to his mother in Mary Webb's *Precious Bane*.

WARTIME FLOWERS BY POST BAN 'UNFAIR'

Florists are protesting against the ban on sending flowers by rail or post, which came into force yesterday and affects both their purchases and sales.

One of them said to me: 'We feel that to restrict the way we sell our enormously reduced stocks is unfair. Flowers may be a luxury, but so are cosmetics and jewellery, and traders in them may receive their stock by post and send it away by post.'

A tour round London yesterday at midday found the shops poorly stocked. There were no flower-sellers outside hospitals and no 'lovely violets' at Piccadilly Circus.

Lord Aberconway, presiding at the Royal Horticultural Society's annual meeting yesterday, said that at an interview with Lord Leathers, Ministry of War Transport, he had put in a plea for flowers generally and for their transport to shows. He had met with no success.

The restrictions on the transport, he said, were a great hardship to those without gardens and to flower growers. The society was unable to hold any flower shows this year.

12.
'An invitation to find the secrets beyond'

Space and Grace in the Garden

Feeling small can be beautiful

By Dan Pearson

A garden is at its most profuse at this time of year, teetering on the edge of the next season. Sunflowers peer down, their flowers way out of reach, fuelled by several months of this wet, lush summer, and runner beans writhe wildly, having outgrown their tripods. The garden could not be more different from the beginning of the season. This is especially obvious for those with town gardens, where clear views from a window or back door have been replaced by cascades of growth and, where just a couple of months ago you were able to look down upon your subjects, it is now a case of feeling dwarfed.

Some feel overwhelmed by this moment but I like to play to it for the change and drama that it can bring. Gardening, as I do, with a predominance of perennials, this change also has the assurance that in just a month things will begin to thin and, by the end of autumn, transparency will be restored. It is an easy game to play as many perennials will rush from nought to 10 in just a matter of weeks, with the added advantage that there's no waiting for an accumulation of growth as there might be with shrubs, nor are you lumbered with them in the long term.

I have always loved the larger-growing perennials. Plants such as *Rheum palmatum* and the giant hogweed, *Heracleum mantegazzianum*, delighted me as a child, such was their rapid responses to tender loving care. The excitement lives on – so much so that I have recently designed a children's garden in Tokyo where the plants have been chosen for their height. Miscanthus have been used close to the paths so that a child can stand under a cascade of growth, while the parasol leaves of *Tetrapanax papyrifer* will provide shelter. Paths weave between wild *Hemerocallis fulva var. littorea* with stems that arch up to 1.5m (5ft); and giant *Salvia guaranitica* will paint a great blue swathe above head height.

Gardening with plants that soar does not mean that you need masses of space, as many will go up and not necessarily out. Not all need rich living, either, and plants such as *Verbascum bombyciferum*, the giant *Ferula communis* or the common teasle will take their space over your head but not at ground level. Their ascent is all about reaching above their neighbours to get the attention of the pollinating insects.

Being self-supporting if you are tall is most important, as a giant crashing down will cut quite a swathe in a summer garden. I had to give up on my beloved rudbeckia 'Autumn Sun' in London because it started to fall over in early summer. Given enough sunlight, this is usually self-supporting and I love to have it where I can for its 2.1m (7ft) splashes of gold. Cardoons – *Cynara cardunculus* – also suffer from the same problem, leaning dramatically towards light.

Cimicifuga (now rather annoyingly re-named actaea) are well adapted to loftiness with a basal clump of dissected foliage which, in late summer, sends up tall tapers of white flower. The snake roots are among the most elegant of all late-flowering perennials, provided you have a cool, damp spot in which to grow them. The north side of a wall is ideal or, better still, some damp leafmouldy ground on the edge of woodland where the air is humid. I have failed with the lovely copper-leaved *C. simplex* 'Brunette' in London, even with lashings of compost and leafmould. The air must be too dry in the city. But, this year, the green-leaved *C. racemosa var. cordifolia* is doing well in the same place, proving that it's always worth giving another variety a try if you fail first time with something you love.

Thalictrum delavayi is another plant that does not thrive here for what I assume are the same reasons, as it loves a deep, moist soil – but that does not dampen my enthusiasm. This and its close relative, the even taller *T. rochebruneanum* are gentle giants, a delicate cage of stems supporting pin-pricks of lilac flower. Related to the aquilegias, these plants make great companions because they demand little in the way of space, but provide a cloud of blossom in mid-air. I love using them with larger-leafed plants such as *Macleaya cordata* for the dramatic change in scale.

Some grasses are also wonderful this late in the season. *Molinia arundinacea* 'Windspiel' (literally 'wind play') is one of my favourites at 2m (7ft) or so, living up to its name and with more to come, as it turns apricot then butter-yellow in October. However, the tallest of all the grasses is *Miscanthus floridulus*, which is an acoustic delight as its foliage swishes against itself in the slightest breeze. Rushing vertically up from the ground in spring, it forms a great 3m (10ft) fountain of sea-green foliage. This wonderful plant is perfect for providing instant screening and immediate height in a young garden. Our summers are not long enough for it to flower in this country, but there is an enormous array of *Miscanthus sinensis* that send up plumes of flowers. 'Silberfeder' is a sparkling, light-catching wonder and 'Malepartus', its smoky counterpart, are two of the most striking.

If you have room, or need plants for their bulk, there are a few self-supporting giants that it would be a shame not to use. Late-flowering *Eupatorium purpureum* 'Atropurpureum' is one of the most dramatic of all the perennials, forming vast sprays of butterfly-attracting flowers. Given a good, deep soil and plenty of sun, it will make a great companion to the biggest of all the persicarias, the cream-flowered *P. polymorpha*. Last but not least, I would not want to be without *Inula magnifica*, a plant tough enough to thrive in rough grassland. If you do grow it in grass, it will scale up the meadow with its with huge paddle-shaped leaves and candelabras of giant dark-centred daisies. Standing among them at full throttle, it is clear that sometimes, it is just great to feel small.

4 JULY 1982

The grey garden – more exciting than it sounds

By Robert Pearson

I have become increasingly conscious in recent years of the value of grey in the garden – used with discretion, of course, as a counterbalance to more forceful colours, and as a means of highlighting the beauty of other colours.

Greens of every hue can, for example, be made lovelier by its presence, and soft colours generally come into their own with such a foil. The stronger elements of the colour spectrum can often be made even more dramatic with a leavening of grey-foliaged plants near them. Grey is, too, a sophisticated colour, and in terms of the overall impression that a garden makes on the eye that is important.

If I were pressed to name my favourite grey-leaved plant I would plump for the weeping willow-leaved pear, *Pyrus salicifolia pendula*, which might have been 'purpose-made' for the smallish gardens that many homes have nowadays. And how enormously attractive it is with its height of 15 to 25ft, depending on circumstances, its pronounced weeping habit and lance-shaped leaves up to 3½in long. These start the season a striking silvery-grey which, on the upper surface of the leaf, slowly converts to glossy green. Clusters of white flowers are borne in April. The common name is highly appropriate, for the leaves are willow-like and most attractive.

I have stressed the value of this tree for small gardens (including those of patio size), but you often encounter it in very large gardens, looking every bit the master of all it surveys. All it needs is a setting (natural or created) that will bring out its gracefulness and charm. It is at its best in a lawn setting, possibly with a darkish coloured background such as conifers would provide – but the possibilities with associates, with regard to grey plants generally, are almost endless.

Thanks to garden centres, which offer it container-grown, *Pyrus salicifolia pendula* is now well known – which is rather a breakthrough, for once it was not, even though the tree was introduced from its native Caucasus in 1780. Culturally, it is easily pleased, growing happily in any soil of reasonable quality with adequate drainage.

That, too, goes for another small tree, in this case from western Asia, which could well be considered as an alternative to the willow-leaved pear. This is *Elaeagnus angustifolia*, which has willow-like leaves coloured silver on their undersides (the upper surface is a matt green), and, although it can make a larger tree, it would be reasonable to expect it to reach a height of 20ft. It is not weeping in the manner of the pyrus, but it does have a lax-growing habit and is most attractive. It should be more widely known, especially as it was first introduced to Britain in the 16th century. Like others of its kind, it is excellent for seaside districts.

For years there has been confusion as to whether the evergreen senecio grown so widely in gardens and having rounded, grey-felted leaves (which gradually revert to grey-green as the season progresses) should be called *Senecio greyii* or *S. laxifolius*. It seems that what we grow here under either name are invariably crosses deriving from both these similar New Zealand species, now grouped together under the cultivar name 'Sunshine'.

This name 'Sunshine' is now finding its way into the catalogues of leading tree and shrub nurseries, and, as names go, how appropriate it is for panicles of bright-yellow daisy flowers are borne with freedom in early summer. Its height is usually around 4ft, its spread in excess of that (up to 6ft) and it is an extremely valuable shrub for planting in a sunny, well-sheltered position where it can provide a telling foil for other plants and be very pleasing in its own right. Well-drained soil is a necessity.

Shrubs that put on their floral display in late summer are always in demand, and that goes too for *Perovskia atriplicifolia* 'Blue Spire', a particularly fine variety of another Asian plant that comes from the western Himalayan region with a territory taking in both Tibet and Afghanistan. Really, I should have described it as a sub-shrub, for it is only semi-woody and the usual practice is to prune the stems to near ground level each spring. Grey, aromatic sage-like leaves (it is a member of the sage family and is known as Russian sage) provide just the right foil for the very attractive foot-long panicles of rich deep blue flowers. Its height is 3 to 4ft. Especially good soil drainage is the prime need, so lighter soils are most suitable, and it needs as sunny a position as can possibly be provided. Then it will delight in August and September.

Taking lessons from Versailles

By Fred Whitsey

L et us explore an aspect of the absurd: like the fool's quips it could have a valuable nugget of truth in it. What have the vast spaces of Versailles, those disappearing vistas, to do with the garden at home? Or the scenic circuit of Stourhead. Has that any relevance? Plenty. In both are fragments of the art of garden-making worth pondering at the end of this long weather-enforced interval before we get back to work.

Le Nôtre's avenues and allées can be read as a heavily underlined lesson that if you want your garden to look bigger than it really is, or are only intent on realising its potential, the sovereign method is to exploit the longest possible view the site offers. Give a view a frame also, and its extremity will at once seem further off still. Add one or two surprise incidents off to one side or the other, each at the end of its own short view, and you will humanise it by arousing curiosity.

In the same way, you can follow a principle laid down at Stourhead, that half-park, half-garden National Trust property in Somerset created with cunning simplicity. Here you follow a path through woods and out into repeated clearings that echoes the outline of the lake lying just below and at intervals you come upon suddenly a series of quite different views across the whole scheme as though you were on a revolving stage.

Now I raise the point at this moment for several reasons. First because the bedraggled look with which gardens have emerged from their cruel winter torment is a spur to doing some replanning, which will quicken the sense of renewal that comes with impending spring.

Next because the weather over the past year has shown how essential in our climate it is to have a path that can take you dry shod round the whole area, large or small. And then because this early time of year and the next couple of months can bring such a bounty of treasures to a garden that are enhanced when you come upon them suddenly. Many of them enjoy either the shade or the protection of other plants.

Many, too, retire quickly after they have bloomed, as for instance, hellebores sink into insignificance when their day is done, and you do not want either their relics or the empty spaces to be on show for the rest of the season. Besides, their known presence out there is an inducement to explore, watching for their return, when otherwise the garden might be abandoned to uncomfortable weather.

If your garden is bounded by fences – or walls! – you doubtless see these as scope for embellishment with climbing plants and low bushes that benefit from their shelter or shade. You will want to enjoy these at close quarters, not from beyond the edge of a broad bed in front. If the boundaries are screened by hedges and you have already discovered how valuable are hedge bottoms for certain communities of plants, like hardy cyclamen and some ferns, you will want to keep on intimate terms with these also.

So a path, I say, following roughly the course of the perimeter, taking you through borders rather than alongside them, between shrubs like tallish rhododendrons or cotoneasters which, as you pass, conceal the view across the open garden. The experience can be like strolling slowly along the side aisles of some cathedral, emerging at moments into the flooding light of the transepts, the incidents passed on the way corresponding to side chapels or some striking window.

Deep borders of hardy perennial plants can be spectacular at their supreme moment in the season, and thick plantings of shrubs can provide effective screens against noise as well as the common gaze. But you only know and enjoy your plants as individuals when you can get on close terms with them, as such a scheme permits.

I do not mean an unbroken path of slabs securely cemented in but one that meanders a little and is no more solid than enough to provide dry walking. It could be of stepping stones, or even of gravel or coarse bark laid over strips of black polythene placed on soil that has been treated with total weedkiller.

I find that each winter and the inevitable enlarging collection of plants one gathers gives reason to make up in this way the rough path that takes a horseshoe-shaped path round our garden and that I often find fresh viewpoints that could do with a little emphasising. Usually they reveal themselves from the way established plants have gone on growing.

The smallest garden has two viewpoints, from the house and from the other end towards it. By creating a main route all round in this fashion one can contrive others. They can be marked by the odd stone ornament, perhaps, but also by plants of architectural outline or unusual colouring as many of the conifers have, as well as by the odd patch of paving to take a seat.

In all this the adroit placing of evergreen bushes is of the first importance. At this time of year, as well as scheming such improvements with pegs and string, one might earmark some already in the garden for being transplanted to more strategic spots. All to the end of achieving more variety within the garden's unity and making it a place that invites you to go for a walk on a winter's day instead of just looking at it as a setpiece from the windows.

Embroidered gardens

By Roy Strong

When evenings have drawn in, and gardening hours have contracted, my horticultural life begins to tread other paths. One of them is stitchery. About 15 years ago I passed out in public through overwork and during convalescence took up tapestry. One floral carpet and too many cat-and-blossom-laden cushions later, I find myself stitching two auriculas, one square panel out of the eight or more other flowers I need to complete before the next carpet arrives.

The relationship of embroidery to gardening has always fascinated me. I recall years ago my surprise when researching for a book on English Renaissance gardens, on discovering a Jacobean writing master who kept a shop in Blackfriars, and whose pattern books included not only design for embroidery but 'For Joyners and Gardeners ... Knots, and Buildings, and Morysies, and Termes'. Anyone who has looked at designs for knot gardens, let alone planted one, which I have, will know how conscious one becomes of the interplay between decorative motifs in any historical period. On visiting an Elizabethan house, one sees those knots turning up again in the plasterwork and marquetry as well as on dresses in portraits. It is an interesting window into the past as to how people got their garden designs, explaining too that wonderful unity of vision which drew together house and garden and which is all too often missing in our own era of design options.

That link of the two arts was to be even stronger in the Baroque century which followed. The supreme garden setpiece was the parterre de broderie, the embroidered parterre, a design in cut turf, clipped box, gravel and coloured stuffs which depicted a formalised pattern of scrolling arabesques, leaf shapes and flowers. Only with the advent of the landscape style did this overt connection between the two arts become less perceptible.

I have been struck by how often people who take to the needle are in fact very good gardeners. I think of the composer William Walton's widow, Susannah, plying her needle across a vast copy of one of the Stoke Edith hangings. These record the formal garden at its height, with fountains, statues, parterres and exotic plants in Chinese blue and white pots. (Stoke Edith, Herefordshire, burned down in the 1920s.) The orginals belong to the V&A, but are at Montacute House, Somerset, a National Trust property, and more than worth a visit. That is her winter work. Outside stretches that masterpiece she and her husband created with the help of Russell Page, La Mortella on Ischia. Then there's Sir Hardy Amies, stitching onto cushions designs for knots which were in the gardens of his heroine, the Winter Queen. Outside there is his own essay in perfect small-garden making. And there's the remarkable Kaffe Fassett, a devoted gardener, who gathers his blossoms and casts them across his extraordinary tapestry designs.

So not for nothing did William Morris, the great Victorian designer, liken embroidery to 'gardening with silk and gold thread'. His gardens were revolutionary in their time, rejecting the gaudy bedding-out of the high Victorian era and choosing to evoke, both at the Red House, Kent, and at Kelmscott Manor, Oxfordshire, gardens of the type he had glimpsed in medieval manuscripts and faded ancient tapestries. His embroidery designs for hangings and cushions were ambassadors for his garden style, popularising interest in wild flowers and old-fashioned native plants. His greatest disciple was Gertrude Jekyll, whose influence is still with us. We often lose sight of that fact that she began her career designing and executing embroideries, abandoning that for garden design only when her eyesight failed her.

Earlier in the century the wife of John Loudon, that prolific garden writer for the new middle classes, pointed out that progression in her book *The Villa Garden*, published in 1850 and a monument to the style Gertrude Jekyll detested. Jane Loudon wrote: 'There is not any lady who can design a pattern and embroider a gown, that might not, in a few hours, be taught to design flower gardens with as much taste and skill as a professional landscape gardener.' Voilà Miss Jekyll.

Both skills call for a strong sense of good design and for a subtle control of colour. Both demand neatness, discipline and order. Winter is a good time if not to take the needle at least to visit museums and galleries with embroidery collections. The whole history of garden design and plants is writ large in tapestries and stumpwork pictures, samplers and bed hangings, upholstery and Berlin woolwork. That such things are an inspiration to the gardener one can gather from the large Flemish tapestry of a Renaissance garden which still hangs immediately above Vita Sackville-West's writing desk at Sissinghurst. How often she must have looked up at it for a fresh green thought over the decades.

A stumpery from scratch

By Carol Klein

E very garden has its dark corners. In town, they may be in the shadow of house walls, the garage or garden shed or the fences, hedges and walls that form the boundaries with next door. In the country, they are more likely to be under trees.

Often such places are lifeless as well as lightless and, being difficult to integrate into the rest of the garden, they tend to be ignored. But if they are given a raison d'etre and seized on as an exciting opportunity, these nooks and crannies can become an aesthetic asset rather than an eyesore.

During the late-Victorian era many of the middle classes built shrubberies, ferneries and grottoes. These were perfect for ferns, which quickly became the height of fashion. Hundreds of new species were introduced from around the world and avid collectors scoured native hedgerows and woods for quirky forms to include in their stumperies and shady corners. The idea of a stumpery is to create a picturesque woodland scene by using stumps and tree trunks surrounded by ferns and woodland flowers.

If dark, unused corners have become repositories for stacks of old pots and garden jumble they can be reclaimed by adopting a scaled-down version of the stumpery. With a little effort and planning even basement steps and gloomy back yards can be transformed into a green and pleasant corner.

Materials

If you live in or near the countryside finding logs and tree stumps should be relatively easy. A group of trunks or branches – or even one on its own – can make a striking arrangement and provide a good environment for woodlanders.

In city or suburban gardens a few pieces of trunk from felled sycamore can be arranged in a dark corner to form the basis for a mini-stumpery. If tree trunks are out of the question there are companies that import waste timber or sell driftwood.

Sawn branches can be sunk into the ground to form small planting areas. If there is no uniformity to their shape and width and their heights are suitably varied they will soon look the part – slosh an occasional layer of liquid comfrey or old yoghurt over them to encourage mosses and lichens to develop.

For a thoroughly modern look, monoliths made from sawn sleepers or old oak floorboards, stacked one on top of the other, provide a marked contrast to rounded clumps of low-growing ferns such as adiantum and the graceful shuttlecocks of matteuccia.

At Glebe Cottage we have several old trunks that are completely unadorned except by moss and lichen. They sit in shady parts of the garden where they make the perfect backdrop for woodland plants.

You can design a stumpery even if you have only a gravelled or paved area – all you need is a tree trunk; the plants accompanying it could live alongside in clay pots.

Preparation

Before arranging the stumpery the area should be thoroughly prepared. In a town garden the soil may be compacted and stagnant. Fork it over and incorporate leaf mould or old compost. Woodland plants dislike rich living so steer clear of manure.

Arrange plants in the spaces provided by the structure of the log, making sure there are plenty in the foreground. If the planting is against a house wall, ensure that the soil level is below the damp course or insert old roofing slates against the wall.

If the stumpery is always in dense shade – as is often the case against buildings – stick to ferns and mosses. The forms and textures of ferns need no other accompaniment.

If there is dappled light under the canopy of deciduous trees you will be able to choose from a much broader range of plants. Mulching with chipped bark or old leaf-litter keeps down weeds, conserves moisture and adds the finishing touch.

Planting ideas

Ferns – *Adiantum pedatum* is a dainty maidenhair fern from North America. Its fragile appearance belies its extreme hardiness. It has a running rootstock and quickly makes a respectable clump. Deciduous; 12in high.

Dryopteris erythrosora makes an outstanding specimen plant. Its tall elegant fronds emerge bright orange and change to lustrous lime-green as they age. Evergreen; 18in–2ft.

Polystichum setiferum, the soft shield fern, is a British native with a mouth-watering assortment of different forms, all intricately divided and ornate. Its fronds stay green all winter until the new ones unfold in the spring; 18in–3ft.

Phyllitis scolopendrium, the 'Hart's Tongue' fern, is also indigenous. It is one of the most adaptable of all ferns, thriving in dry conditions in full light as well as damp, shady sites. Its leathery, upright fronds are evergreen and sculptural; 12–18in.

Athyrium niponicum pictum, the Japanese painted fern, has striking silver and bronze fronds, which light up very dark places. Deciduous; 12–15in.

Woodlanders – Some plants prominent in early spring will be dormant by the summer. Wood anemones and celandines are good examples. They can give way to clumps of primroses, foxgloves and woodland campanulas, and in the autumn to *Kirengeshoma palmata*, *Saxifraga fortunei* and Japanese anemones.

Bulbs – Choose woodland species and plant them in between the ferns and herbaceous plants. Snowdrops are ideal but must be planted 'in the green' – when they have leaves and active roots – not in their dormant state. They prefer damp conditions.

Narcissi will flourish in the same situation. Small, dainty varieties are the ones to go for, especially when space is limited.

25 MAY 2002

Welcome to Never Never Land

By Bunny Guinness

I have been fairly fanatical about gardening since the age of 17. I started creating a garden way before I began to raise a family. By the time my children arrived, it was well under way. So, when I visited friends and saw lawns littered with brightly coloured plastic playthings and chewed-up excuses for flowerbeds, I decided there must be another way. Apart from anything else, clients expect my garden to be a model for the sort of paradise that I am proposing to create for them. There was no way they would be won over by a display that included the usual collection of blue paddling pools, orange swings and yellow slides.

When the children were three and four years old, I hired an entertainer for their party. It was a sunny July day, so he did his bit in our garden next to the pond.

It was bedlam. The children were completely uninterested in Oubly Doubly the Fenland Fool, and spent the time messing around with newts and sludgy aquatic life. As a result, I had no difficulty in deciding what to do for my first Chelsea the following spring: it was to make a garden that was a dream for children, but which adults appreciated, too. *The Wind in the Willows* was to be the theme, enabling me to show how to make water safe (with the use of underwater grids) but accessible (small, shallow rills) for children.

Almost 10 years on, I have found that the garden must be dynamic – changing and developing to keep up with the children. We have dug up the drainable 'natural' paddling pools and scenic sandpits, removed the rustic swings and burnt the home-made Wendy house, as they have all been outgrown. These items, designed for younger children, tended to be close to the house for supervision purposes. Siting them in the garden so they looked appealing yet still worked well was vital.

Now my children are 12 and 14, they spend, if anything, even more time in the garden. The trampoline is undoubtedly the hot favourite – winning hands down against the PlayStation and the television, even after three years of non-stop use from all the family. Needless to say, it is not standing proud and bright blue in my garden. Instead, we sunk it into the ground and asked for a drab, khaki-green surround to the central black mat. This colour costs no extra and merges effortlessly with the garden. Visitors often think it is a pool until they get within 10 yards or so. With the earth that we excavated from the pit, we formed an amphitheatre around the edge, with a timber dragon's head at one end and a tail at the other (carved with a chainsaw). The grassy mound not only helps screen the trampoline but also forms a popular sitting area. It is often used in the evenings when the children, accompanied by a ghetto-blaster and dog, bounce feverishly in the night air. Even small spaces can accommodate trampolines. I have put large (14ft diameter) sunken trampolines into several town gardens and screened them really successfully. They are suitable for just about all ages and, as they can be used (if large enough) by several children and adults at one time, they are great for encouraging your offspring to play together as opposed to bickering about who goes on what.

Now the majority of our play equipment is in a section of woodland that I planted about 17 years ago. The trees went in as tiny transplants less than 2ft high and now support cable runways, hammocks and flying saucers. My son, when aged about 10, decided he wanted to make a new garden and so together we set about developing a designated children's garden here.

If you have room to make a segregated space for them, it does provide an easy solution. Even so, we adults enjoy it, too, and the area is stuffed full of plants, sheets of ferns, honesty, foxgloves, bluebells and other fairly tough, mainly native, woodland ground cover. There is a woven hazel arch to define the entrance and a large, home-made, thatched tree-house (ideal for sleepovers) as the focal point. A cable runway leads from this to a young ash some 72ft away.

This zip wire, or flying fox, as they are also called, is popular, too. We started with one of the smaller 33ft ones slung between two apple trees, but recently the children's aspirations grew. This is one of the least obtrusive items and costs up to £50.

Near the base of the tree-house, we have a fire pit – like water, fire fascinates all ages. I first saw one of these in the United States, where bonfires are lit in many gardens on summer evenings as an attractive heat source and a focus for evenings outside. We cook on ours, a circular sunken hole lined with brick. I have also used stone. They are simple to make and not unattractive.

Our most recent addition is a large wildlife garden in another part of my young wood. This has generated a surprising amount of interest from the children.

We have dug a large 'natural' pool, made a woven tree-seat and a growing arbour, cut glades through sheets of cow parsley and installed a flying saucer. This superb dish, made from woven oak, is 7ft in diameter and suspended about 3ft above the ground. Lying in it, gently floating over the mass of Queen Anne's lace, you can watch the birds and bees on hazy summer days.

Wilder areas in the garden are a dream for many children – to have the luxury of creating private places where they can do their own thing without fear of creating chaos.

Even in small gardens I like to try to include some clumps of hazel, shrub willow or bamboo, perhaps with a network of woven willow tunnels or a small den. Privacy is as important to children as it is to adults, and they relish the freedom of their own secret fantasy world.

🌿 **27 MAY 1962** 🌿

What Mr Whitsey thought of Mr Brookes

By Fred Whitsey

In a week which saw traditional architectural concepts sharply challenged at Coventry, traditionalists were faced with a new approach to design at Chelsea Flower Show.

'Stark', 'crude', 'unfriendly', 'all straight lines', 'un-English', even 'ugly'… All the familiar expressions were used of a garden layout some found unacceptable because it was unsanctified by custom. Other critics, however, described it as 'serene', 'enduring', 'composed'.

The garden which excited comment, if not admiration, at Chelsea was the winning design in a competition organised by the Institute of Landscape Architects and sponsored by trade associations interested in garden construction materials.

The winner was a young landscape designer, Mr John Brookes, whose design pre-supposed a town site which, with almost oriental reticence, he planned for easy maintenance, freely using easily obtained concrete and asbestos-cement components.

Spending much of the past week myself at Chelsea where the thickly crowded show had an overwhelming opulence and variety, I found it a garden one could return to again and again with a sense of relief and tranquillity. Isn't this just what one asks of the garden at home, a retreat from the busy world?

The effect was partly achieved by the interplay of broad plans of turf and concrete slabs, unified by just those straight lines which some critics would like to have seen bent. Slender concrete pillars made a colonnade linked to a small shaded pavilion and added a third dimension.

'Gardening lags far behind some design,' said Mr Brookes when he led me round his garden, 'yet it offers just as much scope for using new and cheap materials in a way that they themselves demand.

'We're still wallowing in rusticity and crazy paving. I rather think Chelsea Flower Show itself encourages this. People are led to copy the displays you see here which, after all, are shop windows. Then they cram far too many different plants into their gardens. Overall form gets little emphasis. Flower shows beguile you with individual plants but give you little idea of how they can be used successfully.

'Yet people show that they do appreciate form by the foliage plants they grow in their houses today. If only it could be translated from the living room and scaled up to the plot outside. It's surprising also that women who show so much taste and restraint in the clothes they wear, forget their sense of colour and style when they plant their gardens.'

As a gardener held in thrall myself simply by plants, I pointed out that many have a collector's interest in plants and enjoy them as individuals. One's knowledge of the plant world was always expanding, and the more plants you learned about the greater your desire to possess them. Gardeners would always be as acquisitive as magpies and as unrepentant.

Was there a conflict here between designer and plantsman that could never be resolved? Were the designer's feeling for unity and the plantsman's inevitable concern with diversity irreconcilable?

'Not, I think, if we carry our basic ideas of design and decoration into the garden. We should think of the outline of the garden as the bare room and the plants as decoration. But the basic design must first be strong enough to support and sustain the wealth of embellishment.'

'A garden must have an underlying unity to be satisfying. Otherwise you're left with the rosy cottage garden vision. You're then living on hope for next week or the doubtful memory of what it might have been like last week. Your effect is never really achieved.'

I asked Mr Brookes how he set about designing a garden. 'First I find what functional details are needed and put these in place – whether there has to be a washing line, somewhere to sit and eat, somewhere for the children to play, especially after rain. I then put the paths in, running them straight from A to B, and never taking them on an unnecessary serpentine course.

'This gives me a basic design. If I like it I exaggerate it. Only then do I fill in with any plants, which represent the detail. Certainly no less than three of any one kind should go together, unless it is a tree or shrub sufficiently individual in character to stand by itself. But always I strive to preserve a background of simplicity.'

I wondered, though, if this really answered the longing every Englishman had in his heart for a fragment of his own countryside outside his backdoor and which the profusion our pot pourri-like gardens helped to provide?

'You can do that just as well with soft colours which blend – unlike the effect made by a lot of lightly coloured annuals and harsh Floribunda roses. You never get anything but pastel shades in nature – not in this country anyway. And any natural scene has some unifying factor of the kind we should start with in our gardens.'

I went home from Chelsea a little troubled by a feeling that somewhere echoes were sounding. I took down the conservative Sir George Sitwell's famous essay, 'On the Making of Gardens'. Yes, here it was: 'Straight lines set off by their monotony the freedom and varieties of natural curves ... flowers will be fairer in formal beds ... irregularity and diversity naturally confuse and bewilder us. ...Symmetry, which gives a sense of rest, will be the law of the garden.'

He was writing in 1909, of gardens made three centuries before his time!

COUPLE'S £100 GARDEN STATUE SELLS FOR £6 MILLION

By Godfrey Barker

An elderly couple yesterday scooped more than £6 million from the sale of a 16th-century bronze statue which they kept in their Sussex garden for 40 years after paying £100 for it.

The Dancing Faun, by the Dutch-born Mannerist Adriaen de Vries, became the most expensive sculpture ever sold at auction when Sotheby's obtained £6.82 million for it.

The buyer was the London dealer Mr Cyril Humphris, who said: 'In my 35 years of dealing this is the greatest sculpture to have come on the market. Adriaen de Vries is now considered to be the greatest sculptor of his age.'

The unnamed sellers, described as 'ordinary people' from Brighton, will collect £6.2 million after commission is paid by the buyer.

Miss Elizabeth Wilson, Sotheby's sculpture expert in London, said: 'The couple are finding it hard to take it in, but they are absolutely thrilled. This is a fairy tale for them.'

The sculpture had originally been destined for sale at a Sussex sale of garden statuary – where its value had been estimated at between £1,200 and £1,800.

It was promptly withdrawn from the garden statuary sale, brought to London for research and found to be the earliest known example of a type of faun sculpture which, with the

Venus de Medici, is seen as the most beautiful survival of the ancient world.

Sotheby's was then aware of The Dancing Faun's importance but, given the comparative obscurity of Adriaen de Vries, estimated it at up to £1.5 million for yesterday's sale.

It is the second coup of its kind in three months. In September Christie's put into a garden statuary sale in Hertfordshire an 18th-century half-length of a goddess with an estimate of £8,000-£12,000.

But it was spotted as a lost early work by the Florentine master Giambologna and sold for £715,000.

13.
'The extent of the crisis'
Drought, Snow and Other Extremes of Weather

Gardening in the worst of droughts

By Robert Pearson

Nobody with a garden in a drought-ridden part of the country, such as the central southern and south-east regions, will be under any illusion about the extent of the crisis. The evidence is there for all to see, in the shape of dessicated plants and burnt-up lawns.

It is distressing beyond words and, with the use of hoses quite rightly banned in many areas, we are looking for ways in which to relieve the agony of much valued plants.

Understandably, those plants which are most at risk are the recently planted trees, shrubs, perennials and so on which have had no opportunity to become firmly established in the present conditions. Even at this late stage it is worth providing the root areas, and perhaps the stems and leaves, of the most vulnerable with shade from cut branches, which could come from yews or cypresses or from an old garden tree where the loss of a few minor branches would be of no consequence. Stopping the sun beating down on such plants for hours every day could mean the difference between demise and survival.

Another thing which could help is to make a saucer-shaped depression round each plant so that any rain which does fall, or water applied from a can, is not immediately dispersed into the parched surrounding soil. Such depressions also help to keep mulching material in place where birds tend to scatter it far and wide, but never apply a mulch over dry soil.

Then there is that useful transplanting spray, Synchemicals S-600 (available from garden stores), which could be pressed into service most effectively in these conditions as a worthwhile palliative. In particular it could help through this difficult period such especially moisture-sensitive shrubs as rhododendrons and azaleas, and hydrangeas. The S-600 liquid dries to form a thin plastic film over stems and foliage, and the manufacturer tells me that it would suggest the weaker of its two recommended dilutions for this purpose, namely one part S-600 in nine parts of water.

Still, it is gratifying to note that nature, in one of its harsher moods, does not have it all its own way. Far too many trees are succumbing to the unequal struggle of making do with totally inadequate moisture supplies (not least the shallow-rooting birch), but there are other deciduous trees (notably maples, beeches and oaks) which are fighting back by going into a state of semi-dormancy. It's a very odd year indeed.

A splendid garden flower which is as likely as any to come sailing through this long, hot summer – indeed, positively relishing the baking it will have been getting in the sheltered, south-facing border it most fittingly resides in every garden where it is grown – is the Algerian iris, *Iris unguicularis* or *I. stylosa* as so many of us still persist in calling it, even many years after its change of name.

For winter colour, through the medium of its delectable lavender-lilac blooms with their touch of yellow on the falls, this Rhizomatous iris is unsurpassed, whether for a snug corner in a bed near the house, with the aspect suggested, or as a cut flower for the home, for which purpose it is also first-rate. But if its blooms are most appreciated in the depths of winter it should be said that they can be enjoyed, in favourable weather, right through in succession from October or November to early spring.

What it needs is plenty of sunshine, warmth and shelter and a preferably poorish soil which must be freely drained. The mass of bold grass-like foliage is an excellent foil for the flowers. September is an optimum time to plant the rhizomes, but be prepared for them to take their time before starting to produce the fine crops at bloom of which they are capable.

The species itself is widely available from hardy plant nurseries, while there are a few not widely available varieties, such as the purplish-violet 'Mary Barnard', which are worth seeking out if you like something rather different. One last thing about this sterling iris – when used as a cut flower it should be placed in a room with a moderate temperature if you want the blooms to have staying power. No trouble there, possibly, now that we are all so conscious of those all-too-frequent fuel bills.

Another sun-loving plant, bulbous in this case, from the other end of the African continent (South Africa) which delights in much the same kind of garden situation as *Iris unguicularis*, is *Nerine bowdenii*, a hardy member of a genus which is otherwise of interest only to the greenhouse gardener in this country. This plant, too, really laps up the sunshine and produces its exquisitely beautiful, narrowly petalled flowers with reflexed tips in umbels of six or more on 2ft stems.

It is a flower which enriches the autumn garden with its colony right up to November. The best time to plant the bulbs, 6in deep, is in early spring – always in soil which is especially well drained – but it can also be done about now. It is a plant to keep in mind for a sunny, warm position.

What the snow did

By Fred Whitsey

Within hours of the snow rolling back, the snowdrops had reached up several inches and were already free of their buds. Another day and there were crocuses waiting for the first flashes of sunshine. Compensation for the destruction around them? Certainly something to be taken as an affirmation that it might not be as bad as all that. Bad, though, it is after the second cruellest February of the century. Too early to assess the full extent of the damage, but certain practical first-aid jobs can be put to hand at once.

In places where the snow was really heavy conifers keeled right over. Where it was just too much for them and they haven't sprung back they need stout sticks now if they are of manageable size. Where a tree is beyond the power of a stake to hold it, four guy wires will be needed anchored to stout pegs hammered deep into the ground.

Conifers that have lost their tips or leading shoots are in danger of growing squat. Cut back to sound-looking wood and train up as the season advances a new shoot rather than attempt to encourage one already there, which may tend to grow outwards rather than upwards. Branches that have splayed out under the weight of snow can be tied in to a main branch, but in some cases it may be better to amputate these branches.

Where shrubs have buckled under the weight of snow – choisya bushes are always candidates for such damage – cut right away half-broken branches and try to tie in others in their place even if it does mean thrusting in canes to hold them.

Hedges that have been bent by the wind when they were heavy with snow are a special problem. They may have to be shored up first with oblique stakes to get them upright and then held in position with heavy stakes hammered into the ground.

So violently did the soil heave when frozen after it was so damp that many newly planted bushes and roses look half pushed out of the ground. They must be trodden back firm, though only after the soil has lost its post-frost stickiness, unless you can put a lot of old leaves over the surface and tread this layer to cushion the force.

Some plants are looking hopelessly bedraggled. Rhododendrons that are still hanging their curled-up leaves will almost certainly recover, though they may yet lose this foliage. Hebes looking as though they have been poisoned will probably die back but produce new shoots low down the old wood, which can later be cut back to these points. Cistus and ceanothus that might have had a blowlamp passed over them will, probably and unhappily, perish, in contrast to scorched pyracanthas that will surely revive.

Nothing at this stage in the season, though, can be pronounced as past hope. Not until we are past Midsummer's Day would it be fair to give up. On the other hand, the impatient may reasonably say that they can't wait upon the chance of recovery and may choose to replace. One point to bear in mind, though: the cut-back bush or climber that does recover from near the ground or below grows twice as fast as it originally did, as though intent on making up for lost time.

It will be interesting to watch the behaviour of those varieties of fuchsia that in the past few years have been judged hardy and adding them to the handful that have proved themselves in specially hard spells in earlier years. My guess is that most of them will come through. They just hadn't been tried out of doors before, so no one could say they weren't hardy enough for an outdoor life and they had remained confined in greenhouses.

I am rather fearful, though, for the safety of the many types of silver-leaved plants that have been planted in the same years. We must expect to lose them and have to start again. So wet had it been before the real cold came that they were heavily charged with moisture. It could have frozen in the cells and ruptured them.

The certainty is that we shall all be talking about the anomalies for seasons to come, puzzled still more by the curious ways of nature. Already I am noting the untouched look of our creeping rosemaries (reckoned the tenderest) while upright bushes nearby look as though they have gone with hypothermia. I rejoice at the greenness of the Australian grevilleas beside the seared cistus. I note that the loquat bush in its corner still has its jade leaves but some camellias not far off have had their foliage turned a chocolate colour. When the reckoning can be made, once again we shall have learned that garden hardiness in the face of winter cold is one of the most inscrutable sides of nature.

31 MARCH 1985

There's dry, there's shady, and there's dry and shady …

By Beth Chatto

Many gardeners make the mistake of thinking that a shady spot or a dry, exposed flowerbed in the garden is an insurmountable problem. And yet with a little extra thought and effort even the most troublesome places can be turned into attractive areas. Plants, like people, do not take kindly to being thrust into the nearest available slot, but if you choose those which are adapted by nature to particular conditions you will be able to make the most of every inch of your garden.

If you have a new house and a new garden, with little or nothing to provide shade, for instance, and the soil is sandy and poor, or gravelly, you will need to think of drought-loving plants. Many of these have grey and silver leaves, protected by a coating of matted felt or silky hairs, enabling them to flourish in open, sunny situations where many conventional garden plants would wither away. These quickly make beautiful soft shapes, as good in winter as in summer. Among my favourite plants of this sort are various forms of Artemisia, ballota and alyssum; lavender, cistus and brooms (genista) will provide an effective background, while *Juniperus communis* 'Hibernica' will add a needed emphasis to the group. *Alstroemeria ligtu* hybrids, most bulbous plants, sea hollies (eryngium) and pinks (dianthus) are just a few of the many flowering plants which would add colour during the summer.

In some gardens shade can be a problem, especially if the conditions tend to be dry as well. As flowering plants tend to grow lank and leggy in this kind of setting, it is best to think less of flowers and, instead, enjoy plants for their beautiful leaves. If there is wall space, a mixture of evergreen and deciduous scramblers can look effective; and think about using ivies (hedera), which come in many shapes, sizes and variations of leaf. Several different kinds of honeysuckle (Lonicera) are also worth considering. Not all will be scented, but all do well in part shade.

On the ground you can create a Persian carpet effect with *Arum Italium* 'Pictum', spotted pulmonarias and the pretty purple-leafed Viola Labradorica. Large evergreen rosettes of *Euphorbia robbiae* will provide bold contrast, or you could use *Bergenia cordifolia* 'Purpurea', whose large, wavy-edged leaves blush to warm reddish tones in winter. Solomon's seal (polygonatum), with ferns like *Polystichum setiferum* 'Acutilobum', together with the invaluable *Iris foetidissima* 'Citrina', lift the scene and add to the woodland effect.

White and yellow foxgloves (digitalis), frothy mauve-pink heads of *Thalictrum aquilegiifolium*, cyclamens and snowdrops are a few of the flowers which will thrive in cool, dimly lit places. But I should not recommend all of these plants in such desperately dry shade as is found beneath a horse-chestnut tree or at the roots of a privet hedge.

While dryness and shade are a problem for some, other gardeners have to cope with a naturally soggy piece of ground. But provided it does not dry to concrete in summer, it can prove to be a blessing. You can look forward to a jungle of fine plants, with one or two shrubby willows as a background. Most have attractive foliage and fluffy catkins, while others contribute to the winter garden with brilliantly coloured stems.

Various forms of water iris and bog primulas thrive in damp soil, as do several other eye-catching herbaceous plants. *Polygonum amplexicaule* makes large bushy plants alight with fine tapers of small crimson flowers. Lysimachias (grand relative of creeping-Jenny) grow more than 1m tall, providing spires of white or yellow flowers for much of the summer.

The problem of heavy clay soil can be considerably alleviated by digging in plenty (I mean barrow-loads) of grit, or even pea-sized gravel bought from local gravel pits, together with all the organic material you can find. When the structure has been improved, the soil becomes more aerated and less sticky in winter, and most plants with thick strong root systems will do well (fibrous rooted plants do not like clay). Flowering plants which can cope with clay include hellebores, hemerocallis, Japanese anemones and those valuable cover plants, the cranesbills. Hostas could be used to dominate the scene, their sculptured leaves softened with frothing skirts of *Alchemilla mollis*.

All of these suggestions will be much more successful if you care for your soil before planting. In a new garden, with hungry soil, save everything which will turn into compost and treat yourself to a load of farmyard manure. Then, remember that hard and compacted soils benefit from deep digging and plenty of humus helps to keep them aerated. Finally, all soils benefit from some kind of mulch (peat, pulverised bark, well-rotted manure or compost) until your maturing plants cover the soil and protect it themselves.

CHELSEA BLOOMS BOYCOTT

By Stephen Bates

This year's Chelsea Flower Show will be boycotted by Newham Council because multi-coloured blooms from South Africa will be on display there, as they have for many years.

Mr John Plant, chairman of the council's leisure services committee, said: 'We are standing by our policy of not taking part in events at which South Africa is represented.'

Newham has been one of the main local authority exhibitors at Chelsea for many years, winning several awards.

A spokesman explained: 'We asked the Royal Horticultural Society to withdraw their invitation to the South Africans, but they decided not to do so. They apparently wish to continue the participation of South Africa more than Newham.'

Mr Alan Sawyer, RHS shows manager, said: 'We had a phone call from Newham's parks manager saying he might not be allowed to take part this year, but we have heard nothing since.'

25 MAY 1988

BLOOMING TOUTS

For the first time in the Chelsea Flower Show's 75-year history, ticket touts were outside the main gates yesterday. Members' Day tickets, at £8 each, were being offered at £60 a pair.

20 APRIL 1963

THIRTY YEARS' MYSTERY

Lady Vansittart saw for the first time at the Royal Horticultural Society's camellia show yesterday the flower named after her 30 years ago by a Guernsey nurseryman. It is white flecked with pink, and the original tree is now 20ft high.

She bought two of the plants, but she still doesn't know why they were named after her.

14.
'The blade should be thrust into the soil vertically so that the shaft tilts forward'

Digging, Pruning, Mulching and Other Jobs of Work

I do it my way: pruning

By Fred Whitsey

Frustration of rising intensity could well be eased by a morning's pruning and burning. But what? Too early for the buddleias and ceanothus. You never know what cold is to come. So I set about the roses. They look butchered, but I think they will be all right.

After all there is a whole school of rosarians who hold that you should not wait until March before you prune your roses and then have to cut away quantities of rising shoots, but that you should do it while the bushes are still dormant. Ah but, say the traditionalists, pruning stimulates growth, and the new shoots may get frosted and you may not have much more branch growth to cut into.

Ah but, reply the modernists, don't we get frosts at the end of March and in April to damage the shoots that follow late pruning? And what about the shoots that come from unpruned bushes and climbers that grow out anyway in the late winter?

It's all an inexact business. No one ever puts it to the real test, and when it has all been done, at whatever time, everyone is too busy to bother about the niceties of the consequences. Growth is so abundant that all wounds are healed. So I say better to get the job done now while the soil is too wet to work. You can always prune from a duckboard.

Prune what and how? Well, on bush and standard roses two types of growth had better go bodily. First the bits thinner than a pencil, which will never produce a flowering twig, and then those old branches too hard in the wood ever to throw out a productive new shoot. You can always tell them by their dark colouring and by the fact that at some time during the winter they have begun to die back from the tip, presaging their fate.

Roses should always be encouraged in their efforts to renew themselves. Remove the old, cherish the new growth is a golden rule. Of course, all varieties are individuals and some are reluctant to make new growth low down. These you have to treat accordingly and gently. Other varieties are only too ready every year to produce strong new growths from near the base of the bush, particularly if they are Floribundas. In such cases you find you have almost a new bush every season.

In between are many degrees of renewal, but it is a sound rule to cut away one old branch, right to the ground, every season. The growths that are left can be cut back by a third to a half as another general rule.

Of course, those untidy crossing branches should be removed altogether. Once the job is done the bushes do look rather sparse, but the astonishing thing about roses is the speed with which they recover in time to enter their big flowering season at the end of June.

Is it important to prune outward-facing buds? To prune buds at all? I am not convinced. Too often the bud to which you prune isn't the one that grows at all. Better to snip where seems convenient. Any of those dying snags that you always get anyway can be cut away later on, as they should be for the health of the bushes.

More important, it seems to me, is nourishing the bushes with some special rose fertiliser. Since it takes some weeks before the plants can use it, this might be a reasonable time to scatter it over the ground so that when it has dissolved and some warmer weather comes the plants will be in a position to take full advantage.

I think fertilising is particularly important for the climbers of the type that make little new wood. They are inclined to be slow, which is all to the good in some ways, but frustrating when you are looking for results like the older more lusty kinds gave, even though they only flowered in summer.

The newer kinds can be encouraged to make their new twigs by arching the branches sideways on their wall or fences, even if this means securing one branch to another. Though this does mean building up a tight mat of growth, it does make for prolific flowering. Of course, you must have some pretty firm basic support or one wet windy day the whole thing will come adrift and you will be presented with a hopeless tangle. Then the sole solution would be to hack mercilessly, knowing that, unlike the bush kinds, growths removed will mean fewer flowers.

The shrub roses are in a somewhat similar category. Prune them hard, like the Floribundas and Hybrid Teas, and you will not get many flowers this summer. Better to ram in three or four stakes and tie to these the whippy branches so that they will be encouraged to throw out the flowering twigs all the way up instead of only at the top, as they will if they are left to grow naturally. They can be wound round the posts in serpentine fashion and again some tied to one another.

Some will undoubtedly say that this is not the way to grow shrub roses. They should be allowed their heads. But if the area is restricted and you want to get around and between them? Corset them as you see them trained in the best National Trust gardens.

Another way is to thrust hoop-like lengths of cane in the ground and train out the whippy branches on these. It makes garlands where otherwise there would be bunches.

To mulch or not to mulch …
is a rhetorical question

By Ken Thompson

Mulch: 'A mixture of wet straw, leaves, etc., spread around (the roots of) a plant to enrich or insulate the soil.' That is the definition in my *Shorter Oxford Dictionary*, which throws into sharp relief the limitations of dictionaries. Neither wet straw nor leaves are necessarily ideal mulch materials, and there's a lot more to mulching than enrichment and insulation.

So what should we be mulching with and what can we expect it to do? For the average gardener, the primary function of mulch is weed control. Indeed, for the gardener determined to eschew herbicides and who does not want to spend all summer hoeing, mulch is the weed-control technique of choice.

Almost anything that covers the soil will control weeds to some extent, and in the world of commercial horticulture, mulch can be almost anything, from plastic to a 'living mulch' such as clover. But plastic is unsightly, and living mulches can cause as many problems as they solve. In a garden context, mulch is usually a layer of some kind of organic material.

Since most weed seeds need light to germinate, any layer thick enough to exclude light will prevent most of them from germinating. It will also kill any weed seedlings that do germinate.

So how thick is enough, or to put it another way, how long is a piece of string? Plenty of weeds have quite small seeds, and for these even an inch is fatal. But weeds with big seeds, goosegrass say, will come through that as though it weren't there, so 4in is a useful minimum to aim for. Wild oat seedlings will come through 8in, so it's just as well wild oat isn't a garden weed, but you get the idea: for weed control, the thicker the better.

Of course, there is nothing to stop seeds of dandelions and willow herb blowing in and growing on top of the mulch, but at least weeds rooted in mulch are easy to uproot. On the other hand, don't even think about trying to control established perennial weeds with mulch. Creeping thistle shoots can emerge from roots at a depth of 3ft or more, so a few extra inches on top is water off a duck's back.

The downside of mulch is that it will also 'control' plants you want to grow. Shrubs aren't a problem, and robust perennials will shrug off 4in of mulch, but don't cover small plants with thick layers.

You are often advised to apply mulch in spring, but this conflicts with a stronger imperative not to dump mulch on top of growing plants, so autumn is better, after herbaceous plants have finished growing, and after some rain but before the winter chill, so the soil under the mulch is moist and still relatively warm.

What to use? Cost, aesthetics and function all come into play. There is such a thing as a free mulch, so start with whatever materials are to hand: garden compost, shredded prunings, lawn mowings, fallen leaves, shredded paper, or a mixture of all of them. If you have a large supply of material – hedge trimmings, for example – a shredder is a worthwhile investment.

Some mulches look nicer than others, so put whatever you prefer on the top, which will often be compost. The appearance of leaves is greatly improved if they are left to rot for a year or two before use. Weed control will be improved by starting with a base layer of a few sheets of unshredded newspaper.

Few gardens produce enough home-grown mulch, so you may decide to buy some.

Despite the dictionary definition, straw is not a good idea. Wet straw may be well behaved, but dry straw isn't, and unless it's certified organic, you never know what may be in it.

Bark mulch looks nice but tree bark is naturally waterproof and does not absorb or retain water. Chipped softwood absorbs water and is generally cheaper, so should be your first choice. Wood is heavy, so distance is the key to cost; shop around locally for the cheapest supplier. If you have a friendly local sawmill and you're prepared to collect it yourself, it may cost very little.

You may also find sawdust available very cheaply, but this should be avoided – it tends to form a compact, water-repellent layer, and it looks awful. Fresh wood chips can be garish, but they soon darken.

Weed control may be your primary aim, but all organic mulches do a lot more than that for your garden. They slowly decay, adding organic matter to your soil, encouraging earthworms and improving soil structure and water-holding capacity. They also physically protect the soil surface from heavy rain, while allowing rainwater to percolate slowly, preventing run-off and erosion. And, while you shouldn't tread on your soil if you can help it, chunky, coarse mulches will also protect it from feet. Even carbon-rich mulches such as wood chips contain small amounts of nutrients that gradually build up the fertility of your soil.

Two final pieces of advice. Don't apply mulch right up to the stems of trees and shrubs; and for permanent weed control, keep an eye on your mulch and top up as necessary to maintain a thick layer.

The last word on gardening tools

By Charles Dowding

Much of what is deemed necessary for gardening is really in the category of gadgets or luxuries, and I hope my recommendations save you money by highlighting the tools and accessories you really need.

My favourite tools are made of copper – or, to be precise, they are 95 per cent copper and five per cent tin: the metal is strong, not magnetic, and does not rust. This is a keen advantage for trowels, hoes and spades where smooth, sharp blades make for effortless use, and there is no need for any regular cleaning or oiling to protect the metal.

Dibber

Invaluable for making holes of about the same size as the root balls of plants grown in plugs and modules, onion sets, garlic cloves and even potato tubers at planting-out time. You can dib holes quickly and then fill them with whatever you are planting, including larger seeds such as peas and beans. The dibbers I recommend are spade handles with a pointed end, usually in wood.

Most dibbers are too short to offer much leverage and also it is difficult to create a pattern of planting holes with so little perspective.

You can make your own quite easily, starting with a wooden handle about 75cm (30in) long: chisel the end and then sand it to make a rounded and pointed end for pushing into soil.

Garden fork

Shorter and fatter prongs than a manure fork mean better durability for jobs like digging out plants and for removing perennial weeds such as couch grass. Look for a sturdy handle that won't snap at the first hint of something firm.

Manure fork

Useful for turning and spreading compost and organic matter generally. Long, thin prongs make it too weak for any kind of digging work.

Hoe

A good hoe has a thin blade with a sharp edge and slides easily through soil. The aim is to cut through all roots of small weeds at a shallow level. Hoes come in many forms: Dutch hoes, draw hoes, onion hoes and swivel hoes, all with blades of varied sizes and at different angles. I recommend trying a few to see which you like. I use a copper swivel hoe: its thin, sharp blade cuts cleanly when both pushing and pulling.

Pocket knife

Often needed in the garden, for cutting string, sticks and flowers, trimming leeks, cabbages and tomato plants, deadheading and many other jobs.

Rake

Handy before sowing seeds, to knock lumps apart and create a smoother tilth, and to fill drills after sowing; also for collecting up surface debris such as leaves and grass. A standard short-pronged version has more uses than long-pronged rakes.

Scythe

More effective and adaptable than often realised, especially when blades are not too long, say 60cm (24in). We use ours to trim grassy edges and for occasional cutting of nettles and brambles. Scything takes some practice but using a short blade helps, and it means you spare your neighbours the noise of a strimmer.

Spade

Even in a no-dig garden, spades have many uses – making holes for trees and large plants, shaping beds, chopping waste matter, digging parsnips. A sharp edge is invaluable: see the tips on sharpening below. Copper or stainless-steel spades are worth the extra money.

Trowel

I use a trowel more than any other tool, for clearing ground, removing perennial weeds and making holes to plant tomatoes, courgettes, potatoes and so forth. Copper trowels are the easiest to use: they retain a sharp edge and slide easily through soil.

Watering can

Choose as large a can as is comfortable to hold when full. You will use a can frequently when propagating plants, for which a smaller one with a fine rose is useful.

Wheelbarrow

Ranking with the bicycle as a supremely cost-effective, energy-efficient and useful invention, a wheelbarrow carries all kinds of materials – to and from the compost heap, above all.

Cloche

A simple and effective way to grow salad in winter, and to warm air and soil in spring. Covering hoops with polythene affords most warmth to plants but means some ventilation and watering is often needed.

Alternatively you can lay fleece or mesh over cloche hoops (see next point), ensuring good ventilation, or directly on plants, which is even simpler and quicker.

Cloche hoops

You can save money by making cloche hoops out of materials such as alkathene water pipe, electrical conduit or wire. They can be up to 1.2m (4ft) wide, to cover whole beds, but wider cloches are also taller, so they need to be strong, according to average wind speeds. Push hoops 10–15cm (4–6in) into the soil and space them about 1m (39in) apart. You can then stretch covers tightly over them and weight them down along the edges with bricks or pegs.

Cold frame

A useful way of starting seedlings and for protecting tender plants, but the edges may harbour slugs: glass-sided frames are best for slug-free growth.

Compost bins

Wooden sides and simple enclosures of old pallets or the cheapest conical plastic bins are effective.

Containers for growing

Use anything that can hold compost and has a drainage hole at the bottom. Larger containers give harvests over a longer period, although it is possible to feed the compost of smaller pots and seed trays, which otherwise run low on nutrients.

Old pots are fine, but terracotta ones need more water than plastic. You can also grow in boxes or crates that have been used for packing foods. Boxes with many holes can be lined with two or three sheets of newspaper.

Fleece and mesh

Both are reusable, and for weather protection a few holes do not matter. Fleece is warmer than mesh and is most valuable in spring, for covering young plants against cold winds. You can also use it as a pest barrier, and for frost protection in winter, when thicker grades or double layers are effective.

Mesh is stronger and useful in summer and autumn for protecting plants from brassica pests, carrot root flies and leek moth. Mesh comes with different-sized holes; for protection against aphids and midges get the finest grade.

These covers can be laid directly on plants, held firm at their edges with a weight every 1m or so. They are light enough for growing leaves to push up, and plants thrive in the environment beneath.

Greenhouse

Glasshouses admit more light and retain more heat than polythene structures and are excellent for raising plants, protecting crops in all seasons, keeping tools dry and so forth: I strongly recommend one if you can afford it. Otherwise a small polytunnel is cheaper, as are lean-to plastic shelters for placing beside a house wall.

I suggest some kind of wooden staging if you use any of these structures for raising plants.

Where space is limited, you could use a portable 'mini greenhouse' on wheels, often sold as a kit with shelving included. I would recommend one of these ahead of a cold frame, which takes up extra room and is all at ground level.

Netting

If pigeons, deer and rabbits are a nuisance, you will need some netting. Mesh size can be as much as 2.5cm (1in), and I find a 4m (13ft) wide roll of heavy-duty black netting is useful for many vegetables: its flexible, diamond-shaped mesh allows for stretching to fit different widths of beds or rows, held up by sticks or cloche hoops, and it can be reused for many years.

Propagating trays

For indoor sowing and potting on, a whole range of products can be bought, or recycled many times. You can also use egg boxes, yogurt pots or any container of a suitable size, as long as it has either a porous base or a hole for excess water to drain out: no plants grow well in waterlogged compost .

Seed trays have no partition and are simple to use. Taking plants out of them involves some root disturbance, however. I find that module trays (also called cell or plug trays) of hard plastic are good as you can push each plant out without damaging the roots and you can reuse the trays. Polystyrene trays are equally good but more expensive. The standard size is 35cm x 22cm (14 x 9in) and may contain 24, 40 or 60 individual holes. The latter are good for growing salad plants, while 40-hole trays are good for brassicas, which benefit from a little more compost.

Shed

You will need some kind of solid shelter for tools and equipment, and also for storing onions, garlic and other harvested vegetables. Few sheds give protection against frost, however, so a shed is not suitable for keeping potatoes and squash through winter.

Stone for sharpening

Invaluable for running smoothly along the blade of spades and edgers, perhaps only twice a year. The aim is to remove jagged edges as much as to sharpen the blade.

Water butt

Useful if there are ways to fill and refill it. Plastic butts of 100–200 litres may have lids and taps, but their water becomes smelly over time from lack of oxygen, and occasional draining out and cleaning is worthwhile.

🌿 16 APRIL 1967 🌿

A nation of composters?

By Fred Whitsey

Lying on the masseur's couch, one was hardly in a position to argue with the theory that you can compost your land and then say a thankful farewell to nature's own agents of destruction, the diseases and the pests that afflict plants. Perhaps it would have been impolite to dispute it, for a health hydro is just the place where such a theory is an article of faith.

Stirred by the cold shower that followed the soothing massage, however, I did rise to what I took as bait. Earnestly I pleaded to know by what sense of fitness a little greenfly would decide to feast on the sickly lettuce and leave the more succulent one untouched. And by what notion of reverence for life it was that a minute flea beetle questing for tiny turnip seedlings would turn away from a patch growing on land that had been manured with compost.

I was left wondering as sorely as old philosophers trying to answer their own proposition of: can a cheese mite see its own leg? Where faith rules it is unwise, as well as impolite, to attempt to reason.

🌿 341 🌿

Plant disease is, of course, a different matter. We all know that you can grow many plants so well that even though they become infected their vigour can be so great that any signs they may show are only vestigial. And this can be achieved only when the land is rich in what gardeners call by the Latin name for ground – 'humus'.

Good gardeners, indeed, are zealous refuse collectors. They are constantly scavenging in their gardens, for every left-over fragment of matter that began life in the soil. They hoard them in heaps that arouse as much pride as an orchid in flower. Nothing is wasted, no spent leaf or withering stem, not the peel of an orange. All is preserved and passed through an artificially contrived process of hastening the decay that nature began. It is not destruction, however, but conversion.

A compost heap is a living thing charged with revitalising power. Yet not eternally. Treat it like the unventuresome man in the parable of the talents and the life-giving bacteria will show offence and go elsewhere, leaving the heap to descend into fibrous decrepitude. Always use your compost in under a year and start afresh.

To make the bacteria work for you night and day you have to concern yourself with certain practical considerations. The smallest-sized heap in which you can hope for a real bacterial population explosion is a 4ft cube. This is made up in layers each about 9in deep, interleaved with soil as you might make a vast sponge sandwich cake. True composters compose it with the same devoted application that a pastrycook with Cordon Bleu standards brings to her task. This is all contained in a wire-netting pen so that it is pressed in on itself as it weathers down instead of spreading out.

And just as any good cook knows just the right touch of liqueur to add and make the difference between an ordinary dish and one that gets conversation flowing faster, the composter has his vital extra to add. The really convinced will add nothing but a herbal activator. (I am not sure if some special incantation goes with it!) Others of us anxious only to produce a really good sample of rotted muck are content to scatter the growing heap occasionally with one of the chemical 'accelerators' that line the shelves of the garden shop.

Of course, if you can get hold of a small quantity of genuine animal manure, there is no better way that it can be used than in a compost heap. If the kitchen waste and garden refuse are not nearly enough to make a heap of adequate size, very good compost can be made by using peat in the stack. In fact, peat that has been composted has a more beneficial influence on the soil than using it direct from the bag or bale.

What you must not add is weed seeds, nor leave lying on the top such weeds as groundsel and dandelions that even in their death throes will mature and produce viable seeds.

Like peat, compost that has thoroughly rotted down can be laid on the surface between plants with a twofold purpose. It will prevent evaporation of moisture through wind and sun, and thus hoard it for the plants. Second, its fibrous relics can be dug in during the succeeding autumn to enhance the texture of soil that its juices will already have enriched.

Just as, say, writings of Shaw, once so revolutionary, are the commonplaces of today, so the compost school has done its work well. No one now countenances the idea that fertility can be achieved with chemicals alone. Everyone realises that at the practical level the soil is a medium to be coaxed with matter of organic origin first. And until horsemanship returns as a leisure pursuit in the way that the Englishman has gone back to his boats, compost is the cheapest and most convenient means of providing the leaven for the lump.

The several ways to weed

By Medwyn Williams

I bought my first house when I got married. It had a large back garden, which I decided to dig over and plant with vegetables. With my father's help, I managed to get it growing away beautifully in the first season. And as soon as the vegetables germinated, Dad taught me my first basic lesson: 'Keep the hoe moving from now on.'

That simple advice has meant that I always get the best possible harvest from any sowing. Weeds can be devastating in the kitchen garden, and are often the reason why people don't persevere with growing their own fresh veg.

It is always better to tackle weeds carefully by hand as soon as they pop their heads through the soil – before they jostle your fragile seedlings and start to suffocate them. The vegetable plants will also probably need thinning out by now, so you can do both jobs at the same time. Hand-weed each row and about 2in on either side: the remaining space between the rows can then be easily cleaned up with the hoe. It is always amazing how, after this initial thinning and weed control, the seedlings romp away and develop into strong, established plants.

There are two kinds of hoe. The basic type is the Dutch hoe, which has been around for many years and works on the push-and-pull theory. It is well-proven and efficient at what it does. My favourite, however, is not a true hoe at all: it's a rather different concept called a swoe. While the hoe has two cutting edges, the swoe has three. You can use it with a push-and-pull action, but it also has a narrow blade on the side that is really useful for getting in between the plants in a row.

And its work starts now. The best way to prepare the ground for next season is by the continuous hoeing of any part of the vegetable plot that will remain empty for the rest of this year. There is an old saying, 'One year's weed is seven years' seed' – in other words, weeds can go on germinating long after their seeds were shed. Thorough soil preparation from now until late autumn will give you a much better chance of controlling weeds next season.

Hoeing is not hard work. Indeed, it can be quite a pleasure, becoming distinctly therapeutic as the blade skims rhythmically back and forth through the crumbly soil. The best time to do it is when the weather is dry and sunny enough to shrivel up all the white, young annual weeds that appear on the surface of the disturbed soil. Hoeing regularly also creates a sort of mulch: a layer 2in or so thick dries out, trapping moisture in the soil beneath.

Hoeing can also work against perennial weeds such as couch grass, thistle and docks, as long as it is done regularly. Like all plants, these weeds need sunlight for the vital process of photosynthesis. So if you continue to knock off the protruding shoots, the plants below will eventually die, starved of nutrients.

There is, however, an easier way to treat perennial weeds – the careful use of herbicides or weedkillers. There are two groups to choose from for use in the vegetable garden: contact killers such as Weedol, which quickly kill off the tops of the plants and are ideal for annual weeds, and the systemic or translocating type, which will invariably contain the chemical Glyphosate (usually sold as Round-up or Round-up Pro Biactive). This latter type can be applied to foliage through a fine rose or a sprayer, but also comes in the form of a gel (for example, Tumbleweed Gel) which you apply directly to the foliage. This is particularly useful for accurate spot application.

The systemic herbicide is so called because the chemical travels through the plant's system right down to the roots, thoroughly eradicating it. Don't be surprised if nothing happens for a fortnight or more: it can take up to three weeks to show any effect. At this point you can speed things up by physically removing the weeds. Any roots left in the ground will already have taken in the chemical and will die off completely over the winter.

Glyphosate kills off any foliage it touches. You can use it between the vegetable rows during the growing season, but you have to be extremely careful not to let it come into contact with your plants. For this reason alone I prefer the hoe. However, Glyphosate does, at least, biodegrade into harmless compounds as soon as it reaches the soil, so you can sow seed as early as the day after spraying. (Never employ a residual weedkiller in the veg plot – the type that is often used on perennial shrub borders – since it leaves dangerous residues.)

Mulching is another excellent way of keeping weeds under control, particularly after the vegetables have grown on from the seedling stage. The soil should be free of weeds prior to applying the mulch and should also be moist. I have found partly rotted straw in between the rows very effective, pulled from the bale in wads about 3in thick. This stops the ground from drying out but it can aggravate slug problems, providing the ideal damp, dark hiding place. If you have vulnerable plants close by, use slug pellets.

An added benefit of a mulch is that it will eventually break down into beneficial humus. However some materials will linger longer than others: for instance, wood-shavings and tree bark can take a considerable time.

A point to remember is that all organic mulches take up nitrogen from the soil as they decay. Replace this element by scattering a couple of ounces of sulphate of ammonia on top of the mulch – just as my father used to do.

My scythe and I

By W. F. Deedes

At one time I viewed with disapproval the growth of stalls displaying machinery at agricultural and garden shows. It seemed to me that the sheep pens or the flower beds grew smaller and the rows of gleaming gadgets longer. With the advancing years, my attitude has changed. My interest is attracted by any new mechanical device designed to save undue physical exertion.

Salesmen offering the latest mechanical refinements for cutting lawns, trimming hedges, felling trees, splitting wood, gathering fallen leaves, slicing through undergrowth or cultivating the vegetable garden have no difficulty in catching my eye.

I would be happier if more of these devices bore British trade marks – goodness knows what the British gardener's import bill amounts to these days – but I am not responsible for this shortcoming. I take what I am offered.

When I was a boy, our extensive tool shed contained no combustion engine. The aged gardener pushed a lawn mower; when the grass was new and thick, a boy with a piece of rope attached to the mower acted as pony.

When big trees had to be cut, two men came with a crosscut saw made of supremely good British steel. I still have an old one hanging in the shed. Hedges were cut with hand clippers; lawn edges trimmed with long-handled clippers. Beds were dug by hand. Hedges were trimmed with a sickle and stick – an art which is dying.

So either we have grown lazier or, as I prefer to see it, our garden work has been made less burdensome. Year by year more and more back-breaking tasks are brought within reach of those long past the age of retirement. This is progress. When I read on some implement a word like 'eezystart' I reach for my cheque book.

All handbooks on garden machines, incidentally, ought to include a passage on how to put them into mothballs for the winter, a precaution which saves hours of frustration in the spring – and a hefty bill for servicing from the dealer.

There remains, however, one old-fashioned implement which defies progress. Nobody has invented anything to replace it, and I doubt they ever will.

Among all the modern gadgets, the old-fashioned scythe stands unchallenged. If it is set right and very sharp, it is still the simplest, smoothest and most relaxing of all garden instruments. Correct setting is not easy, because the old blacksmiths who did it for you have gone. Sharpening with a scythe stone is a knack, which no two people exercise in the same way.

I find a new, full-length blade a shade heavy now, but the work can be done as well with a Turk or short scythe. When the scythe is working smoothly on a keen edge, there is nothing to compare with it.

This is the tool with which men once cut their harvests. Its design enables a man to wield it throughout a summer's day without undue fatigue. It will still perform certain tasks better than any machine.

Many years ago, a woman in my constituency wrote to me, complaining that the county council refused to cut a patch of grass outside her home which bordered the village green. She asked me to nudge the council.

I packed my scythe into the car one Sunday morning, reckoning that a generous act would substitute for divine worship, found the patch and went to work. It represented not much more than two hours' work.

I had not been going long when the lady of the house appeared. Far from being grateful, she was alarmed. What would the neighbours say? They would assume her husband was so idle that the local MP had to do his work for him. But, she pleaded, her husband had a heart condition, which put scything out of bounds for him.

As I finished the job and began to preen myself, the woman reappeared with her sick husband. She wanted me – and the neighbours – to observe the truth of the matter.

Since that experience, I have given up acting the boy scout with my scythe. But within my own curtilage, it has no rival.

17 JANUARY 1981

How to dig

By Fred Whitsey

There are some gardeners who simply grow vegetables to satisfy their pride. I know some who think far more of cabbages than camellias and take much greater delight in growing them. One can understand their sense of achievement, especially when it all begins with wielding a spade on a winter's day, a truly exhilarating process. Though the owner of a garden hopelessly overstocked, like the gardens of most acquisitive plant hoarders, I find myself anxiously watching the vegetable garden soil weekend after weekend, waiting for the day when I can at last get on with the simple, basic business of digging it.

I think bitterly of the frosty nights that could be working on it for me, if only it had already been dug and left rough for cruel weather to refine. For this is truly better than any cultivating, once you have played your part. Equally, I look forward to the spring day when, splintered by hard frost, perhaps fertilised by snow, it will dissolve at the touch of the fork into that fine tilth which is such a joy to anyone who has ever once sown a seed.

First, though, the rough work. Always standing with the back to the wind, one must take out a trench twice the width of the spade and throw the excavated soil to one side. This will simply make the job easier as you then work to and fro across the plot, digging out clods and throwing them forward into the opened trench, twisting them as you go, so that what was formerly covered in snow is now uppermost.

Doubtless some still require double digging – breaking up the lower level before it is covered in – but just try it. You need the strength of a navvy born to it. Time too. I prefer to get into the rhythm that gets the job done quickly, even without rushing at it.

Of course, there are refinements that contribute to this apparently well-oiled performance, details of the kind of simplicity that music teachers and golfing instructors insist on. First you need to sharpen the blade of your spade with a file and, if it has a wooden handle, make this especially smooth with a sheet of fine sandpaper.

The blade should be thrust into the soil vertically so that the shaft tilts forward. Then you reach the greatest possible depth in one stroke. You take fairly thin slices so that you can lift them easily. You bend low so that one hand reaches right down to the top of the blade and as you do lift the least possible strain is imposed on the back. The weight is carried by the hand as you lift and twist the neatly cut slice.

No manure? Not at this stage. To keep stopping to get another barrow-load and then spread it breaks the rhythm that makes light work of it. Besides, manure is scarce and expensive and usually well rotted down in the forms in which you can get hold of it today. Better to spread it over the surface in the spring and integrate it then. It will encourage strong root growth in the seedlings. Anyway, its place may have to be taken by damp peat or composted bark, conditioning agents that will have their greatest value on top.

Suppose, though, you haven't time or energy enough for the process of time-honoured efficacy and which lets the air into the ground to the benefit of whatever is grown there later on? Settle for the fork, especially where you have been diligent in your digging in previous years. Then, even getting out the perennial weeds that have had the autumn in which to re-establish themselves, will be enough, provided you do the job crudely so that the surface is left rough for the frost to work on.

There is another reason, however, for using a fork if the ground is light enough for you to be able to lift and turn the lumps it disturbs. Worms: I am always horrified by massacre of worms that take place inevitably when you prepare a patch of ground with the spade. If they are such friends to man as they undoubtedly are, why execute them as you cut and cut again with it?

FACING THE WIND

Sir, – Mr Fred Whitsey's Saturday gardening columns are long-established comprehensive reading for all interested in gardening and almost without exception his writings contain nothing but sound common (and some uncommon) sense.

That is, until 17 January, when in his article headed 'Spades are trumps' he suggests digging with one's back to the wind.

A more certain recipe for backache, strains, lumbago, and all kindred ills there cannot be.

Button up, face the wind, shelter and protect those vital vulnerable muscles at the bottom of your back and carry on, defy the elements, but don't dig frost in, it takes too long for it to come out.

M. C. D. Pedley
Thirsk, Yorks

POTTING SHED VIGIL GARDENER CLEARED AFTER RAIDER SHOT

A 77-year-old man who slept in an allotment shed for four years to guard his prize tomatoes and geraniums from vandals and thieves was cleared yesterday of wounding an intruder with a shotgun. Mr Ted Newbery surrounded his plot in Ilkeston, Derbyshire, with high fences and barbed wire, Derby Crown Court was told.

He equipped the brick shed with a bed, a television set and a fridge.

Last March, two intruders started kicking the shed door and threatening Mr Newbery, who fired a warning shot through a hole in the door with an unlicensed 12-bore shotgun.

The shot seriously wounded Mark Revill, 22, who crawled with shoulder and chest wounds to a friend's nearby home. But Mr Newbery was acquitted of wounding with intent to cause grievous bodily harm and unlawful wounding.

Judge Brian Woods described the verdict as 'a very honourable outcome'. Mr Newbery said there had been no intruders since the shooting. 'It seems to have done the trick,' he added.

'I shall continue gardening. I've had a lot of support from people who know the hassle I've been going through and I'm just glad it's all over.'

He now sleeps indoors and has surrendered the single-barrel shotgun to the police. 'I am a gardener, not a gunman,' said Mr Newbery of Greenwood Avenue, Ilkeston.

15.

'There are at least four wrong ways to grow daffodils'

The Discreet Charm of the Bulbs and Alpines

Hypnotic blooms

By Robert Pearson

Some years ago, I remember, I came across a marvellous photograph of a no longer young, bowler-hatted visitor to the Chelsea Flower Show who gave the impression of being so absorbed in the orchid blooms a few feet from his nose that if the tent had collapsed around him he would have shrugged it off as an irrelevance.

Now whether I have ever assumed that lost-to-the-world look myself I do not know, but I have certainly seen it on many other faces in similar circumstances. Plants, and especially plants of the quality you find at great flower shows, do tend to have that kind of effect on one. I am glad they do.

There are, of course, plants of many kinds with real charisma, and on this bleak January day how pleasant to reflect on some of the smaller members of the garden fraternity which make one stand and stare.

One such is *Aethionema* 'Warley Rose'. This splendid little alpine plant, a garden-raised hybrid, is a delightful choice for a sink or trough garden, a rock garden or a dry wall where it can revel in all the sunshine that is going and burrow its thin roots down into nourishing, sharply drained, preferably limy soil. This shrubby little plant makes a spreading mass of growth about 4 to 6in high and 1 to 1½ft wide, close-set with pretty blue-grey leaves and, from early May to late June, with a profusion of flower heads in rich rose-pink. Like most good plants, though, it has its foibles – the sensitivity to less than very well-drained conditions I have already referred to, and a keen desire to be left alone once happily settled. Petulance at unseemly disturbance lies only just beneath the surface.

Everybody knows the sea-pink *Armeria maritima*, and most gardeners its relative *A. caespitosa*, a lovely small cushion-forming thrift with a mass of upstanding pink flowers in late spring and early summer, which also needs lots of sunshine and exceptionally well-drained soil. 'Bevan's Variety', a deep-pink form, and 'Beechwood', with more delicate pink colouring and larger flowers, are worth keeping in mind if you're thinking of making a sink garden. So, too, is the even smaller *Dianthus caesius* 'La Bourbrille', barely 2in tall, which pink flowered and grey leaved, is a charming variant of the 'Cheddar Pink'.

A plant I can never keep my eyes off when it is in flower is the carpeting knotweed, *Polygonum affine* 'Donal Lowndes', a better plant in several ways than that other popular variety of this species, 'Darjeeling Red'. It is slightly more compact for a start and the leaves a clearer green, but the main thing which appeals is the appearance of the sturdy, 8in tall, rosy-pink flower spikes which delight for long spells in summer from late May onwards. 'Darjeeling Red' has deep-pink, not red, flowers and these do not put in an appearance until summer is well advanced. For all that, though, both are good plants, as useful for a sunny spot at the front of a border as for the rock garden, their more natural home. Any ordinary soil will do, and if need be they will put up quite happily with light shade.

A favourite with several generations of gardeners has been the sun-loving, ground-hugging *Lithospermum diffusum* 'Heavenly Blue' with star-shaped flowers of the richest possible deep-gentian blue, set off by small, dark-green leaves. For a warm pocket on the rock garden where it can spread its stems it is superb, for these blooms are thickly borne from May to mid-summer and intermittently later in the season. It must, however, be given a lime-free, peaty soil with very free drainage.

Another pretty rock garden plant with blue star flowers also of deep colouring is *Campanula portenschlagiana*, which literally smothers itself in bloom in high summer and puts on another show later in the season, even up to October. Like its similarly named relative, *C. poscharskyana*, it has earned a justified reputation as a strong-growing plant, in sun or light shade and most soils. Indeed, it is a lovely plant which grows about 9in tall had has a spread of several feet and I would hate to be without it in my garden. It is also a splendid wall plant.

The rock garden plant most likely to shut me off from the world, though, is our native pasque flower, *Pulsatilla vulgaris*, in one of its more beautifully coloured forms, for this is a variable plant in flower which may have blooms in colours from reddish-purple and red, through lavender-blue to pale pink. Add to the beauty of these cup-like chalices with their frame of silky hairs the charm of the tufted, fern-like foliage, and you have a plant which competes on more than equal terms with the loveliest of the spring bulbous flowers. This is still another plant which needs much sunshine, first-rate drainage and a soil with plenty of nourishment in it. It revels, too, in limestone soil.

17 APRIL 1976

Planting daffodils the natural way

By Denis Wood

There are at least four wrong ways to grow daffodils. One is in bands along pathways, another is in formal beds treating them like tulips, for whatever the Dutch breeders may do to them daffodils have, and always will have, an ineradicable air of belonging to meadows and long grass. The third way is to buy them mixed by the sackful of different kinds, looking spotty and awful. And the fourth and supreme insult to these beautiful flowers is to stuff them high above eye-level in hanging baskets or containers of some sort, fixed to street lamp-posts as is so disgracefully and insensitively done at St Giles in Oxford.

One right way is to 'naturalise' them – that is to plant them in fairly large groups or drifts in wilder parts of the garden, usually in grass and delectable weeds like cow parsley, which can be allowed to grow long at least until the end of June, because to cut them down earlier would result in the daffodil foliage being sacrificed before it has had time to build up the plants for next season's flowering.

For positions fairly near the house, on a bank of rough grass at the side of a mown lawn, for example, smaller ones only a foot or so high will be in scale, and there are three cyclamineus hybrids which are perfect for this. These are the ones with their perianths (outer petals) ravishingly reflexed, looking like frightened fillies with their ears back. Of these, 'Charity May' is all yellow, 'Jenny' is white all through and 'Dove Wing' has a lemon-yellow cup and white perianth. It is this combination of pale yellow and white which is for me of the essence of spring – it exists in our native wild daffodil, the Lent lily of Housman's poem – and you get it in more developed ones like 'Boswin' or 'Trousseau', which are much taller, from 18 to 20in, and better seen from a distance in orchards or in lawns where the grass is allowed to grow longer at the edges.

A good yellow to make a contrast group is the old but excellent Carlton – a proved naturaliser, which 'King Alfred' is not, incidentally. A good red and yellow to crackle in the spring sunshine is 'Carbineer'. For white drift there is still nothing to touch the flawless 'Cantatrice'. Reversed bicolours are interesting and comparatively new developments. In these the crown or trumpet is paler than the perianth, instead of the other way round. Binkie is one of these – the flower at first clear sulphur yellow but the crown gradually becoming paler, almost pure white. This is another good naturaliser.

For naturalising you must plant them in groups or drifts of one kind only in each drift – different sorts jumbled together look dreadful. You mark out the drifts roughly with canes to make longish groups, and one or two puddle-shaped ones but not too many of these. You calculate at the rate of about 16 per sq. yd. – that is 9in apart on average, but one hopes that few will turn out to be exactly 9in from the next one. You take the bulbs out of the pack and roll them out gently so that they lie haphazard; then, after making a few obvious corrections, you plant them where they lie, faithfully and laboriously with a bulb planter, and with 4in of soil above their noses.

The other way to grow daffodils is in beds in a kitchen garden for cutting and bringing into the house. In Cornwall, where so many of the best daffodils were raised, you could on early spring days see one or two of the new hybrids in specimen glasses on the chimney-piece in the drawing room, the owner standing nonchalantly with his back to them and the fire, too well-mannered to begin a conversation but hoping that you would admire them and inquire for their breeding. One of these must have been 'Greeting', raised at Lanarth in 1934. It is tallish, about 17in, with a really dense white perianth and a small lemon-yellow cap – too small for perfect proportion really, but none the less enchanting. It has an aloof character and is exceedingly beautiful in a vase. One alone in a specimen glass is wonderful.

In general the best daffodils for cutting are the more sophisticated ones which may look a little ill at ease out in the open under stormy skies of spring. 'Matapan' is one of these, having a bright-red centre and a glistening white perianth. Also some of the yellow-and-reds. 'Revelry', for example, with soft yellow petals and flaming-orange centre, and 'Sun Chariot', an enormous flower 5in across, with deep-yellow perianth and orange-red goblet-shaped cup. For many years I used to think that pink daffodils were quite out of character, but they can be remarkably beautiful indoors under soft lighting. One of these is 'Passionale', with pure white shovel-pointed perianth segments with a little wave to them, so that they do not look too formal as if cut out of cardboard.

Then there is 'Ann Abbott', with her apple-blossom pink crown and white pointed 'petals' tending to reflex a little, giving her an air of prim flirtatiousness. This, with 'Chelsea China', was raised by the late George Johnstone, the squire of Trewithen in Cornwall. Mrs J. Abel Smith of Orchard House, Letty Green in Hertfordshire, has preserved some of these with more of her own raising. Many of the others referred to should be obtainable from Kelways of Langport in Somerset or de Jager at Marden in Kent.

The queen of all known alpine plants

By Ursula Buchan

Mention the word 'gentian' in a gathering of gardeners and, more often than not, a frisson will go through the company. For the word conjures up images of short-lived, choice antipodean species, lovingly tended in alpine houses, or Asian species growing in carpets in the acid soils of long-established Scottish or Sussex gardens. There are certainly some pernickety gentians, which are best-suited to the care of enthusiasts, but there are also a number that will settle down reasonably happily in most gardens, provided a few cultivation requirements are met. The spring gentian, *Gentiana verna*, is one of these. Native to mountainous parts of Europe, it is grown in rock beds and troughs in many parts of this country.

In 1906, an advertisement was published in the *Journal of Botany* extolling the virtues of *Gentiana verna* as 'the queen of all known alpine plants in the whole world. It is the only known flower in existence that exhilarates the heart and mind of the fair sex'. Leaving aside such a bizarre claim, this underlines the high esteem in which this plant has long been held, and not just by gardeners. *Gentiana verna* can still be found growing wild in western Ireland, and also on the calcium-rich grasslands of Upper Teesdale in County Durham. Its flowering in late spring and early summer is a great draw to wild-flower enthusiasts, although its very particular habitat and rarity mean that it is strictly protected by law.

The appeal of this plant lies in the intense ultramarine blue of the flat, star-like flowers with their five propeller-shaped petals and white throats. These flowers unfold from pyramid-shaped buds over several weeks in late April and May, and are one of the great joys of the hardy alpine garden in late spring. The flowers may be only 2–3in tall, but the quality and depth of their colour always ensures that they are noticed.

These flowers arise above tufts of mid or grey-green pointed (lanceolate) leaves, which are mainly held in a basal rosette, although there are a few opposite leaves on the short stems. The rosettes can form small mats in time.

Gentiana verna is often found on sale as *G. verna subsp angulosa*, although the purists consider the wild angulosa to be a synonym for *G. verna subsp tergestina*. Dr Christopher Grey-Wilson, the alpines expert, believes that there is great confusion, and that no one knows where 'Angulosa' of gardens arose. Certainly, it is a sturdier plant with longer leaves and holds an Award of Garden Merit from the RHS, and is the plant you are likely to get if you buy *Gentiana verna* from a nursery. It was famously grown by the late Joe Elliott, son of Clarence Elliott, at his nursery at Broadwell, Gloucestershire.

There is also the sub-species *G. verna subsp. balcanica*, a variant from the Balkans with ovate leaves, bigger flowers and broader calyx wings than the type. In the wild, *Gentiana verna* differs in flower colour from white and pale violet to intense blue.

Among other reasonably straightforward gentians, there is the late-spring-flowering, trumpet-shaped *G. acaulis* and the summer-flowering *Gentiana septemfida*, together with its variant lagodechiana. All are quite readily available.

On the trail of the native orchid

By Sarah Raven

W hen I was a child I spent a lot of time going to alpine garden society shows with my father. These were the moments when everyone brought out plants from their alpine houses and set them out on the show bench. People would select the best-looking specimens with the most flowers, wash their terracotta bulb trays and top off the gravel dressing to show the flowers to maximum effect. In early June 'best in show' was always won by the same plant shown by the same man – a vicar from three villages away: an amazing Lady's Slipper orchid, with several flowers on one huge plant. The blooms were extraordinary: tropical-looking balloons with a large, bulbous yellow lip and pinky-purple wings.

Whenever he turned up all the rest of us would groan inwardly: 'Oh no, not him again.'

We all longed for the vicar to be ill on the day so that one of the rest of us stood a chance. We loved to hate his orchid, but I can picture it now nearly 40 years later. It was quite a spectacular thing.

The Lady's Slipper orchid is well known for having only one true wild plant left, guarded night and day when in flower. If you do go to see it – and that is generally thought to be not a good idea – it's in a cage and no one can get near for fear that they'll plonk their tripod on it, or accidentally knock its head off (it's been repeatedly vandalised) and then – whoops – no more Lady's Slipper orchid in the British Isles.

Lady's Slippers can be micropropagated (using plant tissue culture methods in the lab), but decades of attempts to re-establish it in the wild have proved exceptionally difficult, because it needs a special fungus to help it grow. There are some other very rare orchids in the wild in Britain – the Red Helleborine, the Monkey, Frog, Military and the Lizard orchid, all with very few sites where you can see them. However, there are plenty of other orchids that are rare, but easily available to see, and now is the time to make a trip to marvel at what is an incredible array of native orchids.

The one with the biggest wow factor that I have seen this year is the Lady orchid. I thought this was going to be a delicate, exquisite little thing, but in fact it's the biggest British orchid there is. You can spot the best spikes from 100 yards – like a splendid lighthouse of colour amid the short chalk grassland where it grows. Each flower has a dark crimson-scarved head or hood, and then a sparkly white-edged, pink-spotted dress, with a ruched skirt and matching sleeves. They stand a good 18in high, the flower section one-fifth or one-sixth the total height, with eight – at least – 'ladies', each just bigger than my thumbnail, stacked one on top of another. The stem has basal leaves more like a lush-green hosta than a delicate orchid. At least, that's what most of them look like, but this is a very variable orchid.

Most have dark staining under the flowers themselves, which bleeds a bit down the stem, but I have seen one or two that seem a more delicate version, with pure bright-green stems and pale-pink flowers – like a single hedge rose compared with a 'Tuscany Superb', more refined, but with less oomph. The Man orchid, in contrast, is a small and delicate thing with a different sort of strange, other-planet beauty. It has green heads, striped and edged magenta, with a man in trousers – not a skirt – hanging below, his slim arms and legs waving this way and that. I'd been told each also had a willy, but none of mine did.

More extraordinary than beautiful and well worth the hunt is the Fly orchid which, like the lady and man, grows on limey soil, in open grassland or in a wood. In full sun they are tiny, with just two or three flowers. In dappled shade they reach at least a foot, with five or six flowers on a tall, thin stem. Each flower looks like a slim green and conker brown-black fly, but is, in fact, meant to replicate a small female wasp that will attract a male. The orchid's pollen then sticks to the head of the male wasp which carries it from plant to plant in an attempt to mate. Another pair of orchids reaching a peak now is the Greater and Lesser Butterfly – and it seems to be a good year for both. The Greater Butterfly is a magnificent flower, tall, stately and creamy white. Its pale colour and sweet night scent help to draw in the moths that are its pollinators.

Each large individual bloom has a long tongue, which helps to guide in the moths. Where the Greater Butterfly is a beacon on a hillside visible at a hundred feet, the Lesser is as beautiful, but a more delicate thing, found in small clusters rather than in solitary splendour. To tell them apart, you can make sure which you have by looking at the yellowish green pollen sacs (pollinia) in the centre of the flower. In the Greater, these are close together at the top and diverge, wider apart at the bottom. In the Lesser, they are also vertically orientated, but parallel all the way down. If you've yet to plan what to do this weekend, find your nearest area of lime grassland or wood and search for an orchid.

Where to see orchids

These are places where I've seen wild orchids this month, but check the websites of your county's Wildlife Trust and see what riches they offer; all have reserves. Also try National Trust, Plantlife, or Natural England sites.

Wye National Nature Reserve, East Kent (Natural England) – Lady, Man, Fly, Late Spider, plus Common Spotted and Twayblade.

Yockletts Bank, East Kent Downland (Kent Wildlife Trust) – Greater Butterfly, Fly, White Helleborine and Twayblade.

Park Gate Down, East Kent Downland (Kent Wildlife Trust) – Monkey, Fragrant, Fly, Man, Lady, Bee, Greater Butterfly, Late Spider, Musk, Common Spotted and Twayblade.

Denge Wood, East Kent (jointly owned by Forestry Commission, Woodland Trust and an individual) – Greater Butterfly, Lady, Man, White Helleborine, Common Spotted and Twayblade.

Waitby Greenriggs, Kirkby Stephen (Cumbrian Wildlife Trust) – Frog, Lesser Butterfly, Northern Marsh, Marsh Helleborine, Fragrant, Common Spotted and Twayblade.

Ashberry Nature Reserve, near Rievaulx, North York Moors (Yorkshire Wildlife Trust) – Early Marsh, Heath Spotted and the Common Spotted orchid.

'BUYING IN' ROW COLOURS CHELSEA FLOWER SHOW

By Dan Conaghan

The 81st Chelsea Flower Show had its preview day yesterday, with the Royal Horticultural Society insisting it was not 'a horticultural police force' in the debate over exhibitors 'buying in' flowers and plants for their stands.

After some exhibitors admitted they had imported plants from Holland or bought stock from Covent Garden flower market, the RHS wrote to all 700 inviting them to declare the origin of their plants on the displays.

But only a quarter of the 400 growers had yesterday attached notices stating that all the plants had been grown at their own nurseries.

The main protagonists in the debate have been tactfully positioned at opposite ends of the Great Marquee, but it did not stop Mr Joe Ambridge, who has been accused of buying in some of his stock of lillies, calling Mr John Metcalf 'a ratbag' and the whole row 'a bloody disgrace'.

Mr Metcalf, 58, from Norwich and displaying a wide variety of hardy perennials, responded: 'I've spent nearly a year growing plants for my display. Why should someone be allowed to spend a few days buying in stock from a flower market. These people certainly shouldn't be given prize medals.'

Mr Ambridge of Cedarwood Lily Farm, Stoke-on-Trent, disagreed. 'My job is to show people what they can grow in their gardens,' he said. 'I've admitted buying in. If everyone who did it admitted it, you'd see that would be most people here.'

He added: 'The British public are not idiots. They know it is impossible for exhibitors to attend 30 or 40 shows each year without buying in at least some of their plants.'

But the few members of the public accompanying officials and the press seemed disapproving of buying in. Mr Richard Smith, 37, an accountant from St Albans, said: 'Many of us were quite surprised that some plants hadn't been grown by the exhibitors themselves. I think the vast majority of people are unaware that this goes on.'

The Countess Mountbatten of Burma, the show's patron, said: 'I can see no point or fun in buying in something to show here. The whole point of the show is that you produce the exhibits yourself and that it gives you a sense of pride.'

Sir Simon Hornby, RHS president, was unavailable to comment, but his predecessor, Mr Robin Herbert, agreed it was important not to mislead the public. But he said a blanket rule against importing flowers would be impossible to implement.

16.

'One pea that is used in our house for special occasions only . . .'

*Cultivating a Connoisseurial Attitude
Towards Vegetables*

⚜ 6 APRIL 1991 ⚜

Some varieties of vegetable commended

By Beth Chatto

My interest in unusual plants began, curiously, with vegetables. Our first married home was in the house of my mother-in-law, where I inherited from my father-in-law a bed of seakale. This was a new vegetable to me, and it was the beginning of a lifelong interest in unusual vegetables. Today, more than 40 years later, I still have that same stock, propagated from root cuttings about the length and thickness of a pencil which are set in a trench, about 18in apart, in February or early March.

Established crowns are covered just as new shoots are emerging, to blanch the stems and make them tender. Old buckets have done the job well enough, but now my vegetable garden looks very grand, with six terracotta blanching pots, each with a round lid.

I used to throw away the crisp, pink-stained leaves before steaming the stems until I learnt how good they were in an early spring salad. Now the plants I value most in the vegetable garden are salad plants.

The ubiquitous lettuce can now be grown in winter and summer in all shapes and sizes and in a variety of shades, some bronzed, others speckled or splashed with red. But there are other additions to our winter salads that have done much to enliven the northern diet of roots and brassicas. We are still eating the last of the winter chicory. Not the Belgian 'Witloof' variety, but the round, cabbage-shaped varieties, mostly Italian, which turn beetroot-red in autumn and winter. 'Sugar Loaf' or 'Crystal Head' both from large, loose heads, shaped like Cos lettuce. The leaves inside are palest green, with crisp ivory veins.

Chicories are the mainstay of my winter salads. Shredded and mixed with overwintering lettuce and several tasty additions such as American land cress and rocket, they all make a colourful and mouth-watering mixture. Rocket belongs to the Crucifer family. It has striped creamy yellow flowers if allowed to go to seed, but before that, it makes generous helpings of dark-green leaves with a spicy taste, curious to those used to the blandness of lettuce but, like garlic, essential to those who value a rich warm flavour.

Speaking of garlic, the leaves of my young plants are now several inches tall, having been planted as individual cloves in September, in light, well-nourished soil. It is easily grown and can also be planted in spring, but I find that by giving it a longer growing season you can harvest early in August when there is plenty of time to wither the long necks. They must be spread out in a dry, airy place until paper-dry, otherwise they are likely to be attacked by blue mould.

Recently I have been advised to hang my ropes of dry garlic in the light, not in a dark shed or garage, since the light holds back the development of new green shoots. Garden greenhouses are not suitable for storing garlic, as there would be too much humidity. Try the kitchen window.

A variety of onion still crisp and firm in April, with very little inclination to sprout, is the Dutch red onion (*Noordshollandse Bloedrode*). Actually it is a light-purple colour all through, pretty when finely sliced for salads and good to cook. I prefer onions grown from seed. I find they keep better and are less coarse.

I am writing as though drought were never a problem in my kitchen garden, and lettuces never bolted. One answer is to choose a small, fast-growing variety such as 'Little Gem', and to sow small quantities two or three weeks apart. Another is to broadcast a 'Saladisi' mixed salad patch, about a yard square, containing different kinds of lettuce, chicory and chervil. When the seedlings are 2–3in tall, crop with scissors or a knife. If they become tall and coarse, cut them down almost to ground level and they will sprout again.

For those who have very little space, I would recommend growing these mixed salads, or cut-and-come-again varieties of lettuce, in containers – preferably flat and oblong, such as tomato trays or polystyrene fish boxes – stood in a cool place, not in full sun.

As for scarlet runner beans, I have given them up. I preferred the much more prolific purple-podded runner beans because they have such smooth, tender pods, and almost no strings, but now I stick to low-growing beans that do not need stakes. I make two successive sowings to prolong the season, and plant in short rows.

Most of my salads and vegetables are now grown on the short row system. The beds are 4ft wide, so most of the work can be done without treading on the soil, and compacting it. Our problem originally was hungry, gravel-based soil in an area of habitually low rainfall. These beds have now been heavily composted for several years. Light soil devours humus, so it must be applied annually where plants such as salads, peas and beans will be grown – the following year, root vegetables such as carrots, parsnips and onions will do well on the site.

In winter, when the weather is severe, my patches of salad are protected with polythene covers which fit over the width of the bed. I find wider beds are more practical for bulky vegetables such as brassicas and French artichokes. The narrow beds are edged with unplanned planks of wood which were also used to make the two-bay compost bins. The firm edging prevents soil and compost from falling on to the paths and encouraging weeds to grow.

As I do not use herbicides, the paths are kept clean by hoeing: not a difficult task in dry conditions, but at the Henry Doubleday Research

Station near Coventry I was most impressed by the tidy effect of old carpet strips, cut to fit the width of the paths, laid underside uppermost, and fastened along the edges with bent pins made of strong wire.

To conserve moisture, especially with crops such as beans (peas hate very dry summers whatever you do), celeriac, cucumbers (which I find grow best up a wigwam of canes) and courgettes, I mulch with broken-down straw, while all have as much compost as we can provide. Make compost with anything that will break down, even thoroughly wetted newspaper.

Although I have made compost for most of my life, it seems, I was inspired by Dick Kitto's book, *Composting the Organic Way* (Thorsons), to do better. Mr Kitto is a tolerant man, making allowances for those unable to do the ideal thing. But if you stick to his two golden rules, to contain your vegetable waste with solid surrounds to keep it warm and moist (but not soggy), and turn it regularly, you will be amazed at the quick results.

🌿 10 MARCH 2012

Let your palate do the planting

By Mark Diacono

The secret to growing the most delicious food is to forget you are a gardener for a moment. Gardeners think about drawing their patch as a square sub-divided into four, labelled 'Brassicas', 'Roots and Onions' and the like, rather than focusing on flavour.

Instead, pour yourself a glass of whatever you fancy, relax and make a list not of plant groups (who eats plant groups for dinner?) but of flavours, textures and colours that make you excited about eating.

Your list should be uninhibited.

We'll look at ways to adapt your list to any limitations, such as space, later. There is no plant list for the perfect edible garden; tastes differ. But follow these steps and I'm confident you will create a wish list that gets the juices flowing.

Grow what you most like to eat: Your favourite fruit, vegetables, herbs and spices should be the first things on your list. For me that's asparagus, apples, peaches, quince, mulberries, pecans, the very earliest of new potatoes, Moroccan mint, sweet cicely, broad beans and tomatoes. And yours?

Prioritise transformers: You don't need a large space to change every meal you eat. Herbs, spices, garlic and chillies are all short on volume yet long on flavour. Grow just a few pots of herbs and a chilli plant or two and every meal can be transformed for little work, space or expense.

Grow the most expensive crops: Most allotments and veg plots are full of maincrop onions, potatoes and carrots, which are widely available and cheap to buy. Those we grow are often largely indistinguishable from those on offer in the shops. Instead, why not grow the expensive stuff and buy the staples?

Look at your recipe books and your food receipts and identify which fruit, veg and herbs are taking your money: Usually it will be fruit and herbs and any veg that has a short season, such as asparagus, those that are hard to harvest on a commercial scale, such as globe artichokes, or those with a short shelf life, such as salad leaves.

Taste the difference: Many harvests – peas, sweetcorn, and French beans among them – lose some of their essential loveliness within hours, even minutes, of picking. You can taste the difference between this morning's and this afternoon's asparagus, so don't make do with last week's harvest from Peru. Similarly, peaches are a home-grown revelation. Picked a fortnight or more before they ripen, shop-bought peaches soften without development of the sweetness and fragrance that makes a peach so peachy. Home-grown, they areas much a succulent messy drink as a fruit.

Complement the wild harvest: If there are blackberries, elder, wild garlic, rosehips, sloes and crab apples in the hedges and common areas where you live, you may not want to double up on them, but why not grow gooseberries to go beautifully with the elderflower, or apples to go with the blackberries?

Grow some unbuyables: Mulberries, the finest of all fruit, are too soft at their peak to travel, hence I've never seen them for sale. Likewise, courgette flowers, kai lan, medlars, oca, Jerusalem artichokes and Japanese wineberries are all delicious but rarely in the shops.

Equally seductive are the different varieties available to grow: Rather than the half-dozen potato varieties in the shops, you have 6,000 to choose from. It's the same for most fruit, vegetables and herbs. 'Red Rubine' sprouts, 'Crystal Lemon' cucumber and the Japanese 'Black Trifele' tomato are just a few of the many delicious varieties uniquely available to home-growers.

Embrace new flavours: Every year, grow two things you have never eaten before. This rule keeps your mind as well as your taste buds lively and fresh. Salsify, a beautiful pale root that tastes of asparagus, artichoke and faintly of oysters, was my first off–roader and you'll not find a French restaurant worth its salt without it on the menu in season. I'm never without it in my garden now.

And so to the practicalities. Pairing your life with your wish list is the key to making life easy for yourself. Or not. It's up to you.

Choose your scale: Be ambitious about flavour and the quality of your food rather than the size of your plot. It is better to make a small success of a few pots and work up than fail with an acre and scale down. Anyone who tells you that growing food is too much work has simply chosen to grow at the wrong scale for them.

Balance your risks: There are many edibles that, once past seedling stage, virtually grow themselves and offer repeated harvests – courgettes, peas and beans, cut-and-come-again salad crops among them. They should be loved for their easy, inexpensive productivity.

At the other end of the scale are those plants, such as apricots, nectarines and melons, that need particular conditions, a good summer and/or a lot of attention.

Don't let this put you off – after all, main-crop potatoes and tomatoes are liable to blight and you'll see them in most allotments – but do balance the risks with some certainties.

Succession or gluts: With careful selection of varieties and care with sowing times of annual vegetables, it is easy to choose between gluts or a steadier harvest. You can eat home-grown apples for 12 months of the year or have them all ready in the same week to make into cider; rocket can be a year-round treat or a huge haul for making pesto. The choice is yours.

Consider more perennials: Almost all of the fruit and many of the herbs we grow are perennials, producing year after year. Their established root system gives them access to water and nutrients that are unavailable to most shallow rooting annuals, making them more resilient to adverse conditions, including drought. They also tend to be low-maintenance, without the continuous expense and work that goes with growing annuals each year. Asparagus, globe artichokes, sea kale and Jerusalem artichokes are among the many delicious perennial veg to consider.

Make it beautiful: If your garden or allotment is somewhere you are drawn to spend time reading, relaxing or anything but gardening, it is more likely to become a permanent fixture in your life. Whether regimented lines of cabbages please you, or you prefer a tepee of borlotti beans, the lazy habit of a flowering quince or the glorious tower of a Himalayan rhubarb, grow something beautiful.

Variety and natural companions: As well as giving you a more varied harvest, diversity is the best form of pest control. Growing a wide range of plants encourages beneficial insects into the garden to pollinate and predate on potential pests, promoting a more balanced ecology where little gets out of hand. Interplanting is also a great confuser. A big block of carrots is a party invitation to carrot fly, but interplant with spring onions and the sensory message is disguised.

Choose suppliers well: If your partner suggests going out to eat, I imagine you don't just dive into the nearest place that sells food. You'd consider the options, look in through a few windows and peruse the menus. Take similar care when choosing a supplier.

Don't buy your seeds and plants where you buy your paint: Find someone who specialises, online or in person. They can help you overcome many potential limitations. They will know, for example, about dwarf fruit and nut trees that grow little bigger than an umbrella, making a balcony a potential orchard.

Read their catalogues, examine the variety descriptions: These are menus. The plant takes a while to deliver the food, but the wait will be well worth it.

How to cope with drought conditions

Whether growing in pots or the ground, cover the soil. Plant closely where possible, mulch between and sow green manures in any large bare areas.

Nasturtiums are a perfect living mulch, covering the ground rapidly and retaining soil moisture while giving you delicious seeds, young leaves and flowers.

Install a drip irrigation system for containers and individual plants. They are cheap and easy to fit.

Create tiers where you can, growing plants that thrive in shade (for example, veg and herbs that tend to bolt) beneath taller plants.

Use grey water whenever possible.

Look for drought-resistant varieties. Water in the evening rather than the heat of the day to save on loss through transpiration and evaporation.

Consider plants at home in drier conditions, such as Mediterranean herbs.

Top 10 must-grows

Tomato 'Gardener's Delight'

Hugely popular and rightly so. A cherry variety, the small fruit don't need as much of a summer to ripen well. Hard to rival for flavour. Japanese 'Black Trifele' (medium) and 'Costoluto Fiorentino' (large) make an unbeatable trio.

Lettuce 'Reine de Glace'

I grow a lot of cut-and-come-again salad leaves and I'd never be without rocket, 'Green in Snow' and 'Green Oak Leaf', but for a hearting lettuce 'Reine de Glace' takes some beating. Crisp and tasty.

Asparagus 'Gijnlim'

A fantastic early, high-yielding variety producing thick stems of mid-green spears with purple tips.

Nasturtium 'Black Velvet'

A gorgeous dark-flowered variety. Small leaves for salad, larger leaves in risotto, pickle the seeds for a caper-like preserve and eat the incredible rocket honey-mustard-flavoured flowers in salads. An edible mulch, a companion plant and it self-seeds so you only need sow once.

Japanese wineberries

Delicious sweet/sharp, wine-flavoured berries, conveniently at their peak between summer and autumn raspberries.

Moroccan mint

If you have only one mint, let it be this variety. Makes the best mint tea, mint sauce and a fine apple mint Mojito.

Apple 'Veitches Perfection'

Excellent as a cooker or eater. Sweet and sharp in perfect balance, delicious straight from the tree yet keeps like a dream through the winter.

Chilli 'Apricot'

A fruity, aromatic habanero that's as mild as high street coffee. If you like chillies you'll love it and if you think you don't, try this one – it's the converter, I promise. Eat it whole and raw.

Potato 'Shetland Black'

Why grow potatoes you can buy in the shops when you can try something deliciously different? A fine early, floury variety which has a purple skin and white flesh with a distinctive purple ring around the inside of the tuber. A very good and unique flavour.

Dwarf quince 'Lezcovacz'

This is the quince to turn even a balcony into an orchard, as it grows to only 1.3m or so. Aromatic fruit in autumn, perfect for membrillo.

15 JULY 1989

The best ways with peas

By Fred Downham

Every season the largest area in my vegetable patch is taken up by peas. Why? First of all because they are my family's favourites. They are one of the easiest vegetables to freeze and they don't lose flavour, and if you are not sure of your guests' tastes, you can serve peas and be sure that even the children will like them.

On the other hand, peas are not the easiest vegetable to grow; they need relatively weed-free ground. Harvesting and podding them can be time-consuming, which is why I now grow many with edible pods.

You will get the best results from any pea if the soil contains large amounts of humus – if it was heavily manured for a previous crop. This will let it retain moisture in dry periods and drain freely if we get a lot of rain. They will also produce a larger crop if you apply fertiliser with the emphasis on phosphates and potash rather than nitrogen.

Nearly every seed catalogue lists many varieties. So which ones do you choose? The first decision to make is: when are you going to sow? If you want to sow in the autumn so that the plants over-winter and crop early the following season, you must select round-seeded varieties. The same applies if you sow in February or early March before the ground has had a chance to warm up properly. These are much hardier, but you lose out on flavour.

In my opinion, the best two varieties are 'Feltham First' and 'Douce Provence', the latter being the heaviest cropper. In most parts of the country the soil will be warm enough to sow wrinkled seeded varieties in April.

The next consideration is height; peas can grow as low as 15in or reach over 5ft, but however high they grow, they will need supporting. The shorter the plants, the less distance they need between the rows; but the more rows you have, the more seeds you will need. At the end of the season, from a given area, the weight of crop from short or tall varieties will be almost identical. Taller varieties crop over a slightly longer period.

Looking along a row of peas, you can very easily be misled about the weight of actual peas you will be harvesting. There may be plenty of large, fat pods to gather, but what is inside them? For instance, my rows of peas are 22ft long, and from the variety 'Early Onward' I harvested just under 25lbs. Yet when podded there was only 9lb 2oz of only moderately flavoursome peas – 37 per cent of peas to pod. But 'Titania' produced a return of 11lbs of peas from 2lbs 3oz with their pods – just over 50 per cent, and these tasted and looked slightly better than Onward.

One pea that is used in our house for special occasions only is 'Waverex' – a petit pois. They don't produce a very large crop – just 7lbs 2oz from 13lbs 2oz. The pods are only 6cm long and it is a fiddly job podding them. But they are delicious so they are well worth the effort.

To conduct such trials you must have a variety to use as a control, and every year I grow 'Hurst Green Shaft' for this. It grows to 2–3ft, produces large, well-filled pods containing an average of nine bright green peas which, raw or cooked, fresh or from the freezer, beat any others for taste. It does not come out on top for weight, but I have grown it in my present garden for the past 10 years and, whatever the weather, it has never let me down.

Among the edible podded varieties, my favourite is Sugar Snap. Last year, one row yielded over 24lbs, and all they lost in topping and tailing was a couple of pounds. They are 6ft tall, but produce pods only on the top half; remember to pick them at least twice a week. Do this, cook them for about a minute, drain, toss in butter and black pepper, and I'm sure you will want to grow more next year. My favourites are:

'Feltham First': from Dobies, Marshalls, Mr Fothergill's, Suttons, Thompson & Morgan, Unwins

'Douce Provence': Marshalls, Mr Fothergill's

'Early Onward': Dobies, Marshalls, Suttons, Unwins

'Titania': Dobies, Thompson & Morgan. Waverex available from Marshalls, Mr Fothergill's, Suttons, Thompson & Morgan, Unwins

'Hurst Green Shaft': Dobies, Marshalls, Mr Fothergill's, Suttons, Thompson & Morgan, Unwins

'Sugar Snap': Dobies, Marshalls, Mr Fothergill's, Suttons, Thompson & Morgan, Unwins

10 JULY 2010

Foraging on the Lizard

By Sarah Raven

I am used to tramping across a Cretan hillside and finding wild plants that I grow in my garden, but it's fantastic to be able to do the same in the British Isles. Last weekend I went on a botanising walk round the Lizard Peninsula in Cornwall, from Mullion round Predannack and Vellan Head and on round to Kynance Cove. The sea was turquoise, topped with surf, and I found exciting plants in such abundance that it was hard to believe I was not in the plant-rich paradises of the east of Turkey or the Ionian islands of Greece.

Set back from the cliffs you come across a succession of flat plateaux, rocky areas smaller than an average room, each one carpeted with a flower mosaic – tormentil, milkwort, eyebright, centuary, sheep's bit, lady's bedstraw and the delicate burnet rose, already over, but covered in brilliant red galls. There are full, rounded thyme cushions, too, old ant hills, with the extra height and drainage to enable the thyme to thrive, creating brilliant purple pouffes scattered across the moor.

High on my list of exciting finds was wild asparagus, so rare that this is on the endangered plant list, but once you get your eye in you can spot at least one plant every 10th pace. Some are grazed right down, compact mini fir trees, poking out horizontally from the serpentine rocks, but others are more luxurious and run down the boulders like delicate ferny fabric. Cheek by jowl, this was often growing with the lesser meadow rue, not as statuesque and fluffy as its cousin, common meadow rue, but with leaves highly cut and delicate.

You shouldn't even think about picking wild asparagus. We need it to become more abundant, not less, but there are two other sea-cliff plants here in vast abundance that won't be harmed by the odd bit of foraging. Sea beet (also called sea spinach, *Beta vulgaris subsp. maritima*) is the first and you'll find this all over the cliffs and seashore around the British coast. I like the de-stemmed baby leaves of this raw, thrown into a salad with any other quite chunky and strong-tasting leaves. It makes excellent soup and you can also try it in a salad with watercress and purslane topped with a strong blue cheese.

Also here on almost every stretch of cliff and common all over the British coast is rock samphire, *Crithmum maritimum*. This is not related to what most of us call samphire – glasswort (*Salicornia europaea*) – the soft fleshy, mini fir tree plant that covers our coastal mud flats, which you can buy in the fishmonger at this time of year (see recipes).

Rock samphire is an evergreen sea-cliff plant with a herby, slightly lemony flavour, which was hugely popular as a brined and then pickled vegetable in the 16th and 17th centuries. This is at its most tender and delicious before it flowers and I saw lots on my walk in pristine harvesting condition, covered with new growth. Pick this to add to salads, or pickle it in a dill-rich pickle mix, delicious served with a plate of cold meat, or simply served – instead of chutney – with bread and cheese.

In the hollows of cliff-top moorland, where the ground remains slightly damp, there were huge colonies – many hundreds – of Heath Spotted orchid. Some of these had telltale round, black splotches covering their leaves, with others just plain green, every flower a slightly different shade of pale pink blanching to almost white, with their frilly flowers lightly spotted, too.

Walking on a bit, you come across mini fields, short grazed pastures with more pink splats of colour, a distinct pink dish surrounded by the bright green of short, sheep-grazed grass. These dense patches appear, often just one alone, a single sprawling plant of bog pimpernel. You must lie down on your stomach to fully appreciate this relative of the common roadside weed, Scarlet Pimpernel. Each of its small cupped flowers has delicate, darker pink veining, guiding the insects into the centre of the flower and – tiny as it is – this flower is exquisite.

There are breaks in the precipice where the cliff has collapsed and you can climb down over the boulder-strewn slopes. About a mile short of Kynance there was one of these collapses, on what felt like the outermost promontory that appeared lusher than the rest. It was swathed in a river of pink and purple pom-poms, trickling from one section of cliff crevice to a flat section below and then cascading almost into the sea. I know that the cliff tops are a carpet of thrift and kidney vetch in May and assumed that it was thrift until I saw the leaves. These are crinkled, long and thin, but round in cross-section – wild chives.

This is a very rare plant but here on the Lizard, it's there by the thousand, pink globes, purple ones and others almost white, which I'm sure could be snapped up and turned into a desirable herb garden plant. Eat them or not, the plants and flowers on the Lizard are as good as any you can ever hope to see.

23 MAY 1988

Experimental vegetable gardening

By Joy Larkcom

Is there such a thing as avant garde in vegetable growing? I think there is, and that the kitchen garden or vegetable plot of the avant gardener reflects the drift of current culinary, scientific and social ideas, converting them into something down to earth … and edible.

So this is what I would expect to find in the avant gardener's kitchen garden today.

First, there would be lots of salad plants, for salads epitomise modern notions of healthy eating. There would be crisp and crunchy lettuces like 'Little Gem', along with pretty red-leaved lettuces like the old French variety 'Marvel of Four Seasons' and the exquisite culled and frilled 'Red Lollo', a new Italian variety – perhaps coupled with its equally lovely stablemate 'Green Lollo'.

Maybe there'd be a border of the red and green Salad Bowl lettuces. Forming loose heads of oak-shaped leaves, these don't run to seed, so provide pickings over a long season – a valuable quality for the time-pressed gardener of the 20th century.

Coloured lettuce and the stunning Italian red chicory are now almost commonplace in chic restaurants and good supermarkets, but the avant gardener would have several salad plants still unknown to the general public. I'm thinking of the succulent leaved summer purslane and the spicy salad rocket – both popular in the Mediterranean. In winter and spring, there's the dainty round-leaved, mild-flavoured winter purslane or claytonia, known as miner's lettuce or spring beauty in the United States, where it originated, as it was such a health-giving standby for the miners in spring.

Some salad plants in this progressive garden would undoubtedly be growing in attractive little broadcast patches for cut-and-come-again treatment. Possibilities include salad cress, salad rape, perhaps Chinese pak choi, curly endive, spinach and old-fashioned varieties of 'cutting' lettuce, as well as the purslane, claytonia and rocket already mentioned.

These closely grown crops would be cut when the young leaves were no more than 2 or 3in high, at their most nutritious, and tastiest, stage. Moreover, as the seedlings normally re-sprout after cutting, each patch would be cut two or three times, giving wonderful returns in small places.

This old gardening technique was employed in the past to force 'spring saladings' in hot beds and frames for the tables of the gentry. It has found a new niche in the space-starved modern garden.

Avant gardeners scour seed catalogues in search of varieties of vegetables with real flavour. So they would have discovered the super-sweet varieties of sweet corn, such as 'Candle' and 'Extra Early Sweet', which, unlike the traditional varieties, retain their sweetness after picking. But they must be grown apart from the traditional types, or the sweet characteristic will be lost by cross-pollination.

The dwarf French beans should be all varieties with exceptional flavour – purple-podded varieties, the gold wax pods, or the fine, sometimes speckled 'filet' varieties such as 'Aramis'.

There would be several interesting varieties in the pea patch and these would certainly include some mangetout or sugar peas. These are the flat, edible-podded peas – expensive to buy but easy to grow and with a lovely flavour. A new type of mangetout is the American-bred 'Sugar Snap': it combines sweetness with a crunchy texture and, like all the mangetouts, is delicious sliced into salads or lightly cooked.

Another intriguing novelty is the semi-leafless pea, in which most of the leaves have become 'modified' into tendrils. Developed commercially to facilitate the combine harvesting of dry peas, they are a boon to gardeners as they are almost self-supporting. There could even be purple-podded peas in this adventurous garden. They are a tall old variety with striking purple pods though, sadly, the peas are green.

The brassica bed would be interesting, too. Incidentally, you would be unlikely to find a row of anything in the avant gardener's kitchen garden. The owners would have switched to the (old-fashioned) bed system, laying out the garden in 3 or 4ft-wide beds, with plants grown at equidistant spacing in the beds. But I digress. Back to the brassicas.

If space was at a premium, as it tends to be, the avant gardener would spurn slow-growing cabbages and cauliflower and grow instead fast maturing, space-saving brassicas such as 'Sprouting Calabrese' (grown about 10in apart and ready in less than four months). Pride of place should go to the lime-green superbly flavoured variety Romanesco. Another worth trying is the recently introduced Texsel greens, developed from an Ethiopian oil-seed plant. Highly nutritious, it has an excellent, slightly spinachy flavour, and can be grown as a seedling salad crop or like spring greens. Also rated for its nutritional qualities, and also quick growing, is kohlrabi.

I would hope, too, as this is one of my obsessions, that there would be some exciting oriental greens in the garden – perhaps the serrated-leaved Japanese mustard mizuna or the very hardy, mild-flavoured spinach mustard tendergreen, both providing generous pickings over a long season, including autumn, much of winter and spring.

Adventurous vegetable growing and adventurous cooking go hand in hand and the vogue for ethnic cooking – Chinese, Indian and Middle Eastern – would be reflected in the chilli peppers growing in a warm spot or in the greenhouse. In the well-stocked herb garden a few exotics would be found, such as coriander, dill and perhaps the pretty Chinese or garlic chives. Their flat grass-like leaves have a refreshing, subtle, part-onion, part-garlic flavour, and in summer they produce beautiful, white, starry flowers, which can be used for flavouring. Which brings me to the revival of another lost art – the use of flowers in cookery. Surely this garden would be colourful with nasturtiums, old-fashioned pot marigolds, borage – its sweet, clear blue flowers can be sprinkled on salad or entombed dramatically in ice cubes – and more besides.

Common chives would be left to flower; the purple flowerets also look dramatic in salads or in omelettes.

Culinary flowers could give our avant gardener an excuse for embracing another old gardening concept which is returning to fashion – growing flowers and vegetables together, sweeping away the demarcation lines. I should not be in the least surprised to find climbing runner beans, probably the lonely old apple-blossoms variety 'Painted Lady', romping over the garden pergola. And the recently revived dwarf varieties of runner – 'Hammond's Dwarf', 'Pickwick' and 'Gulliver' – would be there too, glowing in the midst of flower beds far prettier than a patch of salvias and quietly nurturing a welcome crop of beans.

23 APRIL 2006

Asparagus tips

By Elspeth Thompson

O ne of the many joys of having a larger garden in the country at this time of year is the possibility of establishing an asparagus bed. It must be satisfying to the point of smugness to step into the garden and return with a trug-full of fresh, tender spears to steam up and eat straight away. Like sweet corn and new potatoes, asparagus tastes heaps better when eaten within an hour of cutting. I have occasionally experienced this, at the houses of friends with the luck to inherit or foresight to establish their own asparagus beds, but the uniquely rich taste made me vow to grow it one day. Asparagus is expensive, even in season, and the price of organically grown spears is astronomical, should you manage to find any. It also needs little attention, once established, to provide a splendid seasonal treat.

So why aren't we all growing it? One reason is the space required. You would need around 30 crowns (or roots) to be able to pick a reasonable bundle of spears at any one time, spaced at least 18in apart. As asparagus is traditionally grown in 4ft-wide beds, that would mean a pretty large patch permanently dedicated to a crop that will yield for only a few weeks every year. I've heard about people growing asparagus in old bathtubs, but have yet to see the results.

Another deterrent is the agonising gap between planting and picking. It's an average of three years before you'll get any sizeable harvest, and though the wait can be cut by purchasing older crowns (those on sale are usually between one and three years old), these are much more tricky to establish. With one-year crowns, the advice tends to be not to cut at all in the first year, and only a very few spears in the second. In this hell-for-leather, have-it-all-now age we live in, few have the patience to wait.

The third reason is the belief that asparagus is hard to grow. Well, it is and it isn't. The difficulty lies in creating the correct growing conditions. Get this right, and the rest should be a doddle. The books are filled with daunting diagrams showing cross-sections of beds, and advise incorporating everything from rubble, grit, leafmould, bonfire ash, sand and crushed cockle shells to improve drainage – asparagus will not tolerate water-logging, but neither does it like getting dry.

The simplest option is a well-dug bed with plenty of organic matter, sand or grit worked in, and a shallow ridge down its length over which the spidery roots of the crowns can be draped. A 4ft-wide bed will take two rows, so dig out a pair of trenches, 12in wide and 18in deep, along each bed, and hump up a shallow ridge down the middle. The crowns should be 18in apart and 4in beneath the surface when filled in, and will need to be watered throughout the first year. From then on, the only care needed is to keep the patch clear of weeds and mulch with well-rotted compost or manure in late winter. The real difficulty will be restraining yourself from cropping that first and second year.

The ideal planting time for asparagus crowns is supposed to be March or early April, but given the cold spring, you can get away with it now. Indeed, there is an argument for later planting, as the crowns are more prone to rot in damp cold soil.

Harvest may seem aeons away as you sow the seed in 6in pots, but it will be here before you know it.

Grow your own and get a life

By Mark Diacono

Life is quite busy enough without creating things to do. There is a certain obsessive-compulsive trait among some gardeners that drives them to seek needy plants. Rather than enjoy summer hours relaxing in the sun, sufferers follow an elaborate timetable of tasks in the hope of coaxing a reluctant harvest from some unwilling plant or other.

Not only that, their partners are asked to look on in wonder in late summer as the resulting gigantic gourd or single polished lemon is placed before them. In case you're wondering, the correct response is to marvel at the horticultural genius that delivered this fine specimen. Or divorce.

I'm not immune to growing the odd high-maintenance plant, but happily my tendency to sloth is stronger, so I fill most of my garden with food that almost grows itself.

If you are keen to grow some of what you eat, but want to keep the focus on enjoying the rewards rather than hard labour, then you need plants that produce fairly quickly, harvest repeatedly and require little of your time while they do it. Allow me to suggest a few.

A new leaf

Kai lan is not a vegetable familiar to everyone, but if I have anything to do with it, it soon will be. In the time it takes to grow just one decent cauliflower, you'll have had many, many lunches off your kai lan. Steamed or stir-fried, it is delicious. In flavour and appearance it resembles the child asparagus might have had if it got together with sprouting broccoli – but you don't have the long wait to harvest as you do with asparagus or broccoli.

The green spears grow about 30in, turning leafy and developing flower heads within two months or so. Every part is edible, even the flowers. Once a root system has established you can slice off whatever parts take your fancy, leaving stumps of 3in or so to grow back. Month after month you can cut off delicious harvests, and although it will die down in the cold, kai lan will survive all but the coldest winters to carry on producing for years.

Know your beans

Borlotti beans taste as good as they look. These climbing beans clamber over anything you grow them against, producing speckled red pods that look as if they were styled by Cath Kidston.

The beans are deliciously nutty and creamy and you get three chances to enjoy them: fresh from the pod in the height of summer they make a fabulous hummus, pasta sauce or the centrepiece of summer soups such as ribollita; any you don't use can be dried and added to winter soups and stews; and any that you haven't eaten by next spring can be sown to give you next year's crop.

Any of the peas and beans family will be similarly productive – the more you pick, the more they'll produce – so each seed will give you many meals.

Squash in

Courgettes have a reputation for being almost tediously productive. This may be largely down to another compulsive disorder afflicting some gardeners: they open a packet of seeds and they have to sow them all. When the dozen or so seeds germinate, we plant them out and then blame the courgette when we are overloaded with produce.

Sow just five seeds for a family of four: assume one won't germinate, one is taken by the slugs and you'll have three plants to harvest from.

The secret to getting the best from courgettes is to pick them small and flavoursome – let the fruit grow larger than a cigar and not only does the flavour decline but your plants become less productive.

Even if you can't eat them when they're cigar-sized, pick them anyway and compost them – focus on keeping the plant perfectly productive rather than guiltily trying to devour each fruit it produces.

Three Sisters planting

If you fancy being more adventurous, with the prospect of even easier rewards, you can combine borlottis and courgettes with sweet corn. In perhaps the most satisfying example of companion planting, this threesome works in harmony when sown together.

The sweet corn provides the scaffold for the bean to clamber through in its search for light and heat, while the courgette leaves spread below, cooling the roots of the other two and helping retain soil moisture.

The bean does as all legumes do – takes nitrogen from the air and makes it available in the soil via nodules in its roots. It uses some of this nutrient to feed itself, leaving any excess for the sweetcorn and courgette, which grow stronger as a result. Placing the three together allows each to thrive.

This American Indian interplanting is known as the Three Sisters, and it works equally well with squash, melons or cucumbers instead of courgettes and any pea or bean in place of the borlottis.

A twist on this is the crafty interplanting of marigolds between rows to deter white fly, and nasturtiums placed as a sacrificial plant near your brassicas: cabbage white caterpillars much prefer them. The flowers of each look great in salads, too.

Spice things up

Chillies can be exceptionally tasty grown on a windowsill, but they are very particular, especially in the early stages. You can sidestep a lot of grief by ordering seedlings from a specialist grower and potting them up when they are delivered in May.

'Fairy Lights', 'Rooster Spur', 'Coffee Bean' and 'Turtle Claw' are fantastic varieties for growing in this way, each throwing out many chillies through the second half of summer and beyond.

If all this still sounds tiring, you can make things even easier by ordering an instant vegetable garden delivered as seedlings. Rocket Gardens will supply a complete veg patch in a box, or try Organic Plants, where you can take a more pick-and-mix approach. The salad mixes are particularly useful.

Focusing on the generous easy winners means you get plenty of reward for your time and money and leaves your evenings and weekends free for whatever else takes your fancy.

Idler's timetable

February
- Order chilli and other seedlings

March
- Start kai lan in modules or Jiffy 7s, or for an easier life, sow direct, from the beginning of March or until September.
- Sow borlotti beans, peas and French beans (any time between now and midsummer) in root trainers or card toilet roll inners to give the roots plenty of room to stretch out as they develop. And/or sow direct.

- Sow cut-and-come-again salad leaves direct and/or plant out seedlings.

April

- Sow and/or plant out a second patch of cut-and-come-again leaves so that one is always productive while the other is recovering.
- Sow sweet corn and courgettes into small pots on your windowsill.
- Plant out kai lan.
- Once the borlotti roots fill the trainer or toilet roll and the top growth has exceeded 6in or so, plant them in the garden.

May

- Take delivery of chilli seedings and pot them up immediately to grow on your sunniest windowsill or patio.
- Plant out sweet corn when seedlings are 3in tall.
- Harvest cut-and-come-again leaves and kai lan.

June

- Harvest cut-and-come-again leaves, kai lan and courgette flowers.

July

- Harvest cut-and-come-again leaves, kai lan, courgettes and (depending on variety) the first chillies and sweet corn.
- Sow/plant more cut-and-come-again leaves.

Supersize that pumpkin

By Toby Buckland

In the run-up to a competition, professional athletes pay attention to the 'onepercenters' – their diet, rest and time spent in the sun – small things, but together they make a big difference to performance. And so it is when growing a prize pumpkin.

If you sow the seed of a variety bred to be big, such as 'Atlantic Giant', in the rich soil next to the compost heap, chances are you'll have a 3 stone gourd by autumn. But watch those 'one-percenters' and you can achieve a 20 stone prize-winner the size of Cinderella's carriage.

The groundwork for a big pumpkin starts in February with a planting hole lavished with a minimum of one ton of well-rotted horse manure and the sourcing of 'thoroughbred' seed from the internet. The best seed will cost from £5–£50 a pop but, if you start with the progeny of a former champion, you're more likely to top the podium come harvest time.

During March, sow seed in a pot, as you would a courgette, in the warmth of the greenhouse and it'll be up and ready to plant atop the settled manure-rich midden when the risk of frost has passed.

As the plant grows, remove all but one pumpkin fruit so all the energy gathered by the leaves is focused on the development of one superfruit.

If two are the same size, choose the one that's roughly 10ft from the roots and growing from a main stem, not a side shoot.

On a large plant, culling all the pumpkins requires almost daily attention. Early in the year, the blowsy yellow female flowers – you can spot them by the marble-sized bulge at their base – are quick to set and can grow to tennis-ball size in a day.

I find the best tool for this job is a telescopic tree pruner – basically a pair of secateurs on a retractable 10ft pole – that allows me to pick off rival fruits from a distance without trampling the stems.

I must say, though, that cutting pumpkins before their prime does go against the grain. The upside is they make for far better eating – sliced, oiled, salted and baked with garlic – than when they're big and as tasty as an overripe cucumber.

When your chosen pumpkin reaches the size of a football, set the fruit on a 4in bed of straw to protect the skin from stones in the soil and spread the pumpkin's weight as it swells. Position so that the pumpkin reclines with the stalk and the stem to one side, then carefully bend the stem into a 'U' shape to give the pumpkin as much growth space as possible. Moving a pumpkin is a delicate operation, particularly while it is in fast growth: the skin is so thin a fingernail will cause sap to bleed from the wound.

If this happens – or worse, a bird pecks your prize-winner – sprinkle with fungicidal sulphur dust to cauterise the cut and prevent infection from entering.

Water is by far the most important influence on a potential prize-winner, accounting for a fluctuating 90 per cent of the weight. During dry weather, the leaves draw moisture out from the fruit to keep growing, which reduces the size of the pumpkin.

So keeping the roots hydrated is key. Do this with a hose or water butt set to drip alongside where the main stem meets the soil, or, better still, with soaker-hose laid in a spiral beneath the leaves and plumbed to the garden tap.

With the hose left to run for an hour every day – more if the weather is hot – the pumpkin will quickly start to plump up. During the most vigorous growth phase, a champion can bulk up 24lb a day. Yours might not gain weight this quickly, but the difference in growth from day to day will almost certainly be noticeable.

When watering, avoid wetting the foliage – this invariably leads to an attack of powdery mildew fungus that appears as a talclike white coating on the leaves. Although the fungus won't spread to the fruit, it curbs the capacity of affected leaves to photosynthesise, thereby reducing the growth of the pumpkin. Removing badly affected leaves and pruning side shoots that are crowded together and encroaching on your pumpkin will help to reduce this, as will feeding.

Early in the year, nitrogen-rich pelleted chicken manure is good for encouraging fast, leafy growth but when the days shorten, it's time to switch to high-potash feeds to help fruit development.

I use liquid tomato fertiliser – a can every other day – as it is quickly taken up by the plant and has a balance of major nutrients that keeps the leaves looking lush, along with a weekly dose of dilute seaweed. Packed with micronutrients, the seaweed helps thicken up the leaf cuticles, reducing the risk of powdery mildew. It also gives tired pumpkin plants a second wind and encourages them back into growth.

Artificial feeding will only take your pumpkin so far. For a place on the podium, it needs to feed from the soil. Pumpkins root along the ground at the intersections or nodes where the stems and side shoots join. Cover with garden compost enriched with bone meal and mycorrhizae (e.g. Rootgrow).

The warmth and length of the summer has a big effect on the size of your fruit. Shade the skin with a screen during the day and keep it warm at night – it's after dark that a pumpkin grows fastest. A polytunnel over the top is ideal, but if this is too high a price for pumpkin glory, second best are large, water-filled bottles placed around the fruit. These capture the warmth of the sun during the day and release it at night.

Finally, when you harvest your prize-winner and take it to be weighed, sever it from the plant with a 2ft 'T' piece of stem and keep the ends in water like a cut flower, snipping them off moments before your contender is weighed.

Good luck! But fingers crossed it'll be far too heavy to lift.

SITE SEIZED TO GROW FOOD

By Sunday Telegraph Reporter

A group of demonstrators occupied a derelict site in London yesterday to prepare it for crop-growing. The Friends of the Earth believe that Britain is 'acutely vulnerable to food shortages' and should grow more of its own food.

About 30 volunteers took over the site, which is opposite the Old Vic Theatre, Waterloo, and has been vacant since the Second World War. It is owned by the Greater London Council.

The Friends of the Earth claim there are 20,000 acres of derelict land in London, alone, which could yield 200,000 tons of potatoes. A report by the group says dogs and cats eat enough to provide most of the protein needs of 700,000 people.

THE BAREFOOT TRAIL TO ROTHERHITHE

By Clare Dover

A deserted area of London's dockland in and around the Surrey Docks, Rotherhithe, has become a landmark on the hippie trail.

The barefoot trail leads down Rotherhithe Street, past derelict warehouses, and areas of wasteland which have been sealed off with corrugated iron and barbed wire, where the only sign of life is the yellow flowers of the ragwort weed.

It ends in an enormous expanse of waste ground where polythene bag tents have been slung from makeshift frames.

It is called the 'people's habitat – a festival of alternative living', and will be 'open' to visitors until Sunday.

Thronging with people wearing shawls and headbands, and scruffy barefoot children playing in the dust, it could have been a scene from a shantytown in the Indian sub-continent. But all the faces were white.

The visitors took off their shoes at Rotherhithe Tube station. There were not many takers for the 'alternative transport' – roller skates on hire for 10p a pair.

Some of the wasteland is being turned into allotments in a struggle in which nature seems to be winning. In the unhealthy, stony soil, only the cabbages seem able to cope and some of the gardeners have resorted to buying grow-bags to bring on their tomatoes.

In an under-developed country, where there is no alternative to scratching an existence from unyielding soil, one can see the point. In Rotherhithe, one feels that the pressures are unreal since the social security office is nearby.

A 'farm' run by Miss Hilary Peters, a freelance gardener, on a filled-in piece of dockland lent to her on a temporary basis by the Port of London Authority, appears to be working.

Miss Peters has 10 goats, two donkeys, 100 hens, 30 ducks and four geese, which are fed on the proceeds from their produce, and gifts of cabbage leaves, lettuce stalks and stale bread brought by the inhabitants of the nearby council flats.

17.

'All now rather wild, but you could make it lovely'

Some Notable Gardens Described

A garden to vie with the best of them

By Fred Whitsey

S poken in the company of knowing gardeners, Crathes is one of these names that produce a mixture of awe and affection reserved for only the greatest of gardens. There may be a castle there dating back to the 16th century with painted ceilings, a ghost and a hunting horn given by Robert the Bruce, but it is Crathes' garden that brings it fame. Other Scottish gardens reach their finest moments in spring. Crathes waits until summer for its greatest days of glory, and then it is resplendent.

This is not because it is filled with highly coloured bedding plants for those weeks of excitement. Some of its effect is due to contrived colour groupings but these have a resourcefulness which other gardens can rival.

The description you read of the layout of Crathes' garden is misleading in its simplicity. The three-and-a-half-acre walled garden, once the castle's kitchen garden, is certainly divided into a series of pleasing rectangles, each with a planting scheme of its own and divided by straight paths.

But this description misses the essence of the place. It offers no linking of the sense of mystery you get as you wander around, the surprises that make you turn this way or that, only to keep retracing your steps.

There are long vistas between the sections that invite you to follow them. Never, though, can you see one section from another. The trees and shrubs planted in the beds artfully conceal and divide, while you are constantly diverted by some fresh delight at your feet and quickly you look for the label to find its name. Soon, you are lost in enchantment.

The paths by which you entered gave you the first acquaintance with the garden's colour scheme. The flowers on either side are all white but they are seen against a background of the purple-leaved plum grown as twin hedges. It is focused on the largest Portugal laurel tree you are ever likely to see, which marks a point where five paths join, all of them equally inviting.

Take one of them and you find yourself in a little garden where all the leaves are golden. You notice the feathery elder, the yellow-fruited guelder rose, the yellow climbing hop and many other shrubs with leaves of yellow. Very quickly, you find yourself surrounded by red flowers and purple foliage. The effect is achieved with such simple plants as potentilla 'Red Ace', buddleia 'Royal Red', and the purple-leaved rhubarb.

Following one path or another, you are astonished by the variety of plants; yet it does not seem like a mere collection, for nothing is allowed to stray out of its appointed place in a colour scheme. By now you have made your way to the greenhouses where geraniums grow on the walls like climbers and where they house many of the old Malmaison carnations, renowned for their powerful scent.

Nearby is a border filled with tender plants, like the osteospernums, gazanias and the marguerites in the colour forms that have emerged in recent years. By now your notebook is filling up fast with names. It is a relief to come across yew hedges of a vastness that could indicate great age.

Next you find yourself in an area where the colour theme has changed to blue. Again, close to the walls, you notice many that insist on such shelter, like the Californian carpentaria, the grey-leaved honeysuckle and the ruby-flowered *Buddleia colvillei*.

How did it come about, this treasure house of plants set out with so artistic an eye? Until 1952, when the castle and its grounds were handed over to the National Trust for Scotland, the Burnett family had lived there for nearly 400 years. The 13th baronet inherited in 1926 and, with his wife, set about gardening with passionate seriousness. Taking her inspiration from the books of Gertrude Jekyll, Lady Burnett planted as her husband's lady ancestors would have embroidered. Now her work is continued by the present head gardener, David McLean, who, with a staff of six, plants in the same exuberant manner.

'I want people to see very little bare soil,' he said. When I was there, you could see only huge displays of plants set out with an artist's hand.

14 JANUARY 2006

Why Great Dixter must never be a museum

By Christopher Lloyd

Dixter is where I was born, in 1921, and where I was brought up. It has been a family home for the best part of a century. Each generation has left its mark. My father bought it in 1910 and he employed Mr (as he then was) Edwin Lutyens to make the necessary additions and alterations.

A large part of the correspondence between Lloyd and Lutyens has been preserved. My father, born in 1867, was a colour printer in Blackfriars and also owned a bleaching factory in Lancashire. He sold his business to his brother Robin, and came to live with Daisy, his wife, at Dixter, choosing the location largely because it was close to Rye, near to which there is a golf course, where my father played at weekends.

Weekends didn't start, in those days, until midday on Saturday. My father wanted a home within striking distance of his golf. He and my mother had already started a family in London. My eldest brother (12 years older than myself) was born in 1909.

I am the youngest and only survivor of six siblings, five boys, one girl. My father's contribution to Dixter largely centred on design and architecture (which were my weakest attributes; I couldn't draw at all). I was only 12 when he died but he was very understanding and saw where my strengths lay. He would take me to Rye golf course where he introduced me to Arnold the greenkeeper and got me interested in different kinds of grasses, in the small nursery for them that they kept there.

My mother was a passionate, hands-on gardener and I was the only member of the family who followed her in that respect. I would 'help' her when she was sowing seeds, pricking out and the like. She had a great capacity for concentration and was always counting, as I do, to help the job along. After pricking a box out, she would tap it on the side, which was the signal for me to remove it.

Our Sunk Garden was originally a flat area, but after the First World War, my father said to my mother, 'Now let us play,' and he designed this feature with an octagonal pool, with two opposite sides longer than the other six. I mention this because the English garden in Chicago has imitated it but has made a regular octagon, which is less interesting, I think.

Ours was otherwise very regular, but when the garden fell into my care, in the 1950s, I allowed the outlines to become blurred, chiefly by self-sowing plants, such as centaury and bird's foot trefoil. Fergus Garrett, my head gardener, considers that this has made it a much more intimate garden. People stand in it and say, 'If I could have one bit of your garden, it would be this'.

Fergus says that the mark I have left is not just on the garden but also on the people I have been with in it, including himself. I think it is true that I did inspire him at an important stage in his life. Now it works even more strongly in the opposite direction. He has been my head gardener for 15 years or so and he takes the lead. But we still work as a partnership and discuss every proposed change, in situ. Ideas come to both of us as we talk, and this is the way a partnership should be – that is, reciprocal. My mind works slowly, now, but Fergie always wants to include me, never wants to hog it, although he is wonderful at taking responsibility. I'm lucky to have a very supportive and enthusiastic team of helpers who identify with Dixter in just the way that I should wish. They all contribute to creating a family atmosphere.

I think I may say that the garden is dynamic. It changes, but not for the sake of change. Ideas come to us, so we try them out. Fergus is an amazing proselytiser. He believes in what we are doing and spreads the word, in this country and in the US.

The number of visitors bears witness to his success. He can grip an audience right from the start, but he is totally unselfish. As long as he is at the helm, I have no fears for Dixter. He is an incredibly hard worker.

The future is impossible to predict but one can make certain provisions. I don't want the place to become a museum but it always wants to be respected and every generation must play its role. The garden is sure to change. It has changed a lot in my time and so has the house. That's fine, so long as it is appreciated as it deserves.

The practicalities of securing Dixter's future are complicated but we have formed a trust – the Great Dixter Charitable Trust – which will take over.

Dixter will change but it will go on. If it always remains loved and retains its own identity, everything else will fall into place.

The Great Dixter Charitable Trust needs to buy the 60 per cent of the estate that I do not own. To achieve this we are calling on our friends and everyone who knows us to help.

30 JUNE 2001

The Barbara Hepworth Sculpture Garden

By Vivian Russell

The Barbara Hepworth Sculpture Garden in St Ives has at last won a much-deserved place on the English Heritage register of parks and gardens of special historic interest.

'I often get up in the night, if there's a full moon,' said Barbara Hepworth in a television documentary made in the 1960s. 'I like to go into the garden and see what kind of new shadows and new forms are revealed in a new light.' In the footage, she is easy to spot in the darkness, wearing a coat patterned with striking black and white diamonds, moving among her monolithic sculptures like an exotic moth drawn to an irresistible flame.

There is nothing in this calm, green oasis of a garden, with its cool white walls, that hints at the 'intense passion' which Hepworth said fuelled her art. She was inspired – 'fired off', she said – by Egyptian art at the age of seven. This compulsion to sculpt was the flame by which she lived, and it was in a fire that she died, 26 years ago.

As a child, she 'loved dancing, music, drawing, painting, and the gorgeous smell of paint'. She absorbed the contours of her native Yorkshire, travelling in her father's car. 'The hills were sculptures, the roads defined form,' she wrote later. 'All my early memories are of forms, shapes, textures. Perhaps what one wants to say is formed in childhood and the rest of one's life is spent in trying to say it.'

These themes were expressed in every piece she carved, and they recur in the garden she made at Trewyn Studio, St Ives, which she bought at the age of 46. It was only then, in 1949, that she spoke of 'putting down roots'.

Before coming to Cornwall, she had lived in London, with her husband Ben Nicholson and their four children, three of them born as triplets. 'My studio was a jumble of children, rocks, sculptures, trees, importunate flowers and washing,' she recalled. The family fled London in 1939, and after four months of living with friends, they moved to a house overlooking Carbis Bay, next to St Ives. 'The day was filled with running a nursery school, double cropping a tiny garden for food, and trying to feed and protect the children. We were picking our salads in the hedgerows and mushrooms in the fields.'

One of the main reasons for buying Trewyn Studio was that it had a garden in which she could show and sell her sculpture, explains Sir Alan Bowness, her friend, son-in-law and executor, and a former director of the Tate Gallery. The studio came with about a third of an acre of land which rose steeply behind a 6m retaining wall in the middle of St Ives. It had been divided from the much larger garden of Trewyn House, which stood further up the hill, and had a few mature trees, a little pool and a small formal rose garden.

Here, Hepworth could carve in the open air, even in winter, and also connect with the community, the chuch, the sea and the landscape – all seminal influences for her work. It was her first real garden, and she called on the help of her dear friend, the neglected but accomplished composer Priaulx Rainier, whose violin concerto was commissioned by Yehudi Menuhin. Rainier was a keen gardener with a small, steep, wild garden which also overlooked St Ives.

'They planned and planted the garden together as a setting for the sculpture,' recalls Bowness. 'Priaulx would spend the morning composing and then come and work in the garden in the afternoon.

'There were always roses, planted near the house, but Barbara didn't like herbaceous plants. She liked the shapes of leaves, but she wasn't particularly interested in flowers – although people would bring her bouquets, which she liked.'

The two women designed a series of terraces, with paths curving around large, informal planting areas in geometric shapes. 'Enclosure' was a key theme in Hepworth's work – the inner and outer world; a nut in its shell; a child in the womb – and to evoke this sense of refuge, she created a protective canopy of trees and shrubs.

She planted flowering cherries, Dawn redwood and *Magnolia grandiflora*. Bowness remembers the day she planted the gingko. 'It is one of the oldest trees in existence,' she told him, 'and I want one in my garden.'

The sculptures were placed by paths or in specially created viewing spaces set off by foliage whose shape she liked – Chusan palms, bamboos, yuccas, phormiums, crinums, agapanthus and cordylines. 'The stone carvings and the bronzes were placed on concrete breeze blocks, so that when they were sold they could be easily moved and then replaced. They came and went all the time,' says Bowness.

By 1965, Hepworth was running out of space, and so she bought what is now the top third of the garden from artist John Milne. But even half an acre was not enough. Shortly before her death, Hepworth felt that the garden was too full and that her *Family of Man* pieces should be moved. They now stand, fittingly, in the Yorkshire Sculpture Park, near

Wakefield. Otherwise, all the other sculptures are just as she left them.

Brian Smith, her secretary and curator during the last 10 years of her life, has his own memories of the garden. 'In June, it was a mass of self-seeding cinerarias, from palest pinks to deepest purples, which looked wonderful with the bronzes.

'One year, there were lots of tulips which looked a bit odd. They were from a Dutch admirer, and she felt she had to plant them. But they didn't come up the next year. She loved the gardens at Tresco Abbey, and many of her plants came from there.'

Hepworth's art was cerebral, but it was also elemental and sensual and she felt people could respond to it more easily in a garden than a museum. 'They are meant to be touched,' she said, and in the garden this is allowed.

There was a St Ives tradition for artists to open their homes to enable townspeople to visit before a show.

'People would come in who perhaps hadn't seen sculpture before,' she said. 'They would all ask me questions, and say: "Well, I don't know anything about it – but this is what I feel." And what they felt was exactly what I was trying to say.'

If it's good enough for Monsieur Blanc...

By Sarah Raven

If you want advice on choosing really fabulous vegetable varieties ask a top chef – preferably one with a kitchen garden. A professional epicure who really cares about food is not going to waste his or her time growing tasteless carrots or tomatoes, however perfect they look; any decent wholesaler can supply those, and probably much cheaper than homegrown. The reason a distinguished chef bothers with a vegetable garden is because he knows that the flavour of the right variety, carefully grown and picked only hours before it appears on a plate, will be in a class of its own.

I have just spent a day with Raymond Blanc's head gardener, Anne-Marie Owens, in the one-and-a-half-acre kitchen garden at Le Manoir aux Quat'Saisons. It fills a beautiful space on a north-east slope and has a huge, perfectly clear pond, fed by chalk land springs that border the garden on the north-west side. Shelter is provided by 80-year-old oaks and willows, and a Cotswold stone wall forms the dividing boundary between this productive area and the formal lawns and spectacular lavender-lined stone paths.

Every few weeks throughout the year head chef Gary Jones sits down with Raymond and Anne-Marie in Le Manoir kitchen to decide between the five or six different varieties of each vegetable they've had on trial that season. Flavour comes first in their list of priorities, but

Anne-Marie's input on reliability and general ease of growth in their organic garden – it has a sandy topsoil and heavier clay bottom – has an important place in the judging scheme. There's no point slaving over some delicious crop if you can't grow enough of it to be of use in a potentially 200-covers-a-day kitchen.

Walking round I was pleased to find that the trio had selected types I was growing too (very reassuring), such as the spinach variety 'Dominant': its excellent flavour and tender texture make the young leaves ideal for eating raw in a salad and for cooking. It's not brilliant in high, hot summer but for the rest of the year it is slow to bolt and suffers from few diseases. Sown outside every fortnight from mid-March until late-August, and inside after that, it will give you baskets of delicious leaves for nine months of the year.

There is Swiss chard in Le Manoir garden too, a vegetable that every single productive patch should include – in winter as well as summer – for its endless months of productivity and superbly strong, earthy taste. Anne-Marie is a firm believer in leaving plenty of room between plants to increase air circulation and decrease problems with fungal diseases – it also makes hoeing the beds to keep them weed-free and productive much easier. She spaces chard 75cm apart and celeriac 'Prinz' at a good 45cm; both double the amount of ground I give them.

To achieve this, the gardeners 'clump sow', placing three or four seeds close together at these wide intervals. You're guaranteed a plant at each station and, if they all germinate, you simply thin the clump to one.

They are also growing great swathes of cut-and-come-again salad leaves, including the pretty oriental green mizuna and the succulent, fleshy-leaved summer purslane. Mizuna is kept covered by horticultural fleece right through from sowing to harvesting. In a no-spray organic garden this is the one sure way of preventing infestation by flea beetle. I've just returned from a week away to find my mizuna in a sorry state, every leaf peppered with tiny holes, which looks ugly on the plate. If I'd protected it with a thin covering of fleece, my crop would be pristine.

Only a couple of lettuces make the grade at the Manoir. One we all know and love is the ever tasty and reliable 'Little Gem', which, as Anne-Marie says, 'is very difficult to upset'. The chefs love it because it is equally good braised or raw. The other is a wonderful old French variety, 'Reine de Glace', a lettuce with lovely crunch and some bitterness in the stem to add a zap to a salad. Its centre is not as tight as many traditional hearting varieties – the 'Webb's Wonderful' and other 'Iceberg' types – and so doesn't brown in the sun.

The five favoured potato varieties are mainly of the salad type: the early Maincrops, 'Belle de Fontenay', 'Ratte', 'Red Duke of York' and 'Charlotte', and the delicious but unpredictable late, 'Pink Fir Apple'. They are also growing great, sweeping 15m lines of a new one on me, 'BF15', which produces a superb, large crop of oval new potatoes with very yellow flesh and a sticking-to-the-knife waxiness that oozes out of the flesh as you cut it on your plate.

One of Raymond's signature dishes is courgette flowers and there are three 30m polytunnels dedicated to just one variety, 'Nero di Milano', to provide enough raw materials for the many Assiette Anne-Marie dishes they make in the kitchen each day. Why this one? Its fruit are firm, tasty and dark, and it is a huge producer of flowers. For perfection, Anne-Marie says pick them just as they open, rather than when they have fully splayed out, and remove the stigma. To achieve an endless supply of courgettes from June until October, they plant three batches. The first crop is sown at the end of February for planting into a polytunnel bed in April. These crop within about six weeks but tire quickly, so sowing new stock every four to six weeks is essential to keep up production.

I'm not generally a fan of turnips but I've been converted by the one and only variety grown at Le Manoir, the long-rooted, pure-white

'Demi-long de Croissy'. Best harvested when tiny, it has a mild flavour, nutty without a hint of bitterness, and is delicious sliced into salads and eaten raw, or poached in butter, with a touch of sugar, salt and pepper, and white wine vinegar.

For the flavour-obsessed vegetable grower like me, Le Manoir garden is heaven – their expert taste trials taught me what could take years of experimenting to discover for myself.

26 MAY 2001

Putting the bloom into Bloomsbury

By Carrie McArdle

In May 1919, Virginia Woolf wrote to her sister, the artist Vanessa Bell: 'I wish you'd leave Wisset and take Charleston. It has a charming garden, with a pond, and fruit trees, and vegetables, all now rather wild, but you could make it lovely.' That autumn, Vanessa moved into the remote South Downs farmhouse with her unconventional household: artist Duncan Grant, writer David 'Bunny' Garnett, and Julian and Quentin, Vanessa's two young sons by her husband Clive Bell.

Beautiful though the place was, conditions were primitive, with no hot water, no electricity and barely any heating. There would also be long hours of farm labour for Duncan and Bunny who, as conscientious objectors, were obliged to undertake this work of 'national importance'.

To turn the house into a home, Vanessa and Duncan embarked on a painting spree, decorating walls, doors, fireplaces and furniture with flowers, figures and fruit. The effect was fresh and spontaneous, sensuous and colourful. Together with the eclectic mix of furnishings that Vanessa brought to the farmhouse, it gave Charleston a special atmosphere.

As Virginia has suggested, the garden had plenty of potential too. The setting was rustic, with an old cattle pond overlooked by timbered barns, lawns, an orchard and a half-acred walled garden. But it was not until the 1920s when the war was long over, that there was time to devote to the walled garden.

This rectangular enclosure was given a formal layout of paths and borders, with a central expanse of lawn gently stepped to create three levels. Enclosed by a santolina hedge, the lawn became the ideal stage for the children's theatrical productions.

The main borders ran away from the house on either side of the French windows. Two rows of apple trees were retained, acting almost as an extra pair of borders at the outside edges of the lawn, and were under-planted with a mixture of Duncan and Vanessa's favourite flowers.

In spring there were vibrant, jewel-coloured wallflowers and tulips in a sea of forget-me-nots, soon followed by bowers of blossom, then the clashing oranges and pinks of oriental poppies and peonies. Summer brought roses in velvety crimson and dark red, spires of midnight-blue delphiniums, drifts of white daises and a wonderful mix of annuals. Statuesque artichokes – adored for their silver foliage – were planted, and roses, figs and fruit were trained up the walls.

The artists planned each year's planting in detail, ordering enthusiastically from catalogues and nurseries. Colour was their inspiration. Describing the garden in August 1930, Vanessa wrote: 'The garden is incredibly beautiful, full of reds of all kinds – scabious and hollyhocks and mallows and every kind of red, from red-lead to black.

'Pokers are coming out. It's all in good order, and we have masses of plums and apples. I have begun by painting some flowers, it seems the inevitable way to begin here.'

Naturally flowers and fruit from Charleston became the subject of still lifes, and the garden became the setting for many portraits. Duncan also introduced art into the overall design, relishing the idea of making it a place for exotic fantasy; he built and painted a gazebo next to the pond, and dreamt of introducing flamingos.

Trained in classical art, he mounted plaster heads of mythological heroes on the garden wall and created Duncan's folly, a courtyard garden, next to his studio.

The most intriguing pieces, however, are by Quentin Bell. His distinctive cement urns are mounted on the entrance gates; in the orchard sits Spink, an incomplete sculpture of a woman in red brick. Nearby, the figure of Pomona, with a bucket of glazed teracotta apples on her head, was inspired by the lemon-gatherers Duncan had painted in Spain.

A leading female figure on the far side of the pond makes a ghostly vision on misty nights; and a Levitating Lady seems to float above the water, supported only by her hair. Less dramatically, Quentin also laid out the Mediterranean-style piazza in the garden, which has mosaics of broken tiles and china, a small pool and fountain.

After Vanessa's death in 1961 and Duncan's in 1978, their daughter, Angelica Garnett, maintained the garden until the early 1980s, when the Charleston Trust was set up. With the help of the landscape architect Sir Peter Shepeard, the Trust restored the garden to look much as it would have done in its heyday in the 1950s.

Today, it is cared for by head gardener Andrew Caverly, who has lived and worked there for six years. During this time, the diaries, letters and memories of family and friends, along with Vanessa's many snapshots, have helped him to recreate the atmosphere of this much-loved place.

✣ 9 MAY 1948 ✣

A day of blossom and flowers

By Vita Sackville-West

Agreeable incidents do continue to occur from time to time, even in 1948; and there still seem to be days when things marvellously go right instead of wrong, rarities to be recorded with gratitude before they can be forgotten.

Such a day, culminating in such an incident, was given to me recently. I had had occasion to drive across 10 miles of Kent, through the orchard country. The apple-blossom was not yet fully out; it was still in that fugitive precious stage of being more of a promise than a fulfilment. Apple-blossom too quickly becomes overblown, whereas its true character is to be as tightly youthful as an 18-year-old poet. There they were, the closed buds just flushing pink, making a faintly roseate haze over the old trees grey with age; closed buds of youth graciously blushing as youth must blush in the presence of age, knowing very well that within a few months they themselves would turn into the apples of autumnal fruit.

But if the apple-blossom was no more than a pink veil thrown over the orchards, the cherry was at its most magnificent. Never has it looked more lavish than this year, nor so white, so candidly white. This heavy whiteness of the cherry, always enhanced by the contrasting blackness of the branches, was on this particular afternoon deepened – if white may be said to deepen – by a pewter-grey sky of storm as a backcloth; and I thought, not for the first time, how perfectly married were these two effects of April: the dazzling blossom and the peculiarly lurid heaven which is only half a menace. Only half, for however wrathful it may pretend to be overhead, there are gleams of light round the edges, with lances of sun striking a church tower somewhere in the landscape. It is not a true threat; it is a temporary threat, put on for its theatrical effect – nature's original of that most strange and beautiful of man's new inventions, flood-lighting.

Enriched by these experiences I came home, expecting no further delight that day; but on arrival I saw a closed van at the front door. Having long awaited some spare parts to repair the boiler, dreary, yet necessary, I walked round to the back of the van thinking how quickly utilitarian life returned to oust beauty, and with a sigh prepared to investigate some graceless assortment of pieces of iron whose function would be incomprehensible to me. But there was no such thing. Instead, a smiling young man confronted me saying he did not know if I would be interested, but he had brought these ... and opened the van as he spoke.

'These' were giant pansies, thousands and thousands of them. The van's dark interior was a cavern of colour. Some royal hand had flung rugs of velvet over the stacks of wooden trays. Purples were there: and subtler colours than purple: bronze and greenish-yellow and claret and rose-red, all in their queer cat-faces of crumpled velvet. I stood amazed. What an imaginative young man, I thought, to hawk this giant strain round the countryside, selling his plants to any buyer. When I questioned him, he said, modestly, that he hoped people would not be able to resist them.

He was probably right, and I wish him good luck in his enterprise. As for those whose houses do not lie on his road, a packet of seed should serve the purpose, and by next spring the ground should appear as though spread with the most sumptuous carpet from Isfahan.

Heroic, eccentric, beautiful

By David Wheeler

The sum of Plâs Brondanw is greater than its parts. This early 20th-century masterpiece is a blueprint for anyone interested in learning how to link garden to landscape, how to create drama using very few varieties of plant, how best to deploy garden statuary and how to create those most potent yet elusive of desirables, tranquillity and privacy.

Clough Williams-Ellis was given the Brondanw estate in north-west Wales by his father in 1908 when he was 25 and he devoted himself to it until his death 70 years later. 'It was for its sake that I worked and stinted, for its sake that I chiefly hoped to prosper,' he wrote in his autobiography.

Williams-Ellis was an architect and, while some of his clients could afford to splash out large amounts of money on their projects all in one go, he had to fashion his own garden bit by bit.

'A cheque for £10 would come in and I would order yew hedging, a cheque for £20 and I would pave a further piece of terrace,' he wrote. Unlike Portmeirion, the Italianate fantasy village he designed a few miles away on the Dwyryd estuary, Brondanw (the Welsh 'w' is pronounced 'oo') is dominated by Snowdonia's craggy peaks; the garden itself is presided over by the severe, four-storey, granite Caroline house.

Williams-Ellis and Brondanw appear to have been destined for each other. For his purposes it could not have been better positioned, occupying just the ideal classical site as defined by Alberti, the fifth-century father of the Italian Renaissance garden: 'a delicacy of gardens' should stand in the foreground, overlooking ' … the owner's land or a great plain, and familiar hills and mountains'. Sir Clough Williams-Ellis (he was knighted in 1972) had them all.

With its lichen-encrusted slate and stone, mature hedges and towering topiary the garden has a timeless patina; its design, however, roots it firmly in the Arts and Crafts style that flourished 100 years earlier. Unlike many formal gardens of the period, which had paths and allées aligned on the windows and doors of the house, Brondanw comprises an intricate set of garden rooms that had to be built or, rather, grown. Made of yew and box, colonnaded by pleached limes, furnished with evergreen shrubs and curtains of ivy, and prettified with a rich assortment of sculpture and uplifting artefacts – a whimsy that came to be known as 'Cloughing it up' – these rooms huddle together at one end of a long fillet of land at the core of the estate. For the past 40 years it has been maintained by Ron Roberts who, now in semi-retirement, continues to help with hedge and topiary cutting.

Williams-Ellis terminated some views with follies and spectacles beyond the garden walls, but it is his long, bold vistas – shooting several miles towards mountain peaks – that place him in the heroic league.

The main axis opens from the little raised belvedere at the southern end, cuts straight through the garden by way of a rectangular pond and slips between 6m-high firs (clipped pencil-thin to mimic Mediterranean cypresses), aiming directly at Cnicht, a Snowdonia peak five miles away.

Another equally dramatic vista begins at a wall with three arched recesses, runs north, between yew hedges, and through a high triple-arched yew screen topped by topiary finials. The figure of a woman, whose features have been eroded by the elements, stands forlornly in the central arch. Her back is set against another Snowdonia peak, Moel Hebog, which rises beyond the reclaimed saltmarsh that spreads across the valley floor below the garden.

Williams-Ellis built the elegant, French-looking orangery within a few years of being handed the estate. The outlook tower, a picturesque 'ruin' on high ground with views to the sea at Porthmadog, was built with funds subscribed by his fellow officers in the Welsh Guards to celebrate his marriage to Amabel Strachey in 1915. Steps proliferate; handrails, benches and all manner of ornamental ironwork are painted in the estate colour – a milky turquoise known as Portmeirion Green – highlighted with gold trim.

The presence of water is impossible to ignore in North Wales. It sustains a pelt of moss on Brondanw's lawns and is responsible for the lichen that overlays both masonry and trees. Pools sit comfortably in the garden and its most shallow piece of water – a rectangle within a cloister of pleached limes among beds of pink mophead hydrangeas – constitutes the heart and soul of Plâs Brondanw.

Like the ribbons of orange crocosmias that now weave between the garden's many hedges, the pink hydrangeas post-date Williams-Ellis, who favoured white-flowering plants – Japanese anemones, viburnum and a few roses. While gardens must learn to march to a different tune when their makers move on, in the quarter century since Sir Clough Williams-Ellis's death far from being challenged, the genius of his creation has been more fully appreciated.

Bluffer's guide to showing off your garden

By Fred Whitsey

Urgent telephone call: Mr Graham Thomas, Britain's most eminent gardener, is on a progress through the region and wishes to call and see the garden. What can it mean? Has some joker put it about that in a frenzied moment of anti-Thatcherism I have decided to emigrate? Has the National Trust, whom he counsels on gardens, then got interested in the future of this overplanted plot with more than its fair share of our native flora too? The fancy wanders, Hadrian VII had no more awesome hour when he heard they wanted him for Pope.

How shall we prepare for his coming? The wettest spring anyone remembers, when little work was done while the rain poured down and everything grew with abandon, has left the place looking as though the owner had already slammed the gate and turned his back on it for ever. At least it throws into sharper focus the problems of trying to maintain a garden too big for you, of the shadow of anxiety descending visitors throw before them and of the industry demanded of those who open their gardens for charity.

Happily, the conservation movement comes to your aid very handsomely these days. No longer do you have to apologise for the weeds. You airily say 'We're leaving these nettles for the bees', or 'You don't see many campions round here now. We're hoping they'll re-establish if we let them seed', 'We always say buttercups are the best ground cover', 'Willowherb makes quite a robust little wine', 'Don't you think bindweed has the most wonderful sculptural flowers?', 'Didn't you know goldcrests just adore chickweed?' or 'You'll see at dinner why we always let a few dandelions flourish'.

Always make sure to use the imperial first person. It implies that your relationship with the garden staff has the right flavour, even if it only consists of one pensioner who, between getting his pipe alight, prefers to spend most of his half-day clearing out the shed for you.

Or if you are fearful about looking overgrown you can always drop the word that 'Everyone round here does his mowing on Sunday afternoons and they're always having barbecues. We've just had to shut ourselves in.' As for weeds on the lawn: 'I loathe chemicals. I can't bear to think of the pussies licking their paws after walking on them.' On shaggy hedges: 'We never have them cut until all the birds have nested and every fledgling has flown.'

Of course, it depends on whom you are entertaining. Never utter that incantation about being 'here last week' to your gardener friend. He will know that it wasn't any different then. More important to realise that he will reconstruct your vision in his own mind. He will be living on dreams too.

You must be sure of using the word 'project' as often as you can. Gardens are always in the making. They are never made. You can excuse all manner of chaos with the assertion that you're working on a new project for this area or that.

If you want to affirm your status as a true gardener yourself, or at least give the impression, make certain to have close to the door by your wellies a trug basket – wooden, never plastic – with secateurs, a handfork and plastic bags ready in it. 'Just say if there's anything you'd like as we go round.' No matter if he takes you up on it when you come to your greatest and smallest treasure, let him have a cutting or a rooted bit. It might die on you next winter and you will be glad to have somewhere to go to recover the stock.

If you can't get all the mowing done in time, mzow strips through the daisies wide enough for two to talk abreast. Conservation again. 'All the meadows have been ploughed up now. Someone must keep a token of them somewhere. Otherwise young people will never know how romantic they were.'

Do go round the edges, though. That always gives a well-tended illusion. In default of an electric edging tool, using a scythe is the quick way of shaping them. There is no mystery about handling one of these, and they always appeal to those of back-to-nature persuasions. To wield a scythe without harming yourself and your image you need to follow three principles: take thin swathes at a sweep, re-hone the blade often as you work, adding a country sound to the roar of the mowers, and 'keep the 'eel down', as skilled scythes-men always say.

If shame gets the better of you and you cannot comfort yourself with countrified rationalisations, try the navvy's trick of slicing off offending weed growth with a spade made as keen as a carving knife at the edge with a file.

The well-maintained effect which it achieves is heartening. Especially if it is followed up with a mulch of peat or composted bark. Of course, the weeds will come through again, but when they do they'll be much easier to pull out. The effect won't be entirely cosmetic. Nor is it when you cut off any weeds at their source. By depriving them of their leaves you are reducing their power to grow. That's one of the laws of nature.

An alternative to this is a bit of sorcery: lay black polythene over the offending ground and spread the peat on that. Leave it in place long enough and what's underneath will give up. There may be an orchid that flowers underground somewhere in the world but no plant, weed or anything else which we have here can survive without the light. Be careful to blind the visitor with that fragment of wisdom.

THE PLASTICINE GARDEN

By Joanna Fortnam

One of Chelsea's most talked about gardens is made entirely of Plasticine. Yes, the stuff we played with at school that never comes out of the carpet. The fact that the creator of Paradise in Plasticine is James May of *Top Gear* fame (and Telegraph motoring writer), makes it hard not to suspect 'prank', especially as the garden also features in an upcoming BBC Two series, *James May's Toy Stories*.

A picture of innocence, May rejects the notion that he isn't serious: 'I think the RHS liked the novelty of the idea,' he says.

And once he'd convinced production company Plum Pictures to back it, May was set.

Modeller extraordinaire Paul Baker of 3D Studios (famous for his 'foodscapes' created with Carl Warner), ran the pre-show workshop in Twickenham.

'Everything's wired wherever possible so it won't wilt,' says Paul. 'The bushes have a base of polystyrene and steel with a Plasticine overlay wired on — there's a veg patch, grapevine, palm trees, lawn, a rockery, a pond. And, as this is James May world, the tree has both oranges and cherries on it.' Via appeals on YouTube and at the Ideal Home Show, the British public also joined in: 'Schoolchildren made daffodils, Chelsea pensioners made poppies,' says May.

Even Jane Asher made some sunflowers and a cake that forms part of the picnic on a rug on the lawn.

'Coming at it from a science and engineering point of view, I found model making deeply engrossing,' he says. One of May's aims is to persuade children to put down their games consoles and play with their families – so if a Plasticine garden can work that magic, can it be all bad?

18.
'Winter colour is nature's most sophisticated palette'

(Discuss)

Making the best of the limbo period

By Mary Keen

'I t'll be nice when we can get into the garden again,' a neighbour said over Christmas. It's actually nice now.

The limbo between Christmas and the New Year was mild and so was the first week or so of January. At the risk of sounding Pollyanna-ish, the days already seem to last longer and everywhere I peer, there are signs of life.

Snowdrops are starting and there are plenty out. A good one called 'Limetree' is like *G. atkinsii* but even earlier. The green-leaved 'Anglesey Abbey' and 'Diggory' look promising and so do several others. 'Lady Beatrix Stanley' is out, or almost out, in the orchard. If I can see the whites of their flowers, I count them as out. Usually, I dislike doubles but they are good in grass because they are visible from farther away.

Lady B is increasing well. Much better than the *Cyclamen coum* which I moved under an apple tree a couple of years ago. Part-shade is what the textbooks say cyclamen like, but what they like best in this garden is a baking south-facing bank at the end of the lawn.

Ants carry their seeds there from the official cyclamen spot under the limes and the corms are now as thick as sunbathers on a sunny day and their flowers are shocking pink.

In a way, this is the perfect time of year to be gardening. There is so much to welcome back. In summer every task seems urgent. In winter nothing does. Sometimes I just potter about in the sun, examining the faces of hellebores, or checking that the bullfinches have not started on the *Prunus mume* outside the back door. It is a time when the garden teems with promise.

I watch shoots lengthening daily, find buds on the daffodil 'Rijnveld's Early Sensation' and smell the sarcococca on the air. Before Christmas I picked some branches of the winter-flowering cherry and brought them indoors. I have been enjoying their slow opening for weeks and when I add a branch of *Viburnum x bodnantense* 'Dawn' to the vase it smells good too. The advantage of mild days is that the winter viburnums are not browned off by frost.

I thought I preferred 'Charles Lamont' to 'Dawn' but the 'Charles Lamont' flowers look skimpier and whiter than they should. It may be that what I was sold was not what it was supposed to be. I plan to check this with a good gardening friend who claims hers is definitely Mr Lamont.

Scented shrubs really come into their own in winter. I could not imagine a garden without sarcococcas and viburnums, but a big disappointment is that the expensive (£40) *Daphne bholua* 'Gurkha' that I bought at Wisley last spring took the whole summer to die. Might have been rain. Or drought at the start. I can't help the former, but the latter may well have been my fault and this is a plant that I count among my all-time favourites. I had one 10ft tall which packed up in the very cold spell in 2011 and I have twice tried Daphne 'Jacqueline Postill' without success. Even though others say it is better than any other bholua form, it seems less hardy here. Deciduous shrubs look good in winter too, now that I am adopting the French pruning technique that John Massey (of Ashwood Nurseries) taught me last summer.

I missed him when I tackled the *Ligustrum quihoui*. The glamorous privet that flowers in August was far too dominant and dense and made more shade in the summer garden than I wanted. It is now a slender airy creature with space at its feet for growing better things than hardy begonia (*Begonia grandis* subsp. *evansiana*).

Is it better to travel hopefully than to arrive? I love the promise of plants to come. Sometimes winter in the garden has more charms for the pottering gardener than full on, no-time-to-sit-down summer.

 24 SEPTEMBER 1988

A Technicolour winter

By Rosemary Verey

W inter colour is nature's most sophisticated palette – a range dominated by subtle tones, sombre contrasts and striking highlights. As the rich shades of autumn give way to gentler winter hues, it is as though a hand has touched the canvas. Many of the trees and shrubs appear skeletal after the lushness of their summer growth and yet it is these newly shorn textures and stripped torsos that become the background colour in the garden. Whereas before it was the flaming reds and burning golds, now it is the gentler fawns and purples and the multitudinous browns and greens that dominate. For the winter gardener, the challenge is to enhance and build upon this mellow array; you would be wise to think of creating a single muted theme.

Bright blues will have vanished from the garden, until the first scillas appear. Yellows, whites and greys, purples and reds are set now against the deeper shades of green and brown. Flashes of pure, bright colour, artfully placed, come as both a shock and a joy – brightly coloured berries and branches look striking against yews and hollies. When the light is strong, the white trunks of birch and eucalyptus are dramatic, standing in the distance beyond an accent of solid green.

Brown is a colour we tend to think of as autumnal. But the brown of autumn is flamboyant, whereas winter's browns are subtle and full of surprises, now rich, now gentle. Brown is not simply a matter of earth or of mulch. There are also seeds and catkins: the clusters of alder and the willow catkin. The best winter catkin-tree is the Turkish hazel, *Corylus colurna*.

Among my favourite browns are the common teasel, the herbaceous *Phlomis russeliana* (syn. *P. viscosa*), and many of the lovely ornamental grasses, which by winter have turned pale fawn. In my borders the gently browning spikes of *Acanthus mollis* – with their shiny green seeds and greying bracts – stand out distinctively. So do the tall, mushroom-coloured stems of *Macleaya cordata*.

During the winter months we notice and appreciate barks and stems most. For the smaller garden, one of the best is *Acer griseum*, the mahogany-brown skin of which peels off, revealing new cinnamon-coloured bark.

Deciduous shrubs assume an important and different role in winter. They can be successfully integrated into mixed borders, stood alone against dark backgrounds or formed into a solid screen.

The smallest, brightest whites of winter are its flowers. The aristocrats are the Christmas roses, *Helleborus niger*; the lovely blooms of the white *H. orientalis* appear later. Snowdrops provide the common touch and, unlike hellebores, which dislike being disturbed, increase of their own accord or can be divided after they have flowered.

Slightly taller are the blooms of *Leucojum vernum*, the snowflake, which come through in February. Each flower, shaped like a minute Tiffany lamp, is tipped with green. *Iberis sempervirens* has intensely white flowers, closely massed, which can bloom from November until March, and glossy evergreen leaves, making a mound 18in high.

White berries may not be as striking as red, but they are still eye-catching and have the advantage of being less attractive to the birds. The translucent winter berries of the common mistletoe, *Viscum album*, hanging in clusters, are generally ignored by birds until well after Christmas.

Foliage, variegated or uniform, is the principal provider of white and grey in the garden in winter. The white-edged leaf of one of my favourite shrubs, *Prunus lusitanica* 'Variegata', takes on a pretty pink flush in winter to match its ruby-red stems. It clips well, as does the silver form of privet, *Ligustrum sinense* 'Variegatum', but I prefer both untrimmed.

The leaves of *Rhamnus alaternus* 'Argenteovariegata', creamy and white-margined when you look at them closely, are grey from a distance. Used as a bush, this plant will lighten a mixed or shrub border all through the year. As a clipped ball or a standard, it is perfect for tubs during the winter.

Silvery ground-cover plants are a godsend in winter, particularly in darker spots. Ivy, usually thought of as a green climber, has a number of variegated silver forms that make impeccable ground cover and also clipped edging. Top of my list comes *Hedera helix* 'Glacier', with its silver-grey leaves edged with a narrow margin of white. The smaller leaves of *Hedera helix* 'Adam' have an overall silver tinge.

Red and purple are the shock troops of winter. Enjoy them individually, use them to heighten a group of whites and greys and golds, or, for a startling long-distance effect, plant them together – copper trunks, red berries, scarlet stems and rich purple foliage.

Once you start looking for shades of red in the garden in winter, you will begin to see them everywhere. Beautiful reddish-brown bark on the trunks and young branches of trees will begin to seem an essential part of winter. Many of the acers qualify admirably for this role. The variety *Acer pensylvanicum* 'Erythrocladum' was shown at the Royal Horticultural Society in London in the early spring of 1977. It was startling in its beauty. The young shoots are bright shrimp pink with a paler striation, and as a tree it is something to search out and plant.

Among the shrubs with exciting rubicund stems, the willows come first. You do not have to find a damp place for willows but, if you do, they will grow more effectively. The scarlet willow, *Salix alba* 'Britzensis' (syn. S.a. 'Chermesina') also has conspicuous scarlet winter stems, and makes a grand stand along a river or stream. A more exotic touch of red is provided by the bright, hairy stems of *Rubus phoenicolasius*, the Japanese wineberry, which can grow to 6–8ft and looks even better in winter than in summer.

Once the deciduous trees and shrubs have lost their leaves, the berries that crown them become all-important. Massed together, they briefly make cones of brilliant colour. By the time winter is fully fledged, many of them will have disappeared down the throats of the thrushes and blackbirds – the red ones seem to be the first to go.

The broad-leaved evergreen shrubs yield a rich crop of berries. *Viburnum rhytidophyllum* is a wonderful soul barrier and a fast grower (after a few years it will reach a height of 8–10ft); if you have both sexes, you can expect a winter display of red berries which gradually turn black. The red or yellow berries of pyracantha are usually left by the birds until they have first devoured the holly and sorbus fruits, perhaps because they do not ripen so soon.

In the garden, roses have hips to offer, often lowkey, sometimes prolific. Dick Balfour tells me that in his Essex garden the longest lasting – and he grows a great many roses – are those of the repeat-flowering climbers, such as 'Dortmund', 'Pink Perpetue', 'Aloha' and 'Morning Jewel'. Their hips are all upright, but when you look at many of the shrub roses you will find theirs hang down on bending stems. I

enjoy watching the birds feasting on the profusion of juicy hips on my
Rosa rugosa hedge.

If you aim for movement as well as colour in your garden, you must
have grasses. *Molinia caerulea* 'Variegata' makes shapely 2ft tufts with
flower spikes which keep their freshness well into winter. *Miscanthus
sinensis purpurascens*, as its name implies, has leaves turning to a rich
purple in autumn, topped with reddish plumes. Caught in the sunlight
when the wind is blowing, or rising from a bed of snow, they show that
winter has a lighter, less serious touch.

Black and darkest grey are the colours that first come to mind for
most people when they think of winter. For the gardener black is a
marvellous background colour, and an essential factor in creating
dramatic effects. I love the silhouettes of trees, the emphatic nature of
the bare tracery and their strong shadows.

Nature herself has recognised the supporting role of black: there
are very few plants which are black through and through. I can think
of one though – *Ophiopogon planiscapus* 'Nigrescens' – that looks best
surrounded by a sprinkling of pale gravel or chippings to show off
the black leaves. Then there are the less obvious blacks – the stems,
berries and catkins. *Cornus alba* 'Kesselringii' has deep-purple stems
which look black in certain lights. Chestnuts lying on the ground, so
richly mahogany-coloured in autumn, turn black in winter. *Ilex crenata*
has black berries and those on the arborescent ivies become black as
winter moves on.

A winter garden - without having to try too hard

By Tom Stuart-Smith

My garden is not a winter garden. There are no coloured stems, very few berries, no variegation nor spiky phormiums and yuccas to liven things into a state of sub-tropical delusion. How miserable, you probably think – the garden must be a mush of rot and decay, brown on grey. Well – yes and no. I have always wanted the garden in winter to look as though it is in the grip of winter and not in a state of seasonal denial; a dialogue with the country that surrounds it rather than an exotic archipelago. This approach seems to suit this little scrap of Hertfordshire. So, I stop short of pyracantha and stripy elaeagnus and try to achieve some effect by creating contrasts between things that are ordered, clipped or formalised, and others that appear to be more random and natural.

Contrasts of form and space are thrown into much sharper relief by a good bit of cold weather. Most important are the structural bits and pieces – the antidote to the mush of decaying and dormant plants. My cloud-pruned yew forms a loose series of partially enclosed spaces. These bloated caterpillars are magnificent in the frost, with every curve and dip highlighted. This type of hedge is not for everyone, but it suits our slightly wonky, bucolic look – the barn, our main living room, leans precariously away from the prevailing wind. These highly mannered hedges contrast with slim columns of Irish yew and enclosures of square-clipped hornbeam. In retrospect I think I might have used beech because it keeps its dead, russet foliage through the winter and is beautiful when clipped into hedges or domes. Still, the hornbeams suit me well enough: the rows of bare stems are satisfyingly bleak.

If there were nothing but this skeletal neatness and formal, evergreen naturalism, the garden would be pretty dull. The counterpoint is provided by the rustling transience of herbaceous plants in various states of decay.

First of all are the evergreen perennials. On my gravel, shrubby and herbaceous phlomis, some *Euphorbia* subsp. *wulfenii* and the rarely used *E. nicaeensis*, *Helleborus argutifolius*, shrubby sages, lavenders and santolinas are mainstays, but constitute only about five per cent of the planting at most. Where the herbaceous planting is really tall I avoid shrubs, unless they are very open and arching, such as the occasional philadelphus, magnolia or species rose, as they become overcrowded by the herbs and grow leggy.

Among all the herbaceous planting (including grasses) I make sure that half are still standing up well into February and try to get a mix of different colours in the dying leaves and stems. Of the taller plants veronicastrums, *Aster novae-angliae* and *Inula magnifica* are among the most rigid and the darkest when they die. Rudbeckias are also excellent for dark shapes and blackish seedheads but tend to struggle on my dry gravel soil. Rich browns are especially useful to dispel the overall dreariness. I value *Vernonia crinita*, which looks like a 2m (7ft) large-leaved aster and keeps its seed heads while the stems remain a deep foxy brown – very handsome with bleached grasses. At a lower level, sedums are superb for rich browns, especially the pewter-leaved 'Matrona' and smaller, purpler 'Karl Funkelstein'. I covet 'Stewed Rhubarb Mountain'for its Venetian red stems in January. I would love to be able to grow common garden bergamot for the seedheads alone but on my soil its not even worth trying.

About 20 per cent of my garden is made up of clumps and drifts of grasses, with good winter form. They have tremendous architectural presence at this time of year and are more solid than anything offered by other perennials. For tall grasses, miscanthus takes the biscuit. The best, such as *M. sinensis* 'Graziella' combine grace and indestructibility. Then comes Calamagrostis 'Karl Foerster' at 1.5m (5ft) with its tight bunch of stick-vertical straws that looks very architectural.

Panicums generally have a bit more colour and stand up quite well, and the giant oat grass, *Stipa gigantea* is a virtually everlasting 2.1m (7ft) diaphanous starbust – though admittedly a beige one. Perhaps my favourite dead grass in January is the comparatively diminutive *Hakonechloa macra*. In its plain unvariegated form it looks like a slightly exotic version of something you might find at the base of an old hedge in Dorset: glossy, tufty and arching gracefully. It is one of the few grasses to keep some warm colour into the new year.

The balance of grasses and perennials stays fairly constant from year to year but editing is done every year, replanting in autumn and spring, restricting thugs like *Phlomis russeliana* and inexorably swelling clumps of miscanthus, and adding to those which tend to get squeezed out or are on the margins of their tolerance (*Echinacea purpurea*, phlox, *Cirsium rivulare*). A lot of this doesn't really have to be done, but like every gardener I am always thinking about how next year could be better.

Spare a thought for the gardener during the coldest months

By Ursula Buchan

Those who work outside in winter are quickest to notice when the days begin to lengthen. Years ago, when I was a green under-gardener, Mr Willis, my head gardener, told me that he reckoned the days started perceptibly to draw out on January 12 – and he was right. (He was right about most things. He told me a lot of other gems, about gardens, about the natural world and about rural life before the war, as we pruned the glasshouse peach trees or swept leaves together.)

After that, every year that I was employed as a gardener, I would look up on January 12 at a pink, freezing-clear afternoon sky and mark the fact that, for the first time in more than a month, I would be going home while it was light. Now that I no longer have to be outside in the dark days of early January, I have lost that small, but intimate, connection with the turning of the earth.

'As the days lengthen, the cold strengthens' was another piece of wisdom I gathered from Mr Willis, and even recent climatic trends would not have changed his mind entirely. This is the moment when the flowers of my favourite early snowdrop – an enormous *Galanthus elwesii* hybrid called 'Maidwell L' – show their clean, cold whiteness against grey-green, fleshy leaves. This is a sight as warming to my heart as the fieriest of autumn leaves or the sweetest of summer roses. Most years, however, a short freezing snap will cause the *G. elwesii* leaves to flop, as if exhausted by the cold, reviving only when the temperatures rise once more.

I have lost something, I know. If you are paid to be outside working, the trudging nature of gardening in January can be dreary, but it makes the rewards of unfurling aconites, irises and hellebores so much the richer than if you simply view them from the warmth of your sitting-room.

Professional gardeners are there to catch the fugitive, delicious scents of *Lonicera fragrantissima*, of *Hamamelis mollis*, or *Chimonanthus praecox* as they go about their work. January is surprisingly busy for the employed gardener, unless the weather is really wintry: planting bare-root trees, sowing early vegetables under glass, digging, sorting through the potting shed, cleaning and servicing the machinery and tools, making seed lists, washing pots, tending the compost heaps, putting down mole traps, pruning apple and pear trees, laying new paths, renovating borders ... so the list goes on.

Though I have left their ranks, I still find it in me to envy the many hundreds of gardeners working in what was once called 'private service', as well as heritage gardens, botanic gardens and public parks. True, they are badly paid, not always well-managed and often isolated, but they have a distinct esprit that comes from hard-won expertise in a complex, worthwhile profession.

So, when you look out of the window this morning and decide that you won't go outside today, as the weather is not very nice and there is no task really pressing, spare a thought for those gardeners who began their weekend duty hours ago, caring for plants in glasshouses which cannot be neglected, even in winter.

And, especially, spare a thought for the 'single-handed' gardeners whose working life is spent on their own and who do not even have the consolation of someone to talk to, as Mr Willis and I used to talk.